CONFLICT AND RESOURCE DEVELOPMENT IN THE SOUTHERN HIGHLANDS OF PAPUA NEW GUINEA

CONFLICT AND RESOURCE DEVELOPMENT IN THE SOUTHERN HIGHLANDS OF PAPUA NEW GUINEA

Nicole Haley and Ronald J. May (eds)

State, Society and Governance in Melanesia Program
Studies in State and Society in the Pacific, No. 3

ANU

THE AUSTRALIAN NATIONAL UNIVERSITY

E PRESS

E PRESS

Published by ANU E Press
The Australian National University
Canberra ACT 0200, Australia
Email: anuepress@anu.edu.au
This title is also available online at: http://epress.anu.edu.au/conflict_citation.html

National Library of Australia
Cataloguing-in-Publication entry

Conflict and resource development in the Southern Highlands
of Papua New Guinea.

ISBN 9781921313455 (pbk.)
ISBN 9781921313462 (online)

1. Social conflict - Papua New Guinea - Southern Highlands
Province. 2. Intergroup relations - Papua New Guinea -
Southern Highlands Province. 3. Natural resources -
Management. I. Haley, Nicole. II. May, R. J. (Ronald
James), 1939- .

330.99561

This book has been published on the recommendation of the Pacific Editorial Board,
which is convened by the Pacific Centre.

Cover photo: Southern Highlanders view the Nembi landscape (Bryant Allen)
Cover design by ANU E Press

Contents

Figures

Tables

Abbreviations

ADA	Assistant District Administrator
APO	Aid Post Orderly
CA	Community affairs
CBHC	Community-based health care
CHW	Community Health Worker
CIFP	Country indicators for foreign policy
CNGL	Chevron NiuGuini Limited
DPLGA	Department for Provincial and Local Government Affairs
FEED	Front end engineering and design
FHRIP	Family Health and Rural Improvement Program
GTQ	Gas-to-Queensland
HEO	Health Extension Officer
HSES	Health, safety, environment and security
ILG	Incorporated Land Group
LANCO	Landowner Company
LLG	Local-Level Government
LNG	Liquid natural gas
MFFN	Melanesian Farmer First Network
MIGR	Ministry for Inter-Government Relations
MP	Member of Parliament
MPA	Members of the Provincial Assembly
NEC	National Executive Council
NYMP	National Youth Movement Program
OIC	Officer In Change
OLPGLLG	Organic Law on Provincial Governments and Local-level Governments
OSL	Oil Search Ltd
PDL	Petroleum development licence
PJV	Porgera Joint Venture
PMV	Passenger motor vehicle
PPL	Petroleum prospecting licence
RPNGC	Royal Papua New Guinea Constabulary
SDA	Seventh Day Adventist Church
SEIS	Social and economic impact statement
SHP	Southern Highlands Province
SHPG	Southern Highlands Provincial Government
SHRDP	Southern Highlands Rural Development Project

TCS   Tax credit scheme

Measurements

km^2	kilometres squared
tlf	trillion cubic feet
bblspd	barrels per day
$A	Australian dollars
$US	United States dollars
K	PNG Kina

Contributors

Bryant Allen is a Senior Fellow in the Department of Human Geography, Research School of Pacific and Asian Studies, at The Australian National University. He previously taught at the University of Papua New Guinea and worked with the National Research Institute (Papua New Guinea). His recent work has focused on agricultural systems in Papua New Guinea, and has included extensive fieldwork in Tari.

Laurie Bragge has served as Community Affairs Manager and Community Affairs Strategic Planner with Oil Search Ltd. He was a patrol officer/district officer in Papua New Guinea from 1961 to 1978, during which time he served in several provinces, including the Southern Highlands Province. During the 1980s he was involved in the tourism industry in Papua New Guinea.

Stephanie Copus-Campbell is a former Director, Strategies and Program Planning Section, Papua New Guinea Branch of AusAID.

Joseph Dorpar, from Kerowagi in Chimbu Province, is the administrator of Madang Province, where he is working hard to restore services in a setting where the provincial government was largely crippled by unresolved conflict among its leaders. Prior to this he worked with the Ministry for Inter-Government Relations, and before that as Administrator of Chimbu Province.

Laurence Goldman is currently Gas Project Community Affairs Field Manager with Esso Highlands Limited. He also holds an adjunct Associate Professor position in Anthropology at the University of Queensland. Dr Goldman conducted fieldwork among the Huli in the late 1970s, has published extensively on the Southern Highlands, and has had a longstanding academic career in both pure and applied anthropological research.

Nicole Haley is a Postdoctoral Research Fellow with the State, Society and Governance in Melanesia Project, Research School of Pacific and Asian Studies, at The Australian National University. She has extensive field research and consultancy experience in Papua New Guinea, particularly in the Southern Highlands.

Joe Kanekane is a Southern Highlander who was Chief Political and Investigative Reporter with the former Independent newspaper in Papua New Guinea, and chair of the Editors Task Force on War Against Corruption.

Kai Lavu is Manager, Community Affairs, with the Porgera Joint Venture, which operates the Porgera Gold Mine in Enga Province, Papua New Guinea.

Neryl Lewis is currently AusAID's Emergencies Manager. Prior to taking up this position, Neryl managed the PNG Humanitarian Unit, overseeing AusAID support for disaster management, Bougainville and Southern Highlands Province.

She joined AusAID in 2001, after completing a Master of Letters in Peace Studies at the University of New England, and worked on the PNG Program for four years.

Jim Macpherson has taught at universities in Canada, Australia, New Zealand and Papua New Guinea. His recent appointments have been as First Secretary in the Ministry responsible for provincial and local government affairs in Papua New Guinea, and currently, with Sir Peter Barter, First Secretary in the Ministry of Health, Papua New Guinea.

Ronald J. May is a Visiting Fellow in the State, Society and Governance in Melanesia Project, Research School of Pacific and Asian Studies, and Convenor of the Centre for Conflict and Post-Conflict Studies, Asia Pacific, at The Australian National University. He was formerly Director of the National Research Institute (Papua New Guinea).

Philip Moya is a Southern Highlander currently working for Oil Search Limited as a senior community relations officer on the Papua New Guinea Gas Project. He has over 25 years of public service experience. Following the failed elections of 2002 he was appointed as Acting Deputy Provincial Administrator and Regional Coordinator (Western) for Southern Highlands. His chief responsibilities included co-ordinating law and order programs and re-establishing administrative functions in the Hela region.

Maev O'Collins is a Visiting Fellow in the Department of Political and Social Change, Research School of Pacific and Asian Studies, The Australian National University, and Emeritus Professor, University of Papua New Guinea.

John Vail lived in Southern Highlands Province from 1980 to 2000, as a member the Papua New Guinea Institute of Medical Research. Between 1995 and 2000 he managed the Family Health and Rural Improvement Program in Tari, a community-based organisation working to improve health and rural livelihoods. Now an Australian-based consultant, he is a founder member of TerraCircle, an association of people with wide experience in the Pacific which is providing technical support for the Melanesian Farmer First Network, a group of community-based organisations operating in Papua New Guinea, the Solomon Islands and Vanuatu.

Noel H. Walters served as a government officer in Papua New Guinea from 1959 to 1986, first under the Australian colonial administration and then with the Independent government of Papua New Guinea. He was Secretary for the Department of Western Highlands Province for three years from 1983. In 1986 he took up a private sector appointment with the Porgera Joint Venture and was a departmental manager and head of the Community Affairs Department for over a decade.

Chris Warrilow was Petroleum Registrar with the Department of Minerals and Energy/Petroleum and Energy from 1985 to 2000, and in this position was involved in the negotiation of agreements in several of the Southern Highlands project areas. Before this, he served as a patrol officer/district officer in several provinces, including the Southern Highlands.

Acknowledgements

This volume had its genesis in a workshop held at The Australian National University in 2003 with a view to gaining a clearer understanding of the dynamics of politics, development and ongoing conflict in the Southern Highlands of Papua New Guinea. The workshop was sponsored by the Centre for Conflict and Post-Conflict Studies, Asia Pacific and the State, Society and Governance in Melanesia Program within the Research School of Pacific and Asian Studies, and was supported by AusAID.

Unfortunately, due to unforeseeable events in Papua New Guinea several Southern Highlanders who had accepted invitations to the workshop were unable to attend, and several who did participate were unable to provide papers for the book. Other chapters in the volume were added after the workshop. Things move quickly in Papua New Guinea, and although some papers were updated prior to publication, inevitably some have been overtaken by the course of events. Notwithstanding this, we believe that the present collection provides a useful background to recent developments and conflicts in the Southern Highlands and offers some insights into the prospects for conflict resolution or minimisation.

The editors are grateful to AusAID for its support of the project, and to the various contributors for their inputs and patience. They would also like to thank David Hegarty, convenor of the State, Society and Governance in Melanesia Program and Sue Rider, the Program's executive officer. Technical support was efficiently provided by Warren Mayes.

Opening Remarks

Stephanie Copus-Campbell

On behalf of AusAID, it is a pleasure to participate in this project, particularly given that I had the opportunity to work on the Southern Highlands for a short period following the 2002 elections, long enough to realise how much there is to learn about its potential, its complexities and challenges. The Southern Highlands is the economic engine of Papua New Guinea, delivering close to 15 per cent of the country's GDP. It is culturally rich and spectacularly beautiful. It has numerous tribal groups and languages. Tribal fighting is commonplace and complicated by an alarming number of firearms. As in much of Papua New Guinea, there is a growing problem with HIV/AIDS. Southern Highlands is one of the richest provinces in Papua New Guinea if you look at the provincial coffers, but one of the poorest if you consider how resources are spread amongst the population: service delivery is poor, with basic services not reaching a high proportion of the people.

My colleagues and I look forward to learning more about the potential challenges facing the Southern Highlands. We are especially keen to discuss issues of conflict and conflict prevention. Conflict in the Southern Highlands is of concern to Australia for a number of reasons. It has contributed (and has the potential to further contribute) to failed service delivery, and more generally threatens good development outcomes; violence after the 2002 elections, for example, resulted in the closing of schools, hospitals, banks, and trade stores; telephones were down and many roads impassable. There is a potential for conflict to spill over into other areas of Papua New Guinea. Conflict threatens key mineral resource projects that are vital to Papua New Guinea's already cash-strapped national economy.

To date, the Australian aid program has provided assistance to the Southern Highlands largely through national programs, including programs in health, education and law and justice. In 2003, in close consultation and cooperation with the Papua New Guinea government, Australia contributed $A1.4 million to assist with the management of the Southern Highlands supplementary elections. And, at the request of Sir Peter Barter, then Minister for Inter-Government Relations, Australia provided two-way radios in a number of hospitals and aid posts to assist with communications. As the aid program evolves to look at more innovative and effective ways to deliver assistance, we are exploring how we can work more directly at the provincial level, especially in the area of good governance.

We welcome frank discussion on the role the aid program can play in conflict prevention, and more generally in achieving development outcomes. However, in any such discussion it is important to be realistic and remember that the responsibility for achieving positive results ultimately rests with the government of Papua New Guinea and the people of the Southern Highlands.

In writing these opening remarks, I was reminded of a story from my childhood. The local school board refused to accept the introduction of a foreign language into the primary school curriculum because of its concern about undermining cultural values. The primary school children were, at best, the victims of a missed opportunity to expand their horizons and develop a new skill. Worse, they were subjected to a narrow-minded and misinformed cultural view that might have had negative repercussions on the role they would eventually play in a global society.

What is the moral of this story to us today? It reminds me of the importance for donors and other stakeholders of coming to understand the challenges facing the Southern Highlands with an open mind that includes an acceptance and understanding of culture and an attitude that a 'different way of doing things' is quite possibly the 'right way of doing them'. It is also important that before any action is taken there is a thorough understanding of the dynamics of the situation and how donor programs/activities/decisions can, if not well understood and thought through, become part of the problem, rather than the solution.

In this context AusAID welcomes this project, as we continue to develop our approach to addressing issues in the Southern Highlands, and Papua New Guinea more generally.

Introduction: Roots of conflict in the Southern Highlands

Nicole Haley and Ronald J. May

For a number of years the Southern Highlands Province (SHP) has been riven by conflict. Longstanding inter-group rivalries, briefly set aside during the colonial period, have been compounded by competition for the benefits provided by the modern state and by fighting over the distribution of returns from the several big mining and petroleum projects located within the province or impinging upon it.[1] According to some reports, deaths from the various conflicts in the province over the past decade number in the hundreds.[2] As a result of inter-group fighting, criminal activity, vandalism and politically motivated actions, a number of businesses, banks and post offices throughout the province have ceased operating. There are no longer any banking and postal facilities outside the Mendi area. As at September 2004 the Mendi branch of Bank South Pacific was the only remaining commercial banking facility in the province, and several large business houses had shut. Best Buy Mendi and the Coca Cola depot both shut in September 2004, resulting in more than 100 jobs lost. Business leaders attributed these business closures to ongoing law and order problems and a dwindling cash economy (*Post-Courier* 24 September 2004). Schools, vocational and training colleges, health centres, hospitals, and guesthouses have closed, sometimes temporarily, often permanently. As at August 2004, Minister for Inter-Government Relations, Sir Peter Barter, reported that 11 of the 12 high schools and all of the secondary schools in Southern Highlands Province were shut (*Post-Courier* 05 August 2004). Dauli teachers college and the Mendi school of nursing remain shut, and Tari hospital is without a doctor. On several occasions government offices in Mendi and Tari have been burned down or destroyed by the supporters of disgruntled political candidates. In December 2002, for instance, fourteen government offices in Mendi were destroyed by fire (*Post-Courier* 9 December 2002). Roadblocks and ambushes have made travel dangerous in many parts of the province and almost all scheduled passenger flights have been cancelled. Expatriate missionaries, volunteers and aid workers have been withdrawn from the province; and for some time Australia's Department of Foreign Affairs and Trade travel advisories have specifically warned visitors to Papua New Guinea against travel to the Southern Highlands. Very few public servants can be found at their posts (although thousands remain on the payroll), and state services have ground to a halt. Corruption is rife. The authority of the state in the Southern Highlands has been regularly challenged and police are often reluctant to act because they are outnumbered and outgunned. The costs in both human and material terms have been substantial. Minister for Inter-Government Relations, Sir Peter Barter, is reported to have said that SHP is at risk of becoming 'a failed province' (*Post-Courier* 21 October 2002).

The problems that have beset SHP were highlighted during Papua New Guinea's 2002 national elections, which were characterised by violence and malpractice of a scale never before seen in Papua New Guinea (Standish 2000). Even in the context of national elections now characterised by 'gunpoint democracy' (Standish 1996, 2000), the Southern Highlands elections were particularly violent. A number of people (including police) were killed; a high profile candidate was kidnapped and held for ransom; all airstrips in the western end of the province were closed following threats that planes would be shot out of the sky, and people throughout the province were threatened and intimidated by wealthy candidates and their supporters, often armed with high-powered weapons (Haley 2004). In July 2002, following clarification from the Supreme Court of Papua New Guinea, the 2002 national elections were deemed to have failed in six of the SHP's nine electorates, leaving the greater part of the province's population without political representation for some ten months.

The declaration that the SHP elections had failed resulted in widespread confusion and a further escalation of violence throughout the province. Disgruntled electors felled dozens of power pylons between Nogoli and Porgera and production at the Porgera Gold Mine in Enga Province consequently had to be suspended for three months (see Lavu, this volume). Thousands of employees were stood down and much revenue was lost. In the weeks following the election the leading candidates in the six undeclared SHP seats declared themselves to be duly elected to parliament (*Post-Courier* 5 August 2002). They and their supporters subsequently threatened disruption of the province's resource projects and promised to 'bring the nation to its knees' if their demands to be sworn in were not acceded to (*Post-Courier* 9 August 2002). The group of six also wrote to the Prime Minister, Sir Michael Somare, threatening that the SHP would secede. John Honale, a spokesman for the group's supporters, was reported to have said:

> I'm giving the Somare-led government until 4.06 pm tomorrow to declare the remaining six seats … If we don't have a reply [to the above mentioned letter] by 4.06 (close of business) tomorrow, then the Southern Highlanders will become a republic country … More people will die. Roads will be blocked; more bridges will be blown up (*Post-Courier* 9 August 2002).

Despite this pressure, the six leading candidates were not sworn in. They and their supporters were forced to wait a further nine months for fresh elections. During this time much energy was spent restoring law and order within the province, in preparation for the supplementary elections.

Supplementary elections were held in the Southern Highlands in April/May 2003. The Electoral Commission managed these elections with the assistance of 2000 additional police, soldiers and prison warders. Despite the additional security presence, the elections were still marred by violence and irregular voting. Large numbers of extra votes were cast in the Nipa-Kutubu and Koroba-Lake Kopiago electorates and many people were unable to vote due to intimidation or because candidates and their core supporters filled out the ballot papers themselves (*Post-Courier* 12 May 2003). During the count a polling official was beaten in front of international observers (*Post-Courier* 7 May 2003) and three weeks later the same man was killed. Initial reports implicated the security forces in his death (*Post-Courier* 30 May-1 June 2003).

The place of conflict in SHP

Goldman (this volume) reminds us that conflict is an integral part of life in the Southern Highlands: 'fighting is both a recurrent and legitimate means of prosecuting claims or seeking restitution' in many Papua New Guinean societies. Conflict *per se* is not considered inimical to social order. Rather, what is important is the way people engage with, handle, and control conflict in a particular context. When controlled and properly contained, conflict is a major feature of sociality in the Southern Highlands. It is unmediated conflict which is problematic. This is a key to understanding the problems facing the Southern Highlands, for there seems to be a diminished capacity to control and contain conflict in the contemporary context.

During the workshop discussion, James Weiner argued that disjunctures between the state and local conceptions of exchange and personhood have served to exacerbate local tensions, contributing to increasingly unmanageable social relations. He noted that the Foi (Southern Highlanders from the Lake Kutubu area) traditionally responded to conflict and unmanageable social relations by dissolving clan ties and moving or relocating. Social life, he observed, was more fluid prior to the imposition of the state, and people had at their disposal dispute-resolution strategies which allowed them to interrupt or contain conflict. The effects of representative politics and land registration in the context of resource development have, however, countervailed the impulse to disaggregate and increased the potential for conflict.

Moreover, traditional dispute resolution mechanisms are not equipped to counter new forms of fighting, which are larger in scale, more violent, and involve high-powered weapons. Traditional dispute resolution mechanisms are necessarily limited, and incapable of dealing with the widespread nature of modern warfare.

The changing nature of conflict in SHP

Several of the workshop participants, especially those who had worked in Papua New Guinea before independence, noted that the Southern Highlands was relatively quiet through the 1970s and 1980s, and that fighting, when it occurred at that time, was usually contained. This was due in part to the fact that many young men were employed outside the province, initially through the Highlands Labour Scheme and because kiaps continued to coordinate and dominate activities in the Southern Highlands well into the 1970s (Ballard 1983:175).

Throughout the 1990s, however, fighting in the Southern Highlands became increasingly violent and protracted, so much so that lawlessness now prevails in many areas. The upsurge in fighting in SHP seems to have coincided with the advent of large-scale resource development projects. Indeed many of the ongoing conflicts concern the distribution of oil and gas royalties and access to project-related benefits. Concomitant with this, many of the workshop participants observed that in the past 15 years or so new-style leaders have emerged and they, along with the younger generation of which they are a part, have come to disregard the norms, values and mechanisms of dispute settlement upheld by the older generation (see Walters, this volume). This has resulted in a situation in which communities are less able to manage conflict.

In the context of resource development, traditional leadership roles have been reassessed, such that young educated men, perceived to be better able to communicate with company representatives, have assumed leadership roles — in many cases to the detriment of their communities. While these new leaders may well have a good command of English, they often lack the leadership skills needed for effective conflict management. Instead of employing oratory to resolve disputes, they rely increasingly on high-powered weapons. In the Southern Highlands today, the majority of adult men either own or have access to a home-made shot gun if not an imported weapon. The prevalence of high-powered weapons throughout the province has meant that the police are often out-gunned and therefore reluctant to tackle the escalating law and order problems.

The past 15 years have also seen the advent of more insidious forms of violence. Goldman (this volume) observes that new forms of injury, including maiming, are now being perpetrated and that armed *raskol* gangs roam the province. In some cases 'hired guns' have been brought into the conflict by warring groups. Some groups within the Southern Highlands have begun to employ terrorist tactics, such as kidnapping and demanding ransom (Haley 2004).

Roots of conflict in the Southern Highlands

Without exception participants at the workshop agreed, notwithstanding the traditional sociality of conflict, that conflict is a serious impediment to

4

development and that the situation in the Southern Highlands is in urgent need of redress. There is a comprehensive breakdown of law and order, and state service provision has all but ceased. The past 15-20 years have seen public servants move in the first instance to larger centres and more recently to other provinces, where they can secure basic services for their own families.

Why is the situation in the Southern Highlands so poor? One of the recurring observations made by workshop participants was that the problems in SHP do not relate to lack of income as such, but to the distribution and reinvestment of that income. This view is endorsed by Sir Peter Barter. In a press release dated 24 February 2003, he noted that SHP is the richest province 'because of the flow from the oil and gas projects' and the poorest province 'because those resources have been squandered'. The widespread mismanagement and misappropriation of government funds as well as oil and gas royalties has meant that although the Southern Highlands is home to several of Papua New Guinea's successful resource projects, the majority of Southern Highlanders have gained little benefit from the projects being undertaken in their province. This is a source of ongoing discontent within the province. One often hears Southern Highlanders ask: why is SHP so disadvantaged relative to other parts of Papua New Guinea when it is home to many of the country's resource projects? In the words of James Marape, a candidate for the Tari Open electorate in 2002:

> Something has to be done because we are contributing so much to this country's economy and there is no justification in the distribution of government services back into our part of the province (*Independent* 28 August 2002).

Clearly, a major source of conflict in the Southern Highlands is inequitable access to state services and to the 'benefits' of resource development. Other sources of tension and conflict include ethnic divisions, lack of effective administration and governance, and unrealistic expectations about resource development.

Background

SHP, one of Papua New Guinea's largest provinces, and its most populous, comprises eight districts — Koroba-Lake Kopiago, Tari-Pori, Komo-Magarima, Nipa-Kutubu, Mendi, Imbonggu, Ialibu-Pangia and Kagua-Erave — occupying 25,700 km². It is presently home to an estimated 500,000 people.[3] Much of the province is poorly suited to agriculture and more than half the province presently remains unoccupied for this reason (Hanson *et al* 2001 and see Allen, this volume). The Southern Highlands accounts for 11 per cent of Papua New Guinea's rural population (ibid:91) and 10.6 per cent of Papua New Guinea's total population (National Census 2000).

Figure 1.1. Resource development in PNG including Southern Highlands Province

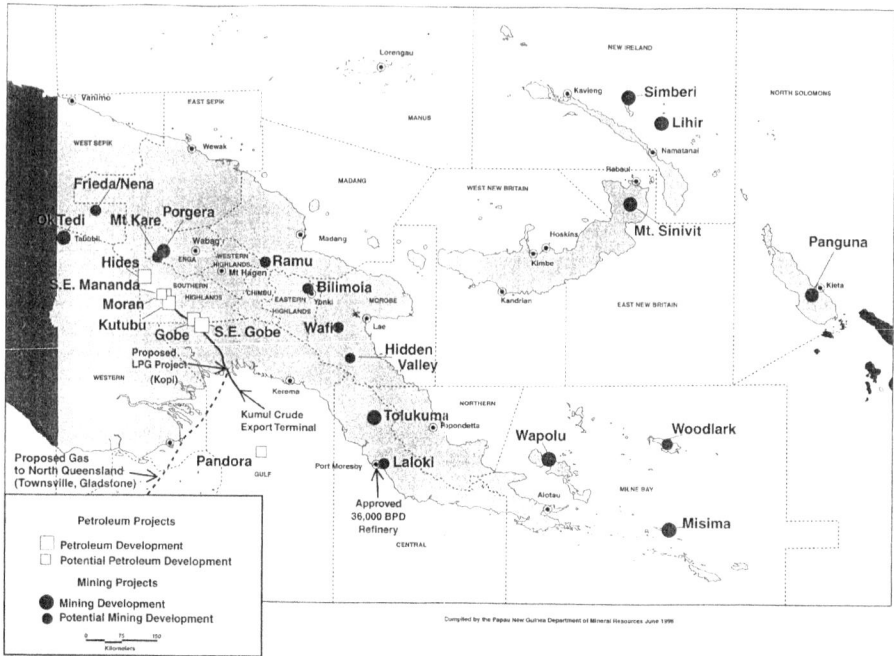

For the most part, the peoples of SHP are concentrated in the central and eastern parts of the province. They tend to live in dispersed households rather than in nucleated settlements or villages, and this makes service delivery somewhat more difficult than in other areas. The Tari Basin and Nembi Plateau are the most densely populated parts of the province (190 persons/km²), closely followed by the Upper Mendi and Lai Valleys (120 persons/km²) (Hanson *et al* 2001:91; Bourke *et al* 1995:27). High density populations (61-100 persons/km²) are also found around Ialibu, between Mendi and Kagua, between Nipa and Magarima, in the Wage Valley, on the Paijaka Plateau and in the Koroba, Komo and Benaria areas. By contrast, the Erave, Bosavi, Kutubu and Lake Kopiago areas, located to the south and northwest of the province, are only moderately populated, while the Lebani Valley, Yeru/Bogaia and Hewa areas are only very sparsely populated (less than 5 persons/km²). The highest populations are found where land potential is the greatest, so there is limited potential for further agricultural growth within the province.

Inequitable access to services

Southern Highlanders experience differential access to services. Nowadays, only the most densely populated areas of the Southern Highlands are connected by the existing road system. The more remote outlying areas are accessed only by air or by foot; in many cases, roads formerly maintained have been allowed to fall into such a state of disrepair that they are no longer open to vehicular traffic. A case in point is the loop road from Koroba to Lake Kopiago.

Twenty per cent of the province's population (approx 100,000 people) now live in places which are accessible only by air.[4] For these people it is increasingly difficult to access their provincial headquarters in Mendi and/or a major service centre such as Mount Hagen. There are no longer regular passenger flights between Mendi and the western end of the province, and the cost of flying has risen astronomically. Whereas people living in the central and eastern end of the province (Mendi, Ialibu and Kagua) can access Mount Hagen in less than three hours by way of a K10 PMV (Passenger Motor Vehicle) ride, people living in Bosavi and the remote western end of the province must rely on air travel which is increasingly beyond their reach. For example, it now costs K388 to fly one-way from Lake Kopiago to Mt Hagen while less than ten years ago it cost only K70 to fly from Lake Kopiago to the provincial headquarters.

To put this further in perspective, incomes throughout the Southern Highlands are typically low to very low, for the most part being less than K20 person/year. The exceptions to this are the areas around Kutubu, Pangia and Mendi, where incomes are moderate, being in the order of K41-100 person/year (Hanson *et al* 2001:91), due to oil and gas royalties, coffee sales and the diversion of government funds respectively. The average person in the Southern Highlands can no longer afford to fly.

Consideration of access and income leads directly to the subject of disadvantage. A recent study by Hanson *et al* (2001) calculated an index of disadvantage for each district of Papua New Guinea, based on five parameters: land potential, agricultural pressure, access to services, income from agriculture, and child malnutrition. The study suggested that people living within the Koroba-Lake Kopiago and Nipa-Kutubu districts were 'extremely disadvantaged' (thirteen districts in the country were classified as 'extremely disadvantaged') and that people living in the Komo-Magarima and Kagua-Erave districts were seriously disadvantaged relative to the national average. The study also observed that the Koroba-Lake Kopiago and Nipa-Kutubu districts have been found to be among the twenty most disadvantaged districts in three separate studies over a 25-year period (Wilson 1974; de Albuquerque and D'Sa 1986; Hanson *et al* 2001).

Thus the 100,000 or so people living in the remote areas of SHP are not just the most disadvantaged and disenfranchised within the province, but are some of the most disadvantaged in Papua New Guinea. These peoples live in poor environments and have low incomes and very poor access to services. They lack schools and health facilities and cannot retain public servants posted there. They are among the most vulnerable in Papua New Guinea with respect to long-term food security (Bourke 2001:11). There are several reasons for this disadvantage, the most significant being demography and remoteness, which conspire to render service provision expensive and difficult. Hanson *et al* (2001:304) note that the most disadvantaged districts tend to be located adjacent to provincial borders, and that the peoples living in such areas tend to be ignored by all provincial administrations. The devaluation of the national currency and the concomitant rise in the cost of air travel have served to further isolate these areas. Local trade stores have ceased to operate due to exorbitant transportation costs, and most of the public servants have absconded. Remoteness, coupled with poor business skills, has contributed to the failure of commercial agricultural ventures such as cattle, coffee and chillies.

The situation in the Lake Kopiago sub-district provides a snapshot of what life is like for Southern Highlanders living in the remote rural parts of the province. As one moves northwest from Tari, what little infrastructure there is in the province completely dissipates. For example, the reasonably well-maintained and graded roads and iron bridges of the Tari and Koroba areas give way to a 4WD track with log bridges, and thence to barely-defined walking tracks. There is no health extension officer at the sub-district health centre, the last one having left in 1996; the local nurses and health workers posted to the area have since relocated to Mount Hagen, as have the school teachers. There are no police or village court magistrates. Health and immunisation patrols have ceased, and formal education is at risk of being completely phased out.

It is now 15 years since Lake-Kopiago Community School (now a top-up primary) has had a full compliment of teachers, and there is a whole generation of children who have had no formal schooling. More critical, though, is the fact that the implementation of an elementary school system has stalled. Years 1, 2 and 3 were suspended in 1999 under the New Education Reforms; no elementary schools have been formally registered and no training of teachers has taken place within the Lake Kopiago sub-district. In fact, there have been no lower-level primary classes in the sub-district for five years. In the remote areas of SHP the education reforms have done nothing more than formally phase out education.

Much has been made of Governor Hami Yawari's free education policy launched in February 2004, but even this has done little to improve the situation in the most remote parts of the province, where schools remain shut due to teacher shortages and absences.

With road closures and the rising cost of air travel, local cash economies have all but ceased to function in many areas. Indeed, whereas in the mid 1990s one could buy all manner of store goods in the half dozen or so large trade stores then operating on Kopiago station, now there is nothing. With the closure of trade stores, local markets have also ceased to function, as there is no incentive for men and women to sell local produce. These developments have important implications for food security, as there is now far less capacity to deal with large-scale environmental hazards, such as drought. As Bourke (2001:11) has observed, low cash incomes represent a major threat to food security in the longer term.

That districts such as Koroba-Lake Kopiago, Komo-Magarima, Nipa-Kutubu and Kagua-Erave rate amongst the poorest in Papua New Guinea, is of concern for many reasons, not least because several resource projects are situated within SHP. This is an ongoing source of discontent at many levels within the province. Southern Highlanders often complain that they have not benefited from the oil and gas production going on in their province. It is this discontent which has fuelled the calls for a Hela Province, and which led to the formation of the United Resources Party (see Haley, this volume). Various groups within the Southern Highlands hold the view that others within the province have benefited disproportionately from resource development projects, and this too is a source of ongoing discontent. In part these complaints can be explained in terms of unrealistic expectations, but it remains the case that the various resource projects within SHP have failed to alleviate rural poverty or reduce the overall level of disadvantage of the districts in which they are situated.[5] Likewise, they have failed to bring about local-level development.

Ethnic tensions and lack of effective administration and governance

A quite different type of conflict both within the province and within individual districts can be attributed to ethnic tensions. Electoral boundaries within SHP do not coincide with ethnic ones. Huli speakers, for instance, are found not only in Tari district, but also in the Koroba-Lake Kopiago, Komo-Magarima and Nipu-Kutubu districts. Likewise, Mendi speakers are found not only in the Mendi district but also in the Nipa-Kutubu and Imbonggu districts. Even smaller groups such as the Duna, who number about 30,000, are split between districts, with three quarters of their population in the Koroba-Lake Kopiago district and the remaining quarter in the Tari district.

There are at least 16 languages spoken within SHP. Of these, the big three — Huli (140,000), Mendi (115,000) and Kewa (100,000) — account for more than 70 per cent of the province's population. This in itself has created much political tension over the years as elected representatives from the various groups have jostled to establish themselves at the top of the province's pecking order. It has also seen the province divide politically, with the Huli-speaking areas of Koroba-Tari-Komo-Magarima in the west, the Mendi-speaking Mendi and Nipa areas in the centre, and Imbonggu and Kewa-speaking Ialibu-Kagua area in the east. These divisions are reflected in current administration policy such that there are assistant provincial administrators for the western end, eastern end and Mendi central area respectively.

Figure 1.2. Southern Highlands agricultural systems and cultural groups

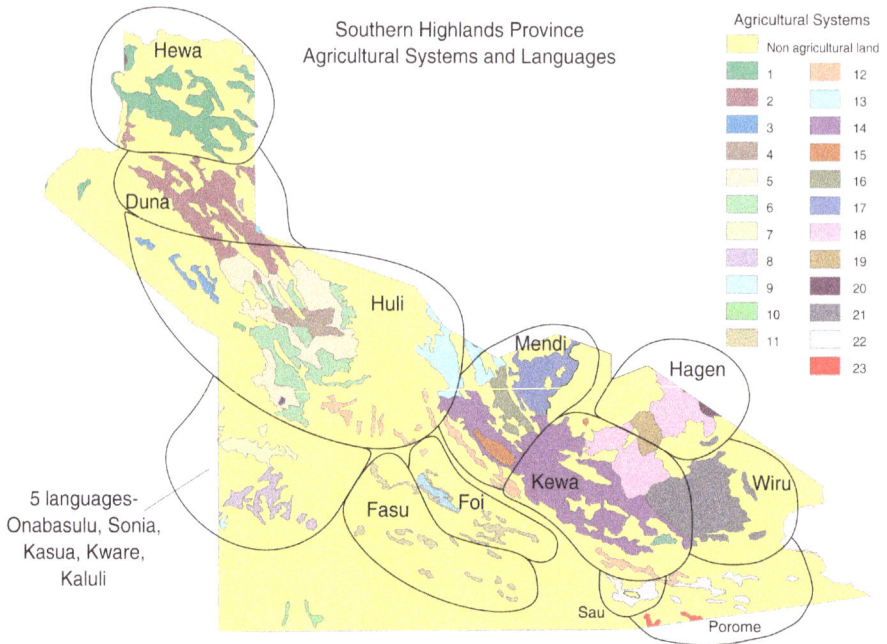

Conflict between the west, the centre, and east of the province has raged for many years, resulting in fighting and road closures in and around Nipa and Magarima. Much of the fighting in recent years has revolved around allegations concerning the death of the former governor, Dick Mune. It was alleged that Mune (from Nipa), who died in a car accident, had in fact been killed by Anderson Agiru, the Huli man who succeeded him as governor in 1997. Specifically, it was rumoured that Anderson Agiru had employed sorcery techniques obtained in the east to bring about Mune's death. Following Mune's death the Nipa people blocked the highway, thereby denying Hulis access to Mendi, the provincial headquarters, and interrupting service provision to the western end of the province.

Such rumour, innuendo and conflict are not entirely new. In July 1980 when the then provincial premier Andrew Andaija died in a plane crash, less than a month after being re-elected, the Huli refused to accept that his death was an unfortunate accident. Instead they blamed the people of Ialibu, Pangia, Kagua and Erave, alleging that some form of sorcery or *poison* had been used to bring the plane down. Andrew Andaija's death, like Dick Mune's, fuelled east-west animosity and resulted in ongoing conflict. In the months following Andaija's death, Hulis attempted to kill the then member for Imbonggu, Glaimi Warena, and were also allegedly responsible for an incident in which Wiwa Korowi was stoned in Port Moresby. At the time, the *Post-Courier* reported that 'east-west animosity between the people of the Southern Highlands is emerging as a serious threat to harmony in the province' (*Post-Courier* 21 August 1980:19).

Ethnic conflicts across the province such as this between the Hulis and Mendis, as well as smaller-scale conflicts at the district level, have proved a significant impediment to effective administration. The result is that the province's ethnic minorities have continually been denied services by their political representatives, who have until now almost always been members of the dominant ethnic groups.[6]

Governance in the Southern Highlands is severely compromised. The past two decades have seen the effectiveness of the courts, police and law enforcement agencies stripped away (see Bragge, Goldman and Warrilow, this volume). The administration has lost the capacity to deal with the province's problems, due in part to ongoing political interference and a lack of administrative accountability.

At the provincial level, jockeying for control of the province between the Huli speakers in the west, the Mendi speakers in the central area and the Kewa-speaking peoples of the east has led to the formation of competing administrations; this has proved an impediment to effective administration and good governance. All too often administrative appointments in the Southern Highlands have been made on the basis of ethnicity and this has resulted in tit-for-tat sackings and reappointments over many years. At present, there are not only new administrative appointees but also people appointed by the two previous governors (Dick Mune and Anderson Agiru) and the various interim administrations of SHP, all of whom claim to hold the same positions. Indeed, at one point not long ago, four different men were being paid as administrator of the SHP. Many people politically aligned with and employed under Dick Mune's administration remain on the government payroll, as do those loyal to and appointed by Anderson Agiru. Under Anderson Agiru's administration many public servants from the western end of the province were transferred into the Ialibu-Pangia area, thereby aggravating tensions between the eastern and central areas. And during the period of the interim administration, people from the eastern end of the province were appointed to positions in the west.

As well as the inevitable tensions this creates, government expenditure is in consequence far greater than it need be, especially when, as is often the case, none of the public servants appointed to a position is actually doing the job he or she is paid for. For example, the Assistant District Administrator (ADA) officially appointed to Lake Kopiago has never taken up his posting there, although he continues to draw his salary as if he were the ADA. He refused to take up his posting to Kopiago, after being threatened by Anderson Agiru's supporters.[7] The man who has for the past six years paraded himself as ADA is a former community school teacher with no administrative training appointed by Anderson Agiru. Most government appointments throughout the province appear to be duplicated in this way, and most are political appointments. During the period 1997-2002 there were two competing administrations in Koroba-Lake Kopiago District — one established by the national MP, Herowa Agiwa, and another by former governor, Anderson Agiru. All the public servants politically appointed during this period appear to continue to draw government salaries.

Added to this is the problem of village-based appointments. This, too, creates local-level tensions. In the absence of the public servants appointed to various positions, local communities have often appointed community leaders to undertake responsibilities. In the Kopiago sub-district, for example, peace and good order committees, village magistrates and lands mediators have been appointed by villagers. None of these people get paid for the work they do. Yet their appointed counterparts sit in Mendi and Mount Hagen and get paid for doing nothing. This creates resentment in the village.

Good governance in the Southern Highlands is also impeded by entrenched corruption at all levels of government, and the presence of high-powered weapons throughout the province. For the most part it is the elected representatives and their fellow candidates who have added the weapons to the mix of ethnic tensions and brewing resentments. In the lead-up to both the 1997 and 2002 national elections, prominent candidates stockpiled weapons and distributed them amongst their supporters. In one case, a prominent candidate flew in cartons of semi-automatic weapons purchased in China while on an official government visit, so that his supporters might usurp control of the elections on polling day. And in the lead-up to polling in the failed 2002 elections, Stanley Kotange, the district administrator for Koroba-Lake Kopiago, wrote to the Mission Aviation Fellowship (MAF), Hevilift and various other air charter companies, warning that local candidates and their supporters were in possession of AK47s, M16s, M202s, SLRs and 303 rifles as well as hand-held rocket launchers and that they intended to shoot down any planes or helicopters attempting to move ballot boxes. Very few of these weapons have been recovered or handed in during the much publicised gun surrenders. Cutting off the flows of money from elected politicians and politically appointed public servants to local militants is crucial to the task of restoring law and order.

Unrealistic expectations about resource development

Many of the workshop participants, particularly those associated with resource developers, felt that inflated landowner expectations were a source of conflict and potential conflict within the province (see Lavu, this volume). Because of the almost complete absence of functioning state services, resource developers within the Southern Highlands, through their community development programs, have taken on the important role of basic service provision. Ken Logan (Porgera Joint Venture, Community Affairs) noted that frustrated and disgruntled landowners often take out their dissatisfaction with the government upon the resource developers. In the period leading up to and following the failed 2002 national elections, Southern Highlanders felled powerlines between Nogoli and Porgera so as to shut down mining operations and hold the government to ransom.

Much of the current conflict associated with resource development projects is directly attributed to state failure: the failure to provide basic services such as health and education; the failure to mediate land and royalty disputes; the failure to address existing law and order problems; the failure to quell unrealistic expectations; and a lack of accountability in relation to the expenditure of funds generated by resource development. Throughout the Southern Highlands one regularly encounters the sentiment that the money being generated through resource development is not being channelled back into rural areas, and this is an ongoing source of discontent.

The state has not only failed to resolve royalty disputes in relation to existing projects, but corrupt politicians and public servants have misused funds generated by the resource projects. An audit of the Southern Highlands administration covering the period 1998 to 2002 revealed a complex pattern of mismanagement and misappropriation involving politicians, public servants, businessmen, and friends of politicians, going back many years. And although this report was released to the fraud squad over two ago, no prosecutions have ensued.

The major resource operations within SHP are now drawing to a close. However, as Lavu (this volume) notes, there is widespread disbelief that this will actually happen. Lavu cites an apparent expectation that the resource developers 'will be there forever' and predicts that such unrealistic expectations will lead not only to disappointment but ongoing conflict. Warrilow (this volume) likewise argues that further resource development on the existing scale is highly unlikely in the current climate, because, although there are several exploration projects underway, there is little likelihood that resource developers will invest, given the current atmosphere of distrust and lawlessness. Future resource development, it seems, will be dependent upon whether the Southern Highlands can be transformed into 'a place where development can take place'.

In the context of resource development, exchange expectations have also been inflated and this has made the management of exchange relations all the more difficult. Compensation and bride price payments have risen exponentially throughout the province, even outside the immediate project areas.

Early predictions

As O'Collins (this volume) points out, much of SHP came under administrative control very late, and as a result was not derestricted until the mid 1960s, or later in the case of the Hewa.[8] Media and government patrol reports from the late 1960s and early 1970s indicate that the majority of Southern Highlanders did not want self-government or independence, and that while patrol officers in other parts of the country were busy introducing new crops, those in the more remote parts of the SHP were preoccupied with contacting, censusing and giving political education talks to the communities within their jurisdiction. In 1970 the patrol officer at Lake Kopiago observed, 'generally the Tumbudu people have shown little interest in or understanding of the House of Assembly, despite political education talks given on every patrol' (Newell 1970:4).

When Papua New Guinea gained independence there were still no schools in the most remote parts of the Southern Highlands. Those in what is now the Koroba-Kopiago district had been operational for only a decade, and the province's first secondary schools had only been operating eight years. By comparison with other parts of Papua New Guinea, SHP lacked the capacity in terms of qualified personnel — its 'educated elite was both small and dispersed' (Ballard 1983:179) — to govern itself and this has been well reflected in the various crises which have beset the province. The problems which have emerged were in fact predicted by the then House of Assembly members and members of the Southern Highlands District Area Authority, who repeatedly rejected self-government and independence as premature. These members made the Constitutional Planning Committee aware of their views and wrote to the Chief Minister, Michael Somare, and the Australian Prime Minister, Gough Whitlam, urging them to conduct a referendum on the issue of independence. They also made their views public. In the lead-up to independence the councillor for Ialibu was reported as saying:

> We aren't ready and don't want it. If we get it now we will go backwards rapidly. Only Moresby and Lae will survive as they will be the last refuges of overseas people, thus the last places with any organisation and efficiency. We in the bush will collapse as the overseas officers leave us (*Post-Courier* 19 June 1974).

Andrew Andaija, the deputy chair of the Southern Highlands District Area Authority, expressed similar sentiments:

> Tari is violently opposed to Independence. All the lying and covering up makes no difference to us. We don't want it and it's no use the Government saying nothing will change after Independence. It obviously will change. Overseas people will leave and we are not capable of replacing them now and won't be for years. Finish the lying and let us get used to self-government and get organised first (*Post-Courier* 19 June 1974).

Matiabe Yuwi, the member for Tari-Komo, likewise endorsed the view that the Southern Highlanders lacked the capacity to govern themselves and effectively administer their own province:

> This is a big matter. Why don't we want it? We are worried, very worried. We aren't stupid and nor do we say we will never have Independence or that we have to keep the white men forever. But think: communications, education, businesses are non-existent and we have no experienced local public servants to take over ...We have self-government and enough power already but we have no judges, competent military services or experienced men in the field. We will never be satisfied without a referendum. Do we have any Highlanders as directors or heads of departments? No, we don't; we see Tolais, Bukas, some Papuans and others in the big jobs but no Highlanders' (*Post-Courier* 19 June 1974).

Andrew Wabiria, the MHA for Koroba-Kopiago, was similarly opposed to independence, and publicly urged the Australian government to reverse its policy of withdrawing expatriate officers. He was quoted in the *Post-Courier* (13 August 1974) as saying, 'experienced expatriate officers are needed in the Southern Highlands District to assist the settlement of land and other disputes'.

That community schools were late to open and have in the past decade closed at an alarming rate, means that literacy levels within the Southern Highlands are low and do not reach more than 50 per cent for males and 30 per cent for females anywhere in SHP (see Allen, this volume). This has ongoing implications for good governance. Throughout much of the Southern Highlands there has been negligible primary education for the past 15 years, resulting in an entire generation of young adults who have missed out on formal schooling. In much of the Southern Highlands literacy levels must be falling, with serious long-term implications for the province.

HIV/AIDS

Also looming is the HIV/AIDS epidemic. Already people in remote areas of the province are dying of AIDS-related illnesses, yet HIV/AIDS awareness and prevention campaigns are yet to reach these areas and there is little scope for future intervention. How are messages about preventative measures to reach the most remote corners of the province when the schools and health centres have shut, and people lack even the most rudimentary health services? In places like Kopiago those most at risk are the generation of young people who have missed out on formal education — a cohort of young people who are neither literate, nor fluent in Tok Pisin.

In rural areas throughout the highlands, people are now dying from AIDS-related illnesses, and these deaths are being blamed on witchcraft and sorcery (*Post-Courier* 13 May 2004). Women in the Southern Highlands and elsewhere in Papua New Guinea are, as a result, being tortured and killed in trials of increasing regularity. In December 2003 one such witch trial occurred at Lake Kopiago (see Haley 2004). During the course of this witch hunt and trial six women were held captive and repeatedly tortured over the space of a fortnight. One woman died as a result and the others sustained horrific disabling injuries. The attackers in this instance were boys in their late teens — boys who have missed out on the opportunity for formal schooling due to school closures and teacher shortages. This event and others in the area have not been formally investigated and it is unlikely that the perpetrators will be punished as there are no police or magistrates in the Kopiago sub-district.

Contemporary witch hunts and trials being reported across the highlands appear to be linked to the burgeoning HIV/AIDS epidemic. The Kopiago witch trial, for example, was precipitated by the first instances of AIDS-related deaths in the area, and the women who were tortured were accused of killing a young man who most likely died of AIDS-related tuberculosis. The link to AIDS, the breakdown of essential services, and the emergent practice of witch hunts in which women accused of witchcraft are violently tortured alerts us to the possibility that Papua New Guinea's HIV/AIDS epidemic not only has huge public health and development implications but that it looms as an unresolved law and order issue.

Conclusion

It is clear that conflict and disorder in the Southern Highlands are not amenable to simple explanations or easy solutions. Fighting appears to have been a historic feature of social relations in the Southern Highlands. But the nature of conflict and the mechanisms available to control conflict and promote reconciliation have been irrevocably changed by the colonial experience, the expansion of inter-group relations which the Australian administration set in train, and the introduction of an overarching state — no matter how tenuous the state's presence might have been in some parts of the province. The intrusion of large resource projects has also had a major, though uneven impact on Southern Highlands' communities, both culturally and materially, by generating new income flows and at times providing community services which the state has been unable to provide.

Despite the revenue generated by these resource projects, there is little evidence of the benefits that this wealth might have been expected to bring. Royalties are consistently alleged to have been misused and squandered and far from improving the well being of Southern Highlands communities, these new sources of revenue have created new sources of friction within and between communities, such that Southern Highlanders are now fighting for access to the limited state delivered services and to the benefits and services resource developers can provide.

At the same time, the declining capacity of the state to assert its authority against *raskol* gangs, local 'warlords' and corrupt politicians has undermined the state's legitimacy and fostered a downward spiral of weak governance, lawlessness and violent conflict. One manifestation of this has been the failure of elections in the province, at both national and local levels, and as a consequence the effective disabling of the provincial assembly.

Unchecked conflict is, of course, a serious impediment to development, and it is all well and good to better understand the roots of conflict in the Southern Highlands, but where does that leave us? What can be done to improve the situation for Southern Highlanders? Hanson *et al* (2001:313) recommend that 'disadvantaged districts' be formally incorporated into national policies so that the inequalities they identified at district levels might be addressed. On the basis of their study Southern Highlands was one of the most disadvantaged provinces with five of the eight districts being rated as either extremely disadvantaged or seriously disadvantaged with respect to the rest of Papua New Guinea.

Until the overall level of disadvantage throughout the Southern Highlands is improved the distribution of resources will remain a source of conflict. The problems facing the Southern Highlands need therefore to be addressed as a matter of urgency, because as the post-election violence which accompanied the 2002 national elections demonstrated, political instability in the highlands can and does affect the flow of resources throughout the country.

The Southern Highlands does of course provide several development conundrums. Good governance relies on public servants being in place and doing their jobs — police, magistrates, teachers and health workers are needed on the ground throughout the province. They need to be supported by a functioning administration. However at present there is negligible infrastructure in the western end of the province, so one of he the first challenges is how to encourage public servants back into these areas.

It is also difficult for donors to provide service delivery in areas which are effectively under siege, and this is another problem presented by SHP. Places such as Mendi and Tari (the two largest population centres) are difficult to work in due to lawlessness and fighting. Whereas more remote places which are relatively safe, miss out on essential services because they are further down the line.

If funds and resources could somehow be channelled into these remote areas, benefits would no doubt flow, because civil society stills exists in these areas, and lawlessness is not the problem it is in the larger centres. This is a real challenge for donors. Small scale community level development focussed on the more remote parts of the province will most likely result in more immediate successes and more general successes throughout the province in the longer term (see Vail, this volume). Indeed many of the workshop participants agreed that the idea of small successes needs to be more fully explored, and that in seeking solutions to the problems which have beset the Southern Highlands we must seek to harness local initiatives and 'aggregate the small successes'.

References

Ballard, J. A. 1983 'Shaping a political arena: The elections in the Southern Highlands'. In D. Hegarty (ed.), *Electoral Politics in Papua New Guinea: Studies on the 1977 National Elections*. Port Moresby: University of Papua New Guinea, pp.174-195.

Bourke, R. M. 2001 'An overview of food security in PNG', in R.M. Bourke, M.G. Allen and J. G. Salisbury (eds), *Food Security in Papua New Guinea*. Canberra: Australian Centre for International Agricultural Research, pp. 5-22.

Bourke, R. M., Allen, B. J., Hide, R. L, Fritsch, D., Grau, R., Hobshawn, P., Konabe, B., Levell, M. P., Lyon, S., and Varvaliu, A. 1995 *Agricultural Systems of Papua New Guinea Working Paper No.11: Southern Highlands Province*. Canberra: The Australian National University.

de Albuquerque, K., and D'Sa, E. 1986 *Spatial Inequalities in Papua New Guinea: A District-Level Analysis*. Port Moresby: Papua New Guinea Institute of Applied Social and Economic Research.

Haley, N. C. 2004 'A failed election: the case of the Koroba-Lake Kopiago Open Electorate', in P. Gibbs, N. Haley and A. McLeod (eds), *Politicking and Voting in the Highlands: The 2002 Papua New Guinea National Elections*. State, Society and Governance in Melanesia Discussion Paper 2004/1. Canberra: State, Society and Governance in Melanesia Project, Research School of Pacific and Asian Studies, Australian National University, pp. 16-26.

Hanson, L. W., Allen, B. J., Bourke, R. M. and McCarthy, T. J. 2001 *Papua New Guinea Rural Development Handbook*. Canberra: The Australian National University.

National Statistical Office, Papua New Guinea (NSO) 2002 *National Thematic Map Tables PNG 2000 National Census on CD-ROM*. Waigani: NSO.

Newell, B. P. 1970 *Lake Kopiago Patrol Report 4-1969/70*.

Standish, B. 1996 'Elections in Simbu: towards gunpoint democracy?', in Y. Saffu (ed.), *The 1992 PNG Election: Change and Continuity in Electoral Politics*. Political and Social Change Monograph 23. Canberra: Department of Political and Social Change, Research School of Pacific and Asian Studies, Australian National University, pp. 277-322.

—— 2000 *Electoral Governance in Papua New Guinea: Chimbu poll diary, June 2002*. Cited at: http://rspas.anu.edu.au/melanesia/pngresourcepage.htm

Wilson, R. K. 1974 *Socio-Economic Indicators Applied to Sub-Districts of Papua New Guinea*. Melbourne: Melbourne University.

ENDNOTES

[1] Southern Highlands Province is home to the highly successful Kutubu, Gobe and Moran Oil Projects and the Hides Gas to Electricity Project, all of which are now operated by Oil Search Limited. These generate cash royalties and other non-cash benefits which are distributed between stakeholders (the national government, the Southern Highlands provincial government, local level governments and the SHP landowners directly). Gas from Hides is purchased by the Porgera Joint Venture (PJV) and used to generate electricity which in turn powers the Porgera Gold Mine located in Enga Province. This electricity is transmitted via a high-tension power line running through SPH. Southern Highlanders with land along the power line easement receive annual occupation fees while those living within the Lagaip-Strickland riverene corridor receive water use payments in respect of tailings, which are released into the river system. Southern Highlanders have benefited from several PJV initiated Tax Credit Scheme funded projects.

[2] Phillip Moiya, SHP's Western Regional administrator, has recently reported that there were 164 conflict-related deaths in the Tari area alone in 2003 and a further 40 such deaths between January and August 2004 (see Lewis, this volume).

[3] The 2000 national census records a population of 546,265 for the Southern Highlands Province, although it is likely that the actual population is much closer to 500,000, based on the extrapolated 1980 census population using the 1980-1990 inter-census growth rate of 3.5 per cent. In several districts within SHP, population figures were inflated for political gain in preparation for the 2002 national election.

[4] This figure is based on calculations from Bourke *et al* (1995).

[5] It should be noted that resource projects elsewhere in Papua New Guinea have also failed to lower the overall level of disadvantage in the districts in which they are situated. For example, the Lagaip-Porgera district, home to the Porgera gold mine, was amongst the thirteen districts ranked as 'extremely disadvantaged' relative to all other districts in Papua New Guinea, as was the North Fly district, in which the Ok Tedi mine is situated. Interestingly, Telefolmin district, which supplies much of Tabubil's workforce, was the equal most-disadvantaged district, alongside Middle Ramu, home to the Ramu nickel mine.

[6] The 2002/2003 national elections produced some electoral results inconsistent with this, in that a Duna candidate won the Koroba-Lake Kopiago seat despite the Huli commanding a huge electoral advantage (see Haley, this volume; 2004) while Hami Yawari (from Kutubu) won the provincial seat.

[7] In 1992 the officially appointed ADA had aligned himself with Herowa Agiwa, so instead of taking up his appointment to Kopiago he spent the last term of government based in Koroba.

[8] The north Hewa area was derestricted in 1971, only two years before self government and four years before independence.

The National Government and the Southern Highlands since the 2002 General Elections

Joseph Dorpar and Jim Macpherson[1]

National government interaction with the Southern Highlands Provincial Government (SHPG) and administration has been based on a commitment to decentralisation, consciousness of the legal roles and limitations of central agencies and line departments, awareness of the political culture of the Southern Highlands Province (SHP), and political pragmatics since the national election in Papua New Guinea in July 2002. This chapter describes: national interventions in the SHP following the national election and in preparation for the supplementary election in April-May 2003; residual activities of the SHP desk in the Ministry for Inter-Government Relations (MIGR) between the supplementary election and the decision of the National Executive Council (NEC) to strengthen intervention in the SHP, made in July 2004; and steps taken since the NEC decision, and their effect.

The analysis focuses on the work of MIGR under the Minister for Inter-Government Relations, Sir Peter Barter, and the department under his ministry, the Department for Provincial and Local Government Affairs (DPLGA). MIGR and DPLGA are responsible for monitoring performance of provincial governments and administrations, and coordinating activities and support of the central agencies and line departments in response to the needs of the provincial government and administration.

The work of DPLGA and MIGR largely depends on implementation of the Organic Law on Provincial Governments and Local-level Governments (OLPGLLG). The analysis shows that the national government has had its authority to intervene limited by gaps in the Constitution, which were not recognised by the authors of the OLPGLLG, and that national agencies have limited capacity and commitment to respond to the special challenges offered by the SHP.

The present analysis complements the analysis by other authors of the present volume. It was written after their drafts were available, and gives the national context in which the developments they describe evolved. The authors of this chapter share concerns about maladministration, breakdown of services and infrastructure, decline of local-level government, breaches of sound governance, breakdown of law and order, and failure to develop a sustainable economy.

The authors are also concerned by the proliferation of weapons, including high-powered firearms, in the hands of certain individuals and their supporters, and intimidation of the public and rival groups. The possession of firearms by one clan or faction is a pretext for another clan or faction believing that they need access to weapons. More broadly, armed hold-ups and confrontation along the highway between Tari and Mendi, and animosity between Nipas and Hela, are an excuse for the Hela people, who occupy the western part of the province, to retain their weapons.

The authors believe that the consequences of prolonged collapse of services and law and order in the SHP are drastic. SHP could continue a downward spiral in services, peace, infrastructure and commerce. Services such as health, education and transport, when provided, legitimate and support the government presence, and offer access to commercial opportunities for villagers. Their absence is a rationale for reverting more to clan-based society, in reaction against a government presence.

The economic problems could be accentuated by premature closure of Kutubu Oil Field and Hides Gas Field, and by the precarious position of the SHP at the end of the Highlands Highway. There are threats, for example, to the power supply from the Hides Gas Field (in Hela) to the Porgera mine (in Enga). These are based on perceptions and allegations of a lack of services to areas adjacent to the gas field, and on poor distribution of benefits. They are backed up by weaponry and felling of the pylons which carry power to Porgera.

The economic consequences could be drastic for the nation. Premature closure of Kutubu Oil Field and Hides Gas Field would reduce government revenue. The light at the end of the pipeline from Papua to Queensland would grow more distant. National income is already under threat as a result of the anticipated closure of major mines in the next decade. Collapse of law and order would deter investment, and give overseas commentators opportunity to stigmatise Papua New Guinea as a 'failing', if not 'failed', state.

There are allegations that provincial corruption induces national corruption by bribing national members of parliament (MPs) to vote a certain way on particular issues, such as the votes of no confidence in the national government, and bribing members of central agencies to make decisions that favour and protect members of the SHP government and their friends and allies.

The authors are besieged by visitors and submissions from the SHP, which are designed to influence decisions by the ministry. They know what they are told, but do not always know the motives of the informants or the relationship between the information and realities within the SHP. The authors also receive numerous allegations of misbehaviour in the SHP. In some instances these allegations have been substantiated by investigations. In almost no case have they resulted in criminal prosecutions; they remain, therefore, allegations.

Specific knowledge comes on the rare occasions when departments (and most notably the national Department of Education) have made systematic surveys.

National government authority between the failed and supplementary elections

Unity and devolution

Papua New Guinea is a unitary state, with functions, powers and finances devolved to the provincial governments and local-level governments (LLGs). The National Parliament retains national authority. It can resume authority devolved to provincial governments and administrations and other lower-level governments, and can, at any time and without consulting provinces, amend or repeal any part of the Constitution or an organic law, or approve a new organic law. The Constitution and the OLPGLLG define the division of functions, powers and finances between the national and provincial governments. The ultimate unitary nature of the Papua New Guinea state is shown also in the authority the national government has to suspend provincial governments or to withdraw functions, powers or finances.

Authority to intervene following the 2002 national election

Failure of the 2002 national election in the SHP was a manifestation of ongoing problems in much of SHP society and culture, and its unacceptable expression in provincial politics. The tension had been expressed earlier in district-based confrontation during the governorship of Dick Mune, and in the unsuccessful attempt in 2000 and 2001 to withdraw functions, powers and finances from the Agiru government.

Inflation of electoral rolls and control of voting and counting of votes by force and threat of force preceded the general election in much of the SHP.

The failure of elections was such that no provincial governor was elected, and elections for LLGs in much of the province were void. There was no quorum for the provincial assembly, and no basis to establish a provincial government — or many LLGs.

The Constitution, OLPGLLG and other legislation had not provided for a failed election. The national government as sovereign power resumed authority until supplementary elections were held, but was obliged by the Organic Law on National and Local-level Elections to hold elections 'as soon as practical'.

The Minister for Inter-Government Relations, Sir Peter Barter, was given overall authority for the SHP. It is indicative of provincial perceptions that Sir Peter, on his frequent visits to the province, was often referred to as governor. However, his authority was temporary, and limited to preparing for smooth running of supplementary elections, in coordination with the Electoral

Commission, the provincial administration and the Royal Papua New Guinea Constabulary (RPNGC).

As possible, and as part of restoration of government presence, Sir Peter Barter also oversaw provision of government services. He was guided by a ministerial committee which included ministers responsible for major service providers and law and order. This committee was complemented by a bureaucratic taskforce composed of senior representatives of the departmental and agency counterparts of the ministers.

A Southern Highlands Office was set up in the MIGR. It was manned by a senior public servant on attachment, an officer surplus to the requirements of the National Museum, who originated in the Hela Region, and another recruited as part of the ministerial staff.

Government services between the failed and supplementary elections

The interim administration in its short life of less than a year was partly successful in restoring services. Good support from the national departments of Health and Education speeded some recovery of health and education services, although this work was necessarily impeded by collapse of transport infrastructure and lack of banks and other financial services outside the provincial capital, Mendi.

Law and order problems were, in part, solved during this interim period. Sir Peter Barter, with good support from churches, women's groups and community-based organisations, and community officers of the Hides Project, achieved large arms surrenders in Hela. A special resource was a police mobile squad based in Tari, with a commander who had a good sense of community outreach. This was accomplished by a cultural *ju jitsu* which used inter-clan connections, self-help projects which transcended the interests of clans and factions, and the display of surrendered arms as a mark of status. Sir Peter's exceptional presence and role was shown in his willingness to meet face-to-face with villagers and dissidents.

A measure of the success of this approach was that police did not need to use weapons during this period. But this success was transitional. Mobile squads are a short-term resource. The RPNGC has fewer police per head of population than any other South Pacific nation, and limited funding.

The absence of any bank in Tari handicapped restoration of services and redevelopment of commerce. Intercessions with banks failed, largely because of perceptions of lack of security, lack of business, and lack of adequate telecommunications. Only late in 2004 was a facsimile of a bank agency to be established in the district offices in Tari.

Community commitment to maintaining law and order declined with unresolved problems in supply of services and maintenance of infrastructure. Sir Peter also had limited time, and his personal intervention could not be repeated. In other parts of the province, 'big man' interventions created unsustainable and unrepeatable precedents. In Mendi, for example, an effort was made to settle disputes which originated from the death of the former governor, Dick Mune, by government agencies paying large sums in compensation and seeking the surrender of weapons. Such measures rewarded those responsible for disputes rather than those who kept the peace, and guaranteed a market for manufacture of homemade guns.

Other aspects of national government intervention were less successful, and lack of success generated further problems. Major problems with delivery of government services have arisen from the absence of staff from their posts and multiple appointments to posts. This has wider ramifications, as lack of services means no government presence and a justification for resistance to the government's presence in other fields.

Absence of staff from their posts in district offices is understandable. Lack of law and order, lack of maintenance of offices, lack of office supplies and equipment, and, in some areas, occupation of housing and offices — or their removal — by customary landowners made work difficult. Receipt of salaries in much of the province became difficult with decline of transport and banking services.

The Department of Personnel Management issued a special general order instructing government workers to return to their posts, or to have salaries cut. This still has to be enforced — although in November 2004, the Education Department in partnership with the Southern Highlands administration was to instruct the dismissal of absent teachers.

Multiple appointments to the same positions have led to problems of high costs, mixed allegiances, and confused command structures. At the top, no fewer than four officers were being paid as provincial administrator. At the middle level, multiple and often politically-motivated appointments of district administrators have created competing lines of command in district administration, and often district administrators have lacked relevant experience and training.

These problems continue in 2004. Sir Peter Barter has attempted to resolve the situation created by Department of Personnel Management inaction and provincial political interference (which is not unique to the Southern Highlands) by restoring authority to appoint provincial and district administrators to DPLGA, and by making provincial and district administrators accountable to the minister and DPLGA. DPLGA, as of November 2004, had still to act.

Election promises accompanied the supplementary elections. On the part of the national governing coalition, these included promises to move towards a separate Hela Province — based on the comparatively large population of the Southern Highlands and culturally-based antipathy between the Hela region and other parts of the province. On the part of the governor elected by the supplementary election, Hami Yawari, promises included the introduction of 'free education', with SHPG paying all school fees.

Neither set of promises has been met entirely. Lack of funding for the Boundaries Commission means that no steps have been taken towards forming a Hela Province — which in any case would need to first resolve tensions between Huli clans and others in the Hela region. The national government has, however, promised funding in 2005. The Hami Yawari government introduced 'free education', but had not planned its implementation or costed it. This is discussed in the next section.

Developments following the supplementary elections

The Provincial Assembly

Under the OLPGLLG, heads of rural LLGs, national MPs, and one head of an urban LLG are *ex officio* members of the Provincial Assembly (MPA). Provincial governors are aware of the need for support in the Provincial Assembly. They need votes of the Provincial Assembly to support legislation, and to elect a deputy governor who supports the governor's policies and interests, and they need to avoid a vote of no confidence.

Election of heads of LLGs is under the authority of the PNG Electoral Commission. However, the governor or his staff altered the approved lists of elected heads of LLG in order to pack the Assembly with his supporters. The ousted heads of LLGs, where they had the money for court cases (which by their reports could cost up to K150,000), have contested their lack of recognition in the courts. The governor has use of state funds to contest their applications. The outcome has been a court order in November 2003 for admission of heads of LLGs. This was overturned by the argument that the instruction was invalid because it conflicted with a sitting of National Parliament — although no MP need be present for the swearing-in of MPAs, and the Provincial Assembly need not be convened. In mid November 2004, duly elected heads of LLGs still had not been admitted to the Provincial Assembly, and the governor's nominees were still receiving entitlements as MPAs.[2] The lawyer representing the heads of LLGs was anticipating a full court hearing in March 2005 — well after the passage of the provincial budget.

Flow-on effects to local-level government and administration

No precise survey has been made either of the meetings of the Provincial Assembly or of local-level governments in the SHP. Reasons for this are discussed below. There is, nonetheless, considerable anecdotal evidence of the confusion of having, in effect, two heads for each of 17 LLGs. As funding goes in two distinct routes, accountability for funding is jeopardised. The incipient strife which already occurs when there is more than one approved district administrator is doubled when there is more than one head of an LLG.

There are allegations of the governor handing out large cheques to village representatives outside the LLG system, without accountability and proper process. There is thus less and less ability to deliver services at district level. By some reports, this has been compounded by the absence of members of the administration and government who are in Port Moresby for much of the time, and a breakdown in accountability, morale, and equipment at provincial headquarters in Mendi.

Implementation of 'free education'

School fees have increasingly blocked access to education in the SHP, more especially in the higher grades, and from areas without access to mineral royalties. The governor's promise of 'free education' in his campaign for election therefore attracted considerable support.

The problem with 'free education' is in implementation. The provincial administration's estimates of the possible cost fell far below actual costs. The provincial administration also had no enforceable policy on admission of students. The results were grossly inflated enrolments, which pushed up institutional costs. The maintenance of schools and school housing, too, had been lacking, and no extra provision was made for it. Staff and student accommodation and teaching areas were sometimes unusable.

By mid 2004, there were reports of schools closing down, disgruntled parents attacking teachers, unpaid suppliers threatening principals, and even of idle students holding up traffic.

DPLGA from July 2003 to June 2004

Suspension and withdrawal of functions, powers and finances from provincial governments

The OLPGLLG, when it came into effect in 1995 with accompanying constitutional amendments, reduced the grounds for a national government to suspend a provincial government. It transferred most grounds[3] to a new provision for 'withdrawal of functions, powers and finances from provincial governments'.

There was justification for the enacted changes. Some suspensions of provincial governments under the previous Organic Law on Provincial Governments had been politically motivated. The new provisions allowed selective withdrawal, and steady and public pressure for the provincial government and administration to reform and thereby institutionalise good governance and administration, and it ensured accountability through the National Parliament.

Unfortunately, the authors of the OLPGLLG had not considered the constitutional changes required to validate an organic law to enable the national government to withdraw functions, powers and finances. On 8 October 2001, in a case involving the then governor of the Southern Highlands Province, the Supreme Court — without taking into account substantive issues — ruled that Section 51 of the OLPGLLG was invalid.[4] The authority to withdraw functions, powers and finances needed to be specifically mandated by the Constitution. The authors of the OLPGLLG had not amended the Constitution to enable the national government to withdraw functions, powers and finances from provincial governments.

The consequences for the national government's relations with provincial governments are radical. The national government now has only two legal grounds for suspension of a provincial government: a challenge to the authority of the National Parliament[5] and declaration of a state of emergency, where that state of emergency includes 'action taken, or immediately threatened, by any person that is of such a nature, and on so extensive a scale, as to be likely to endanger the public safety'.[6] The former has never been explored. A declaration of a state of emergency in the Southern Highlands risks considerable negative publicity, which might again deter investors.

DPLGA did not advise Sir Peter Barter of this court decision, for almost a year after he became minister. Indeed, DPLGA may have been unaware of the decision, as a number of its lawyers had resigned or were facing disciplinary charges. MIGR, on independently discovering the invalidation of Section 51 of the OLPGLLG, attempted to have the department prepare drafting instructions to close the gap in the Constitution and amend the OLPGLLG. For a long time, copies of the court decision were unavailable; the ministry obtained a partial copy from the University of the South Pacific and eventually DPLGA found a complete copy. After waiting for DPLGA action, MIGR composed the drafting instructions. It then took DPLGA eight months to steer the drafting instructions through other departments and the Central Agencies Co-ordinating Committee. The NEC promptly endorsed the drafting instructions. On latest news, amendments will go to parliament in March 2005.

These delays have left the national government only an unexplored ground for suspending a provincial government, which is a substantial breach of sound government and administration. Provincial governments know that they can disregard injunctions of national agencies to conform to good practice, that they can delay court procedures by technicalities, and, allegedly, that they can bribe the central agencies for favourable decisions.

The Southern Highlands Office in MIGR

The SHP Office in MIGR has been maintained with a single officer. This unattached senior public servant, although of undoubted ability, has suffered health problems and has been unable to make a full-time commitment to the office. Consequently, a full review of developments in the SHP has not been undertaken, relations of central agencies and line departments with the SHPG have not been well coordinated, and preparation of strategies for enhanced intervention has been slow.

Intervention in the Southern Highlands, February 2004

By January-February 2004, there were constant complaints from the SHP about the collapse of services, the decline of law and order, and the growth of misappropriation. Undoubtedly some complaints had a narrow political or personal agenda; nonetheless, there were enough substantiated reports to give rise to serious concern.

In March 2004 MIGR, in consultation with DPLGA, prepared a policy paper for the National Security Council (a council of ministries concerned with state security), and cabinet. National Security Council approved the submission in April, for NEC to consider.

The paper recommended a hierarchy of interventions concerned with institutionalising sound government and administration. Proposed strategies in order of priority were:

- enhanced administrative procedures for ensuring sound administration and delivery of government services;
- SHP members of parliament to use their dual role as MPAs to activate public accountability at provincial and local levels;
- MIGR to use authority given by the OLPGLLG under suspension provisions to secure accountability of the governor of the SHP; and
- the possibility, as a last resort, of moving to suspend the SHPG.

Delayed approval

The National Security Council and the National Security Advisory Committee strongly endorsed the proposed intervention plan. The plan, in the form of a cabinet submission, had then to be taken by the secretary for Provincial and Local Government Affairs through the Central Agencies Co-ordinating Committee. This was delayed until the end of July 2004 largely because the DPLGA had not taken steps to obtain responses from concerned ministries and agencies. Cabinet approved the submission in late July 2004.

Establishment of the SH Office in DPLGA

The Southern Highlands (SH) Office was to have been re-established in DPLGA. Funding did not arrive until mid October. The same unattached officer continues to fill the position, when he is not absent (he still has not been paid his outstanding entitlements by DPM). No other officers have been recruited, nor have definitive proposals for staffing the office been approved.

The funding allocated by NEC for the operations of the SH Office was transferred during October 2004, but no plans have been made to use the money. Delays in the establishment of the office mean a continuation of *ad hoc* responses from DPLGA staff, who have other tasks and other priorities.

Recommendation for establishment of the SHP Task Force

The bureaucratic SHP Task Force has been convened twice since July 2004, facilitating progress towards intervention (see below).

The same departments which had been present during the consultations leading to the development and approval of the submission continued their pro-active engagement with the SHP government; those which had been absent, including the Department of Personnel Management and the Department of the Attorney-General, remained absent.

Recommendations for enhanced administrative interaction

The national government's normal mode for interaction with the SHPG is to support, strengthen and institutionalise good governance by the SHPG and sound administration by the SHP administration in order to ensure delivery of services and honest and transparent use of government resources.

Where normal patterns of monitoring and support fail, the national government can strengthen the pattern of monitoring and support by line departments and central agencies. The effectiveness of such administrative interaction depends on coordination of the work of central agencies and line departments, and the capacity and commitment of those agencies and departments. The response from some line departments, and especially the Department of Education, was strong. Other agencies, including the Department of Personnel Management, were unwilling or incapable of acting.

Recommendations for activating referral agencies

The plan as approved asked for accelerated preparation of prosecutions for well-documented cases of misappropriation. The success of administrative intervention also depends on the effectiveness of referral agencies such as the Police Fraud Squad, and the Ombudsman Commission.

The plan reflected concerns that referral agencies either lacked commitment or capacity to undertake investigations and take appropriate action. In some instances, where evidence of large-scale misappropriation seemed strong, people wondered whether corruption at the provincial level had metastasised to the national level.

The RPNGC reports that prosecutions are being prepared. As of mid November 2004, no case had come to court.

Recommendations for activating provincial democracy

Provincial politicians may work as members of the Provincial Executive Council, as MPAs, or through national or local publicity of issues.

Assumptions which underlie use of MPAs include: willingness and capacity of national MPs to be effective MPAs supporting sound government, and proper representation of heads of LLGs as MPAs.

All these interventions are problematic. Some national MPs are allies of the provincial government. Some national MPs have allegedly not been sworn into the Provincial Assembly, or have been disqualified by failure to attend Assembly meetings. The provincial governor has allegedly chosen his supporters as MPAs, without regard to their election as heads of LLGs.

The minister for justice was asked to prioritise the hearing of election-related cases. Nonetheless, cases related to the swearing-in of heads of LLGs as MPAs have yet to be finalised.

Recommendations for improving law and order

RPNGC, the Corrective Institutions Service and the Ministry for Justice act as a partnership. While law and order problems are undoubtedly endemic, there is as yet little government support for Defence Force and the National Intelligence Organisation involvement in the development of short-term and long-term strategies for law and order in the SHPG. Major developments have included:

- proposals to rectify the very low constabulary: population ratio, and achieve long-term development, based on analysis by the RPNGC;
- support from the SHPG for training of community police;
- the re-opening of prisons in the SHP by the Corrective Institutions Service; and
- the revival of magisterial services.

Interim intervention

The Minister for Inter-Government Relations used his authority under Section 187E(1) of the national Constitution to require accountability of the SHP governor; to encourage good governance and sound administration in the SHP, and to establish grounds for possible suspension of the SHPG. The procedures to be followed are specified in the OLPGLLG. Section 56 states that:

> When the minister responsible for provincial government ... is of the opinion that the ground for suspension of a provincial government ... exists or may exist, he may ... require ... the provincial governor ... to appear before him and give an explanation of any matters which have come to the attention of the minister.

The looseness of wording of this section allowed the Minister for Inter-Government Relations to summon the governor of the Southern Highlands to his office, and there require him to explain, before the minister and secretary for Education, the governor's 'free education' policy. This in turn led to a partnership between the SHP government and the Department of Education which has led to repeal of the SHP government's free education policy and substantial rebuilding of the provincial education system.

Application of grounds for suspension

The attorney-general has not been represented at meetings of the SHP Technical Task Force, and has not responded to instructions from NEC to detail considerations affecting the application of the grounds for suspension under Sections 187(E)1 and 187(E)4 of the Constitution. MIGR has prepared a draft statement of application and procedures, for comment.

Other recent developments

The SHP government has taken steps which suggest a longer-term orientation. These include a program for development of cash crops as a sustainable replacement for the oilfields as they close down. It has also contributed to training of community police, with an emphasis on project sites.

Some moves by members of the SHP government resemble earlier models of misappropriation and corruption. The SHP government, although it has no legal right to do so, has set up its own Kutubu LLG Special Purpose Authority, to substitute for the Special Purpose Authority properly recognised by DPLGA. It hoped thereby to obtain control of benefits from the Kutubu oilfields. This attempt has been publicly and effectively countered.

The national government has moved for substantive appointment of a SHP provincial administrator, with the object of ensuring an independent and impartial source of authoritative advice for the SHP government. An apparent attempt by a senior officer to bribe his way to a substantive appointment as provincial administrator has been foiled by reference to the Public Service Commission.

There have been strong and public calls by SHP leaders of the principal governing party, the National Alliance, for suspension of the SHP government. These have proposed declaration of a national emergency under Section 187(E)4 of the Constitution, even though this is open to legal challenge and is only a short-term alternative.

The governor has switched his allegiance from the opposition in the National Parliament to the government, in the context of an impending vote of no confidence. His reasons for changing are not known. However, as at November 2004 steps to explore possible suspension of the SHP government are on hold.

References

Kwa, E. L, Gelu, A. and Golman, W. 2003 *The Judicial Scrutiny of the Electoral Process in a Developing Democratic State*. Waigani: University of Papua New Guinea, NCD.

ENDNOTES

[1] Although the authors work with the Ministry for Inter-Government Relations, opinions expressed here are personal opinions. Shortage of time and other work-related pressures have prevented us consulting with the minister for Inter-Government Relations and other stakeholders as this paper was being written. This — most emphatically has not been because of lack of respect for their views. The shortage of time for a multiplicity of tasks is one aspect of work in the Ministry for Inter-Government Relations. Concerns with the Southern Highlands provincial government are embedded in work with the other provinces, including Bougainville, the National Capital District, and Emergency and Fire Services.

[2] The problems of delayed court decisions are general in Papua New Guinea, rather than specific to the Southern Highlands. See Kwa, Gelu and Golman (2003).

[3] Section 51 of the OLPGLLG defines these grounds:

- corruption or abuse of power within a Provincial Government … so as to render the government either ineffective or lacking in public respect and confidence; or
- failure by a Provincial Government … to keep or cause to be kept proper accounts and records of transactions or dealings; or
- a Provincial Government … has an ineffective internal control system; or
- a Provincial Government … has failed to submit reports as required by law; or
- there has been a breakdown in the administration of a province; or
- there has been deliberate and persistent frustration of or failure to comply with lawful directions of the National Government; or
- a Provincial Government … has deliberately and persistently disobeyed applicable laws, including the Constitution, an Organic Law (including this Organic Law) or any national legislation applicable to the province …; or
- there has been a failure to carry out functions in accordance with the development policies and standards of the National Government.

[4] SCR No. 04 of 2000, in the matter of Section 18(1) of the Constitution, in the matter of application by Anderson Agiru, Waigani: before Amet CJ, Kapi DCJ, Los J, Salika J, Sevua J., 2001: 26 April, 8 October.

[5] Section 187E(1) of the Constitution.

[6] Section 187E(4) of the Constitution.

The Setting: Land, economics and development in the Southern Highlands

Bryant Allen

Southern Highlands Province (SHP) is located almost in the middle of the mainland of Papua New Guinea. It is on the south-western end of the Highlands Highway and subject to the vicissitudes of landslides, bridge failures, potholes and criminal activity along the whole 600 km of the highway to Lae.

The province is 25,698 km^2 in area and is the eighth largest province in terms of land area in Papua New Guinea. Land in the SHP ranges from below 600 m to over 2800 m in altitude. Land above 2800 m is not used for agriculture in Papua New Guinea and is usually not permanently occupied, although it is used extensively for hunting and harvesting pandanus, an important seasonal food source. Around 14 per cent of SHP is below 600 m altitude and just over five per cent is above 2800 m (Table 3.1).

Seventy-two per cent of SHP land is not in use for agriculture. It is either too high too cold, too cloudy, too steep or receives too much rain. Agriculture is concentrated between 1200 m and 2400 m above sea level (Table 3.1). Although only 30 per cent of the total land area is located between 1200 and 1800 m above sea level, 54 per cent of the land in use for agriculture is found in this altitude zone. Similarly, only 14 per cent of the province is between 1800 and 2400 m above sea level, but 22 per cent of the land in use is at this altitude. Conversely, of the 3600 km^2 of land below 600 m, only 219 km^2, or three per cent, is in use. People are even more concentrated by altitude zone, with just over 90 per cent of the province population living between 1200 m and 2400 m above sea level. Highest population densities occur between 1800 m and 2800 m above sea level, where land is occupied at around 100 persons per square kilometre.

Table 3.1. Altitude ranges in SHP, by land area, population, and population density on land used for agriculture, 2000

Altitude (m)	Land area (km²)	% Land area	Land in use (km²)	% Land in use	Population in 2000	% Pop.	Population Density per/km²
0-600	3660	14.2	219	3.08	5205	0.95	24
600-1200	7854	36.6	1299	18.26	32,983	6.04	25
1200-1800	7821	30.4	3878	54.53	328,964	60.22	85
1800-2400	3840	14.9	1582	22.24	165,964	30.38	105
2400-2800	1095	4.3	134	1.88	13,149	2.41	98
2800 +	1427	5.6	0	0.00	0	0.00	No pop.
Total Area	25,698	100.0	7112	100.00	546,265	100.00	77

Source: PNG Resource Information System (PNGRIS); PNG National Census 2000 (NSO 2002).

Two-thirds of SHP is made up of mountains or hills and almost one third is of volcanic origins (Table 3.2). A broad curving band of limestone influences the landforms of much of the province. A number of large Pleistocene volcanoes have forced their way through the limestone to build large cones; Mt Giluwe is the second highest point in Papua New Guinea at 4160 m, and Mt Ambua and Mt Kerewa are both over 3600 m high. Other prominent volcanic cones are Mt Ialibu and in the south, rising out of the lowlands, Mt Bosavi. A large elongated lake, Lake Kutubu, lies in a limestone depression in the southeast.

Table 3.2. Landforms in SHP by land area, population, and population density on land used for agriculture, 2000

Landform	Land area (km²)	% Land area	Land in use (km²)	% Land in use	Population	% Pop.	Population Density per/km²
Mountains & hills	16,803	65.4	4433	62.33	318,822	58.36	72
Volcanic	7513	29.2	2293	32.24	179,173	32.80	78
Plains & plateaux	894	3.5	276	3.88	38,523	7.05	140
Floodplains	488	1.9	110	1.55	9747	1.78	89
Total Area	25,698	100	7112	100	546,265	100	77

Source: PNGRIS; PNG National Census 2000 (NSO 2002).

Agricultural land use follows closely the pattern of landforms, with 95 per cent of agricultural land being on mountains and hills and volcanic landforms. Similarly, 90 per cent of the population of SHP live on these landforms. Population densities are highest on floodplains, but only seven per cent of people live on floodplains. Population densities are relatively high at around 80 people per square kilometre on all landforms.

Table 3.3. Average population growth rates (% per year), 1966 to 2000: Southern Highlands compared with other Papua New Guinea regions

	1966-1971	1971-1980	1980-1990	1990-2000	1966-2000
Southern Highlands	0.51	4.04	2.99	5.48	3.07
Southern Region	3.35	1.81	2.72	0.21	1.84
Highlands Region	2.07	1.95	2.05	3.65	2.49
Momase Region	2.35	2.30	1.82	3.36	2.48
Islands Region	3.59	2.40	2.90	2.30	2.69
Papua New Guinea	2.61	2.09	2.25	3.24	2.55

Notes:

Growth rates are calculated as follows: LogN(Pn)-LogN(P0)/inter-censual period × 100. The inter-censual periods used are 1966-1971, 5 years; 1971-1980, 9.1 years; 1980-1990 9.92 years; 1990-2000, 9.92 years; 1966-2000, 33.94 years.

National Capital District is included in Southern Region from 1966-1980 and is excluded after that.

Sources: 1966-1990: DNPN (1999); PNG National Census 2000 (NSO 2002).

The 2000 National Census suggests that the SHP population is the largest provincial population in the country. However censuses in SHP have been problematic for some decades, with the provincial population fluctuating wildly between censuses (Table 3.3; Figure 3.1). The rapid increase between 1966 and 1971 is explained by a large number of communities being censused for the first time, but the 1980 to 1990 decrease in population is probably the result of a serious undercount in 1990. The addition of 229,000 people in the 10 years between 1990 and 2000 would appear to be the outcome of a combination of an undercount in 1990 and an over count in 2000. An increase in the population of more than 42 per cent in the 10 years between 1990 and 2000 is not possible, especially as other census information indicates that at least since 1980, when the first data is available, SHP has lost more people from migration than it has gained.

Figure 3.1. Average population growth rates (% per year), 1966 to 2000: Southern Highlands compared with Papua New Guinea regions

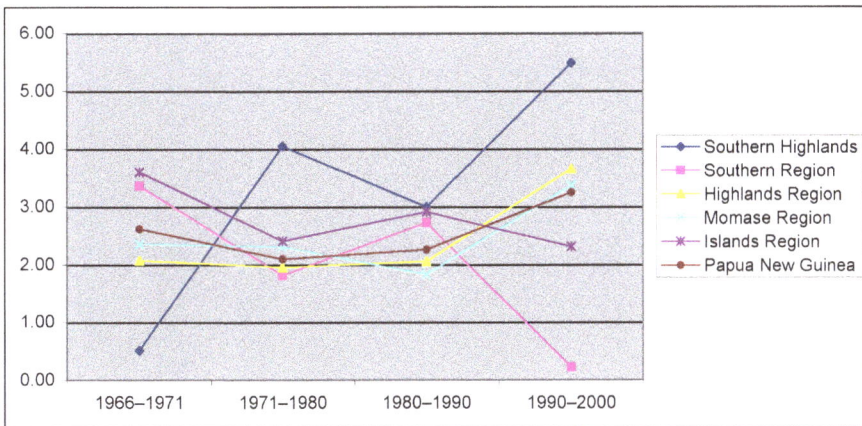

Source: DNPM (1999: Appendix A4); PNG National Census 2000 (NSO 2002).

The sources of this over-counting can be guessed at if the 1980 SHP district populations are projected at 1.5 per cent per year and the projected populations are compared with the censused populations in 2000 (Figure 3.2). The 2000 populations of Ialibu-Pangia and Tari-Pori are smaller in 2000 than the projection suggests they should be. On the other hand, the 2000 censused populations of Mendi-Munihu and Nipa-Kutubu are significantly larger than predicted by their 1980 populations, so it would be appear that the over-counting occurred mainly in these districts.

Sixteen linguistic groups occupy SHP. In the far west are the Hewa, who live in small and relatively mobile communities in the upper Strickland Valley. To their south are the large and related Duna, and Huli speakers in the Kopiago area and in the Tari Basin and surrounding uplands and valleys. More people speak Huli in SHP than any other language. The Huli cross a major physical divide formed by Mt Ambua into the Nembi Valley where they border the Mendi speakers who extend east into the Lai and Mendi valleys and uplands. To their east, the Kewa, Wiru and Hagen speakers live along the southern side of Mt Giluwe and around Mt Ialbu. The Hagen speakers go northeast into Western Highlands Province. In the south of the province in the lowlands[1] live the Onabasulu, Sonia, Kasua, Kaluli around Mt Bosavi and the Fasu and Foi around Lake Kutubu. In the southwest are Sau and Porome speakers, small groups living in rugged and isolated limestone valleys. Political schisms occur along language boundaries but geography is also important. Serious political struggles have developed between Duna and Huli speakers in the west, who have threatened to form their own province (see Haley, this volume), Mendi speakers in the centre and Kewa and Wiru speakers in the east. Small and isolated language groups like the Hewa and Onabasulu have no power or representation, although the discovery of gas at Lake Kutubu has recently catapulted Fasu and Foi speakers into provincial and national prominence.

Figure 3.2. SHP Districts: Predicted population change 1980-2000 verses censused population in 2000

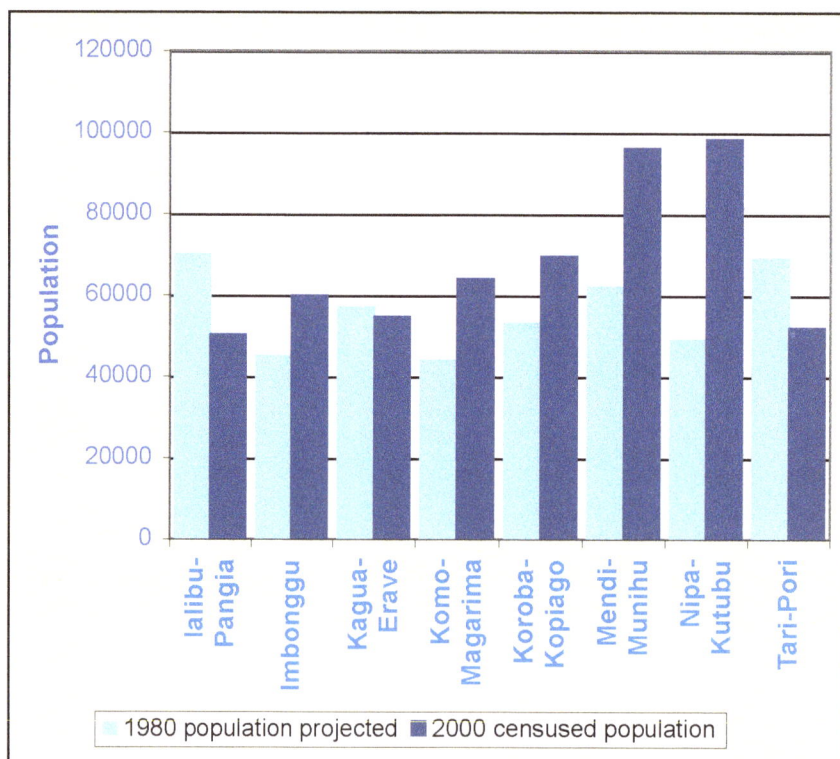

Source: PNGRIS; PNG National Census 2000 (NSO 2002).

More than 80 per cent of the SHP is of very low or low quality for the production of sweet potato (Table 3.4, Figure 3.3). Less than two per cent of the total land area of SHP is high quality land. More than 75 per cent of the SHP population, however, is concentrated on low and medium quality land, with a further 10 per cent on high or very high quality land.

Table 3.4. Land quality by land area and populations

Land quality	Land Area (km²)	% of land area	Population	% of Population
Very low	6583	25.6	71,327	13.1
Low	14,848	57.8	271,214	49.6
Moderate	3877	15.1	139,518	25.5
High	356	1.4	52,152	9.5
Very High	35	0.1	12,054	2.2
Total	25,698	100	546,265	100

Source: PNGRIS; PNG National Census 2000 (NSO 2002).

The higher quality land in SHP is predominantly located in the Ialibu-Pangia district, with other smaller areas of high quality land being found in and around Tari, in the Mendi district and in the Koroba-Lake Kopiago district.

Figure 3.3. Land quality

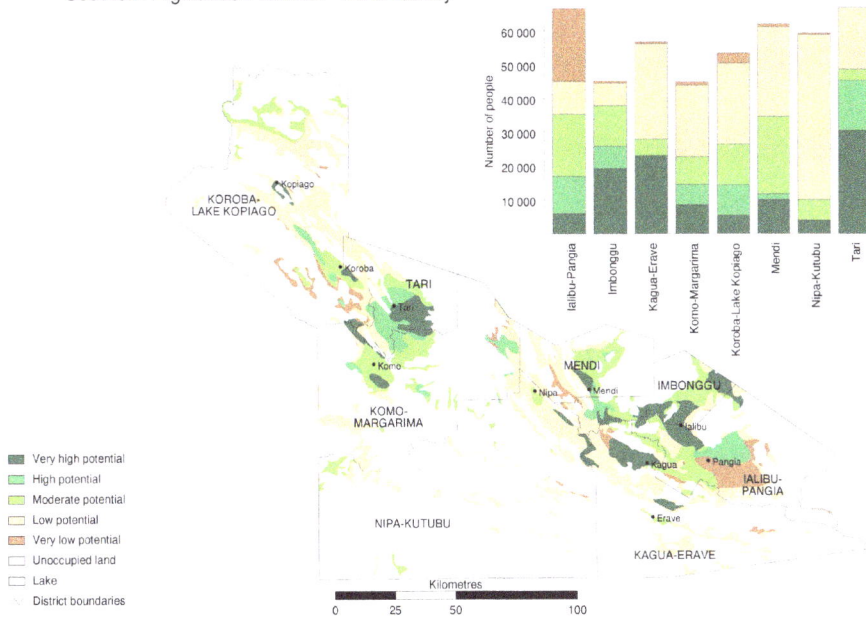

Source: Hanson *et al* (2001:95)

SHP agriculturalists improve low and medium quality land by drainage, mounding and composting, enabling them to produce enough sweet potatoes to support high human population densities and large pig herds. Their ingenuity, however, cannot overcome cold temperatures at altitudes above 2800 m, steep slopes and cloudiness. SHP is one the cloudiest provinces in Papua New Guinea and agricultural production is constrained by lack of sunshine in many parts of the province.

SHP agriculture (Figure 3.4) is dominated by high intensity sweet potato production for pigs and food. It ranges in intensity from continuous cultivation at Tari, where composted mounds are used, to cultivation periods of up to twenty years at Nembi, Mendi, Ialibu, Kagua and Erave, where circular mounds and long beds without composting are used to grow sweet potato. To the northwest and the southeast, agriculture is low intensity shifting cultivation, but is still dominated by sweet potato. Only in the south is agriculture not the most important source of food. There sago is the most important food, supplemented by very low intensity shifting cultivation.

Figure 3.4. Agricultural systems

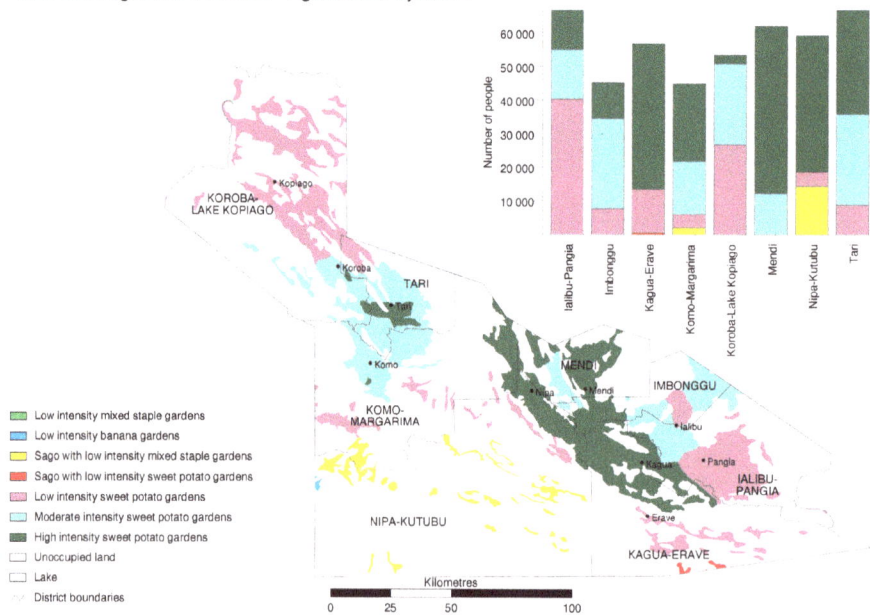

Southern Highlands Province - Agricultural Systems

Source: Hanson *et al* (2001:94)

Unlike many of the agricultural systems to the east in the Wahgi Valley, and to the north in Enga, SHP systems have yet to develop strong cash cropping components. Coffee is only important in the east, close to Mt Hagen. Small coffee gardens exist at Tari and in the Mendi and Lai valleys, but production is very low and coffee husbandry of poor quality.

This inability of SHP agricultural systems to generate cash incomes is a serious constraint on rural development in the province. The World Bank-funded Southern Highlands Rural Development Project planted large areas of coffee and tea in various parts of the province in the 1970s, but today none of these areas is productive. This means that the great majority of rural people in SHP receive estimated cash incomes of less than K20 per year (Figure 3.5). The only places where rural incomes are higher are the Ialibu area, where people have coffee and good access to the Mount Hagen fresh food markets, and around Lake Katubu, where people receive royalty monies from the local oil and gas projects.

Figure 3.5. Estimated rural cash incomes 1996

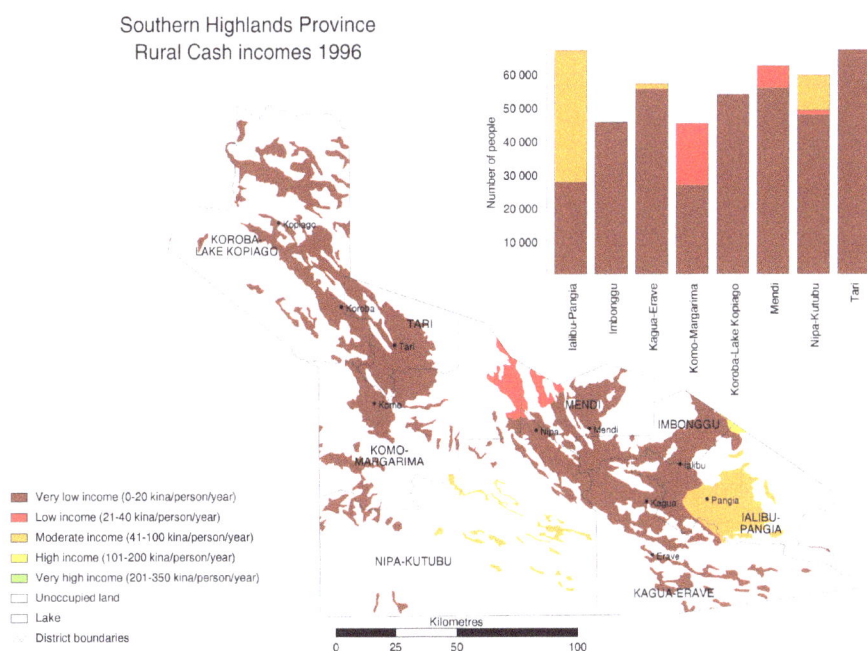

Source: MASP; Hanson *et al* (2001:93)

Royalty moneys aside, cash incomes in SHP are closely associated with accessibility to markets and services centres, which is in turn associated with the location of roads (Figure 3.6). People living in the northwest, southwest and southeast corners of the province are more than one day's travel from any service centre. By contrast, people in the northeast are within four hours' travel of a major service centre, namely Mendi or Mount Hagen. The central parts of the province are within eight hours' travel of a service centre.

Figure 3.6. Access to service centres and markets

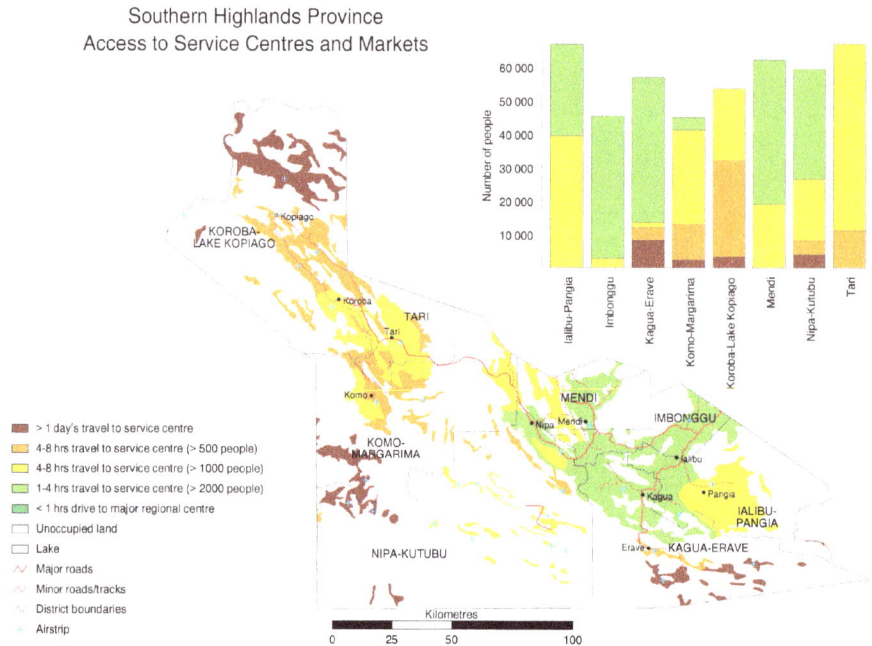

Southern Highlands Province
Access to Service Centres and Markets

> 1 day's travel to service centre
4-8 hrs travel to service centre (> 500 people)
4-8 hrs travel to service centre (> 1000 people)
1-4 hrs travel to service centre (> 2000 people)
< 1 hrs drive to major regional centre
Unoccupied land
Lake
Major roads
Minor roads/tracks
District boundaries
Airstrip

Source: Hanson *et al* (2001:92)

The combination of relatively high population densities, high-intensity agriculture and poor environments is resulting in pressure on land in some parts of SHP that will lead to land degradation in the short to medium future. The most critical areas of land pressure occur in the Mendi, Nipa-Kutubu and Komo-Magarima districts (Figure 3.7). On the other hand, there are areas at Tari, Kagua, Erave, Komo and Mendi that could support higher-intensity land use.

The combination of relatively poor environments and low cash incomes is also reflected in patterns of child malnutrition. The most recent survey of malnutrition in children under five years of age in SHP was the National Nutrition Survey of 1982-83 (Heywood *et al* 1988). When the results of this sample survey are extrapolated over the whole of Papua New Guinea and recalculated into the 2000 districts, SHP children are shorter for their age than most other children in Papua New Guinea, but are reasonably heavy for their length. Stunting, significantly low length-for-age, is an indication of long-term or chronic malnutrition, whereas low weight is an indication of short-term nutritional problems. In 1982-83, children in Koroba-Lake Kopiago District were the shortest children in Papua New Guinea, but for their length they were the heaviest. Komo-Magarima and Mendi children were also among the shortest children in Papua New Guinea but were also heavier than most children of their length.

Notably, the only children in SHP that were of average height and were above average weight were those in Ialibu-Pangia and Imbonggu districts, where cash incomes are highest and there is better access to services and markets. This association between malnutrition and environment has also been shown to exist on a more local scale; at Tari, children whose mothers live in poorer environments are born on average 300 g lighter than children whose mothers live in better environments (Allen 2002).

Figure 3.7. Agricultural pressure and potential

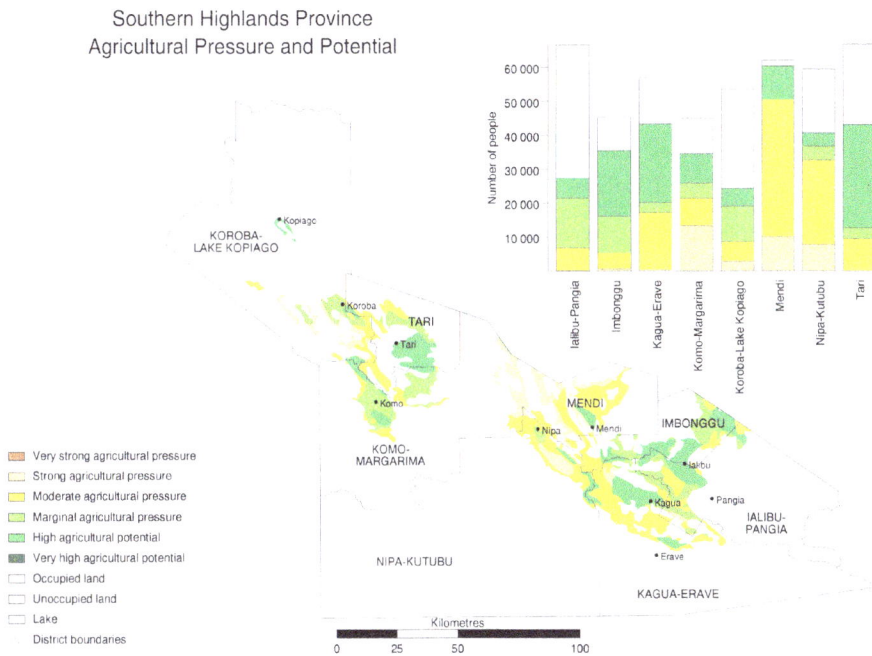

Source: Hanson *et al* (2001:96)

Trends in child nutrition are also reflected in literacy rates in SHP. Everywhere in the province more men than women are literate, and a greater proportion of adults, male and female, are literate in Ialibu-Pangia and Imbonggu districts, than elsewhere in the province (PNG 2000 National Census, household data files). However, nowhere in SHP are more than 50 per cent of adults literate.

Figure 3.8. Literacy rates by district

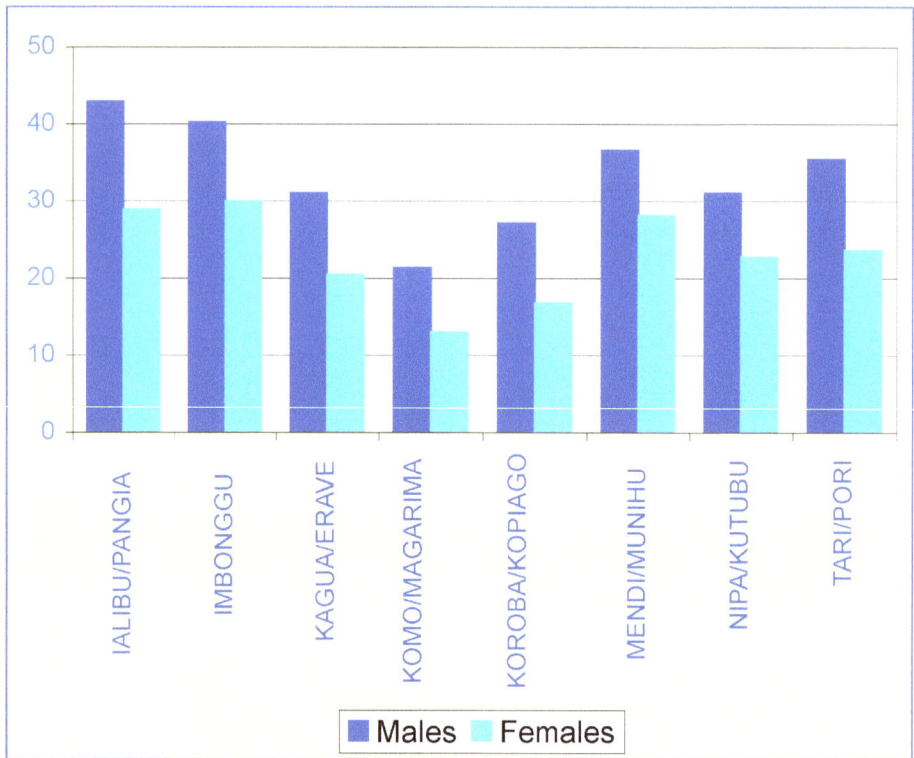

Source: PNG National Census 2000 (NSO 2002)

The three major components of disadvantage — poor environment, low cash incomes and poor access to markets and services — are summarised in Figure 3.9. This shows areas of 'disadvantage' in SHP (Hanson *et al* 2001). The most disadvantaged people in SHP are those on the Nembi Plateau and in the higher fringes of the Mendi Basin, where agricultural pressure on land is strong, incomes are very low, and population densities are high. People in these areas are vulnerable to land shortages and subsistence food shortages, and have little cash available to buy supplementary foods. Large numbers of people in the Wage and Lai valleys face similar disadvantages, but their incomes are slightly higher. The upper fringe areas of the Tari Basin earn low incomes and have moderate pressure on their land. Smaller numbers of people in the Lagaip Valley in the northwest, in the lower Erave Valley and in the Mt Bosavi area in the southwest, have poor access to services and poor agricultural environments, but populations are small and there is little pressure on land. Few opportunities to improve livelihoods exist in these areas. The Kopiago area is also an area of disadvantage. With the exception of the wetland areas surrounding Lake Kopiago, the environment is poor, as is access to services. Added to this, incomes are very low.

Figure 3.9. Disadvantaged areas

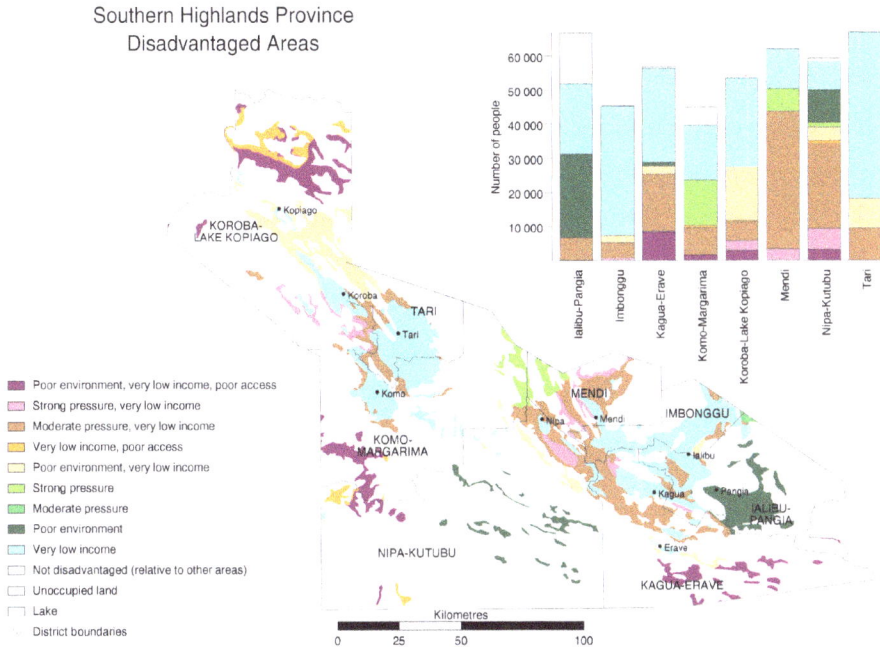

Southern Highlands Province
Disadvantaged Areas

Poor environment, very low income, poor access
Strong pressure, very low income
Moderate pressure, very low income
Very low income, poor access
Poor environment, very low income
Strong pressure
Moderate pressure
Poor environment
Very low income
Not disadvantaged (relative to other areas)
Unoccupied land
Lake
District boundaries

Source: Hanson *et al.* (2001:97)

Conclusion

Large numbers of people in SHP are increasingly vulnerable to declining crop yields and food shortages, due to a combination of poor agricultural environments, high population densities and intensive agriculture. Compared with their counterparts elsewhere in Papua New Guinea, many Southern Highlanders are particularly disadvantaged: incomes are low throughout the province and most people lack the capacity to purchase supplementary food. Compounding this is the fact that cash crop development is hindered by major environmental constraints and very poor access to markets.

References

Allen, B. J. 2002 'Birthweight and environment at Tari', *Papua New Guinea Medical Journal* 45(1-2):88-98.

Department of National Planning and Monitoring (DNPM), Papua New Guinea. 1999 *Papua New Guinea National Population Policy 2000-2001*. Waigani: Population and Human Resources Branch, Sectoral Coordination Division, DNPM.

Hanson, L. W., Allen, B. J, Bourke, R. M. and. McCarthy, T. J. 2001 *Papua New Guinea Rural Development Handbook*. Land Management Group, The Australian National University. Canberra.

Heywood, P., Singleton N. and Ross, J. 1988 'Nutritional status of young children — the 1982/83 National Nutrition Survey', *Papua New Guinea Medical Journal* 31:91-101.

National Statistical Office, Papua New Guinea (NSO). 2002 *National Thematic Map Tables, PNG 2000 National Census on CD-ROM*. Waigani: NSO.

Wurm, S. and Hattori, S. 1981-83 *Language Atlas of the Pacific Area*. Linguistics Series C, Part 1. Canberra: Australian Academy of the Humanities.

ENDNOTES

[1] Foe in current Papua New Guinea government usage.

The Southern Highlands: A hasty transition from unknown to riches and chaos

Joe R. Kanekane

The late Mathew Kohai, a health adviser with the Department of Southern Highlands, still could not accept the recent developments in Mendi. Having lived there all his life, the Manus Islander was baffled that the once peaceful province is now a place of lawlessness. He sought answers, attempting to identify a particular cause, but could not find one. He recalled the days when systems were functional and public servants like himself were keen to work in the province. He was adamant that things would improve and had no intention of being transferred elsewhere.

The rest of the province is still banking on the hope that the province will return to normalcy. In the meantime, Mendi is still facing petty crime. Tari is constantly being tormented by armed thugs. Despite police presence, lawlessness continues on the peripheries, though in Ialibu, Kagua, Erave, and Pangia the law and order challenges are less. Public servants are fearful for their lives, and people have migrated to Port Moresby and elsewhere in the country.

The Southern Highlands Province has moved from an unknown province to an important source of revenue for the country. In the early 1990s successive governments placed emphasis on the discovery of oil and gas. Along with this came the opening up of new roads to wealth and influence, as well as social disharmony. The eastern end of the province[1] has better road access to neighbouring Western Highlands Province, has enjoyed better health and government services, and has greater business opportunities. Lawlessness, anarchy and a general deterioration of government services have occurred more in the central and western ends of the province, which include Mendi and Nipa, where there have been roadblocks and tribal feuds, and Tari, which has been characterised by vandalism and lack of respect for law and order. The province's wealth is also concentrated in the central and western end of the province, which are blessed with natural resources and enjoy a lion's share of the proceeds from them through royalties and tax credit scheme funded infrastructural projects.

This paper will provide an overview of the province, seek to establish the causes of the present unrest, and examine what needs to be done to resolve the problems. However, it is not easy to find quick solutions.

History and geography

It is believed that the Southern Highlands was settled nearly 20,000 years ago, based upon the dating of grinding tools found in Mendi. It was not until the mid-1930s, however, that exploratory patrols visited the Southern Highlands and opened it to the world.

Clarke (1982:15) notes that the first school in the province was established at Lake Kubutu in 1953, some eighteen years after first patrols entered the area. Schools were subsequently established at Mendi, Tari and Ialibu, and thence the more remote parts of the province. It was not until 1967 that the first secondary school in the province was established.

As the Southern Highlands was a slow starter, prominent Southern Highlanders travelled elsewhere for their education. Former politicians Sir Wiwa Korowi (Southern Highlands provincial member 1977-1982 and 1987-1991) and Peter Peipul (MP for Imbonggu 1997-2000) received their education at Awaba High School in the Western Province. Three-term Ialibu-Pangia MP, Roy Yaki (1987-2002) went to the Asaroka Lutheran High School. Other prominent Southern Highlanders were educated in the Western Highlands.

Little by little, development came to the province under the colonial administration. The Australian Army established an engineers' base in Mendi, and was involved in much of the province's civil and infrastructure development until their departure in 1996. According to Terry Boyce, who was a commanding officer of the unit and provincial works manager, the army was often asked to mediate disputes (quoted in Marjen 1981). The army engineers did an excellent job; at one stage, Southern Highlands was said to have the best Works department in the entire country.

Early leadership

Respect and esteem was accorded to traditional leaders, who established their reputations by giving pigs or other valuables in exchanges with other tribes (Wiessner and Tumu 1998:253). Crocombe (1983: Chapter 11) expounds on the concept of the Melanesian leader, arguing that political power was achieved through skills in production, organisational politics and war (also see Chao 1984). Melanesian bigmen plan productive activities, mobilise the resources of the group, and create wider groupings, at least temporarily, for inter-group cooperation through ceremonial events.

When the colonial administration introduced the positions of *luluai* and *tultul*,[2] the traditional leaders were a natural choice. They assisted the administration, especially in its efforts to understand custom and tradition. In the Southern Highlands, men like Turi Wari (MP for Ialibu-Pangia 1968-1977) and Matiabe Yuwi (MP for Tari-Pori 1968-1982) played this role. Prominent kiap Ron Neville made an early transition to politics, and became one of the first white men to serve as a member for the Southern Highlands. On the basis of his experience as a kiap and the respect he commanded, he represented the province from 1964-1977. Papua New Guinea's first Prime Minister, Sir Michael Somare, in his book *Sana*, records that Neville was a critic of Pangu's stand on colonial rule and had a memorable encounter with one of Pangu's stalwarts, the late Sir Albert Moari Kiki, during a session of the 1972 parliament (Somare 1975:63).

With Neville at the helm, and with a group of seasoned traditional leaders, including Paiele Elo (Koroba-Kopiago), Momei Pangial (Mendi) and Tegi Ebial (Nipa-Kutubu), the province was making steady progress towards its ultimate goal of electing more local leaders. Matiabe Yuwi was involved with the Constitutional Planning Committee, while the rest were involved in parliamentary committees. Yano Belo (Kagua-Erave) subsequently joined them, and was made a government minister soon after. Dame Rachel Cleland (1985) wrote of the potential of two Southern Highlands leaders, Andrew Wabiria and Momei Pangial. She was awed by their patience and willingness to understand the ways of the white man. Dinnen (1998:48) also gives credit to these leaders, noting that the 1972 election marked the beginning of the opening of the state to local participation.

It also marked the emergence of indigenous politicians as a significant new category of power broker, linking local power structures to economic institutions of the state. The election of former diplomat and high school teacher, Wiwa Korowi, who defeated Ron Neville in the provincial seat in the 1977 elections, was a major turnaround. Korowi, who had been a diplomat in Nigeria and Asia, was called on by Southern Highlanders to play a key role. He became Minister for Health, Public Utilities and Minerals and Energy under Michael Somare (1977-1980) and Sir Julius Chan (1980-1982). During this time he was successful in bringing the Pauanda and the Tari hydro power plants to the province. He upgraded health centres to hospitals and connected districts by telephone. The significance of the government's presence, and especially the role of elected leaders, was beginning to register with electors. Korowi also travelled extensively around the province, educating people about the changes taking place. This gave people a clearer picture of the government's objectives, and importantly let them get to know the province's regional member. Korowi lost the 1982 elections but was re-elected in 1987, defeating Francis Pusal. He remained in parliament for four years, resigning in 1991 to successfully contest for the office of governor general.

At the provincial level, outspoken Tari leader Andrew Andaija was elected interim premier of Southern Highlands. His interim cabinet contained seasoned provincial politicians. However, Andaija died in a plane crash in 1980; he was replaced by Tegi Ebial from Nipa. From 1980 to 1985 Ebial maintained the *status quo*, juxtaposing his cultural roots as a traditional leader with selective modern ideas. His experience in the House of Assembly helped him run the province. Ebial was defeated in 1985 by Yaungtine Koromba, who was premier until 1991. It was during Koromba's reign that the news of oil and gas discovery started shaking the province. Koromba played a key role during his time, signing on behalf of the provincial government its agreement to participate in the Kutubu Oil and Hides Gas projects.

Albert Mokai, an Arts graduate from the University of Papua New Guinea (UPNG), was elected premier in 1992, however his tenure was short-lived: the Southern Highlands provincial government was suspended and an administrator was appointed. When the suspension was lifted in 1994, Francis Awesa, a former provincial secretary, was elected premier. Awesa, a law graduate from UPNG, brought with him experience from the PNG Electricity Commission and the corporate circles where he was an executive. It was during Awesa's tenure that the royalty benefits from the projects were reviewed, paving the way for increased benefits. Awesa had been in office for only one year when the Chan-Haiveta government's provincial and local-level government reforms were passed. Awesa was relegated to deputy governor while regional MP Dick Mune (who had replaced Wiwa Korowi in a by-election in 1991) became governor. Disagreements between Mune and Awesa saw the latter sacked as deputy governor.

The premier's job was thus shared amongst leaders from all corners: Andaija from the west, Ebial from central, Mokai from the west, Koromba from central and Awesa from the east. On the national front, leaders like Glami Warena (MP for Imbonggu 1977-1987), Aruru Matiabe (1982-1992), Philemon Embel (Nipa-Kutubu 1987-2002), Anthony Temo (Imbonggu 1987-1997), and Michael Nali (Mendi 1992-2004) also played key roles as ministers.

The transition from traditional leaders to younger and more educated ones started in the mid 1980s. But despite the growing political maturity, Southern Highlands still lagged behind neighbouring Western Highlands and the other highlands provinces. Scores of labourers were hired by rich Western Highlands coffee and tea entrepreneurs to work on their plantations. Despite the discovery of oil, opportunities were restricted and Southern Highlanders found themselves increasingly marginalised and were prompted to seek opportunities elsewhere. Many of these labourers are still living on plantations, despite the collapse of coffee and tea estates, because they have access to better lives and services.

Provincial and local level government reforms

There is no doubt that the reforms vigorously advocated by the PPP-Pangu-led government in 1995 have been a failure. Acceptance of the new system came slowly, and the way the governors were able to position themselves was damaging. When Dick Mune[3] realised his powers, he did not hesitate to use them. He sacked Francis Awesa as deputy governor and the member for Koroba-Kopiago, Herowa Agiwa, was elected by the assembly to replace him. Awesa maintains that he is still not aware of the reasons for his premature departure from politics (personal interview 2001).

Mune was a big-spending governor, who bought Land Cruisers for his council presidents and rewarded those who were aligned with him. There was talk that funds were starting to disappear. Under Mune, access to funds, materials and services that were previously restricted was freed up. Bogus invoices and other claims were forwarded to the provincial government. People of the Southern Highlands woke up to the fact that funds were available to those aligned with the ruling regime. Crowds of people started congregating around the Mune camp, and people from all parts of the province looked to him as the man with the money. He surpassed his predecessors in changing people's perceptions. Council presidents became powerful in their constituencies. Cash flowed into the peripheries, and people saw Mune was a true leader. He was, in many respects: he had several wives and concubines, he was a village leader and a very powerful orator, and, above all, he was a grass-roots-oriented person and people found it easy to deal with him. John Opengi, former lord mayor of Mendi town, once gave Mune the title of 'action man'; the people's money, he said, was now in their own hands. Robert Tawa, Ialibu Basin local level government president, echoed this sentiment, asserting that Mune did not care how much he gave, as long as it served a greater number of Southern Highlanders (personal interviews, 1997).

During the 1997 election campaign, Dick Mune held a rally at the Nipa station. Hundreds of supporters from around the province showed up to express their support. They gave cash and verbal pledges, and spoke of a new style of leadership that had dawned on the province. They urged voters to grant Dick Mune a second term. Prime minister, Sir Julius Chan, and Constitutional Development Commission chairman, Ben Micah, staunch PPP front-liners, praised Mune's leadership. Sir Julius in particular asked supporters to vote for Mune for a second term so that the PPP legacy could continue. He described Mune as a strong highlands leader, and said that after 1997 people like him would take the PPP reins. He also named Nipa (Mune's local area) as 'Number Two Namatanai',[4] which delighted the crowd. On that occasion Mune slaughtered more then 500 pigs, which were distributed to those that attended. But despite his great popularity and his campaign strategies, Mune lost the 1997 election to the independent Huli candidate, Anderson Agiru.

The Court of Disputed Returns

When Mune lost the election, the dreams of his supporters were shattered.[5] They did not know what to do, other than to rally behind Mune as he proceeded to contest his loss, filing a petition with the Court of Disputed Returns against

Agiru's win. As a result of the dispute, Agiru — who was from the Tari district in the Hela area — refused to stay in Mendi; he claimed his life was in danger and chose to live in Moresby, governing the province from there.

As the court battle dragged on, tensions grew between the Hulis and the people of Nipa. The discontent of the Nipas began to show in small roadblocks, and the harassing of PMVs and commuters. When Mune lost his life in a car accident in 1999, people blamed Agiru. The argument was that Mune had won the election fairly, but because of Agiru's disputed win was forced to seek legal redress, which resulted in his death. Some went so far as to accuse Agiru of sorcery both in winning the election and in causing Mune's car to crash.

Faced with such accusations, Agiru chose to remain permanently in Port Moresby, although he assisted in Mune's funeral arrangements. He dealt with the provincial administration but was never there to see the people. If he travelled to the province, he was there briefly and then returned to Port Moresby. His administration, too, spent long periods in Port Moresby seeking directives from Agiru. Deputy Governor Wambi Nondi remained in the province, apart from sojourns to Port Moresby, but was not as influential as Agiru. Agiru's absence provoked a lot of people, and the law and order situation in Nipa started getting out of hand, with frequent roadblocks.

After the Skate government lost a vote of no confidence in 2000 and Sir Mekere Morauta became prime minister, the provincial government's powers were withdrawn and the incoming PDM government appointed one of its experienced party men, Pila Niningi, as administrator. Niningi, who was from Ialibu, ran the province for a short while before being displaced.

The boom period initiated by Mune had come to an end; people looked to Agiru to continue the flow of money, but it did not happen. Agiru's absence from the province contributed to their frustration. Even in Agiru's district of Tari, violent crime started to increase. Mendi followed, and by 2001 Southern Highlands had major law and order problems. Some argued that had Agiru remained in the province, travelling and conversing with the people, the situation would have been different. However it is not clear that this would have been the case: a spontaneous development of violence took place in the province, exerting pressure on government services. In project areas such as Hides and Kutubu, landowner tensions were rising: power pylons were being brought down, and roadblocks were apparent in the Hides project area. Mendi became a fighting zone in 2001, with businesses shutting down, the school of nursing closed, public servants fleeing, and anarchy prevalent. A tribal feud between the Tunjup and Unjumap groups escalated; the death toll rose with the proliferation of high-powered weapons, and the hiring of mercenaries becoming increasingly common. Southern Highlands was in the news daily, with reports of violence and mayhem. Police and the Morauta government tried to do something, but Mendi's woes increased, and for some time the town was almost deserted. However, Agiru left a legacy: the six-storey Agiru Centre in the middle of Mendi town.

The churches' role in peace mediation

Bishop Stephen Reichert of the Mendi Diocese, and Bishop Clarence Kapali from the United Church said they both felt obliged to do something to discourage fighting and promote peace mediation in the Southern Highlands. In separate interviews they described their efforts to solve the tribal fight in Mendi. The subsequent truce in Mendi was a credit to the two of them, but also to Francis Awesa, the former premier. In a separate interview he said that something had to be done about the state of affairs in the province. Awesa was particularly concerned that, as a local leader from Mendi, he had an obligation to assist the peace process. Along with the two church leaders, he helped organise the first surrender ceremony, which was witnessed by hundreds of warring clansmen. The ceremony was hailed as a success, though Awesa admits spending his own money to get the process under way. He also enlisted the tribal leaders and acknowledged their courage and willingness to stop the fighting. However the initial impetus, and the fine work done by the two churchmen, assisted government agencies to sustain the peace efforts. Both Bishop Reichert and Kapali have been held up or threatened by *raskols* a number of times. However they have persisted and as a result Mendi is slowly getting back to normalcy.

Tari is also experiencing some problems, but it is hoped that the presence of police will improve the situation. Former Tari police station commander, Simon Nigi believes people are willing to assist the peace process. He says the challenge is for leaders to bring themselves down to the people's level so that they can understand how the challenges are being met. Police are working around the clock and Simon Nigi has travelled extensively and talked with people, hoping that, by understanding the people, he can devise practical means to deal with the challenges.

Prominent Southern Highlander and former diplomat Dominic Diya believes the absence of competent administrators in the province has had negative results (personal interview 2001). He is adamant that unless competent administrators are on the job, the province cannot prosper. Diya, who was once provincial administrator, argues the province can be managed with limited funds, if professionals are appointed to the top posts. However, people have become used to getting handouts. The Southern Highlands desk within the Finance Department is having a nightmare sorting invoices and claims amounting to hundreds of thousands of kina.

As Whiteman (1984:38) argues: 'culture changes when the ideas that people hold in common change. Change begins with individuals and their ideas and as these new ideas spread throughout society culture begins to change'. People have aligned themselves with the governor or politicians in order to gain something for themselves. During his tenure, Mune promoted this. It has made for a difficult transition.

The future

Utting *et al* (1995:168) suggests a broad framework within which law and order problems can be addressed: if people are to interact with their neighbours on equal terms and participate in the political process, access to public services is essential. We have seen the failings of Agiru's leadership style and that of the late Dick Mune, which have brought about the present state of affairs in the province. People use a variety of means to show their frustration with governments, but if they receive the services they need — health, education, roads and so on — such frustration can be overcome.

Many communities are now being asked to take on new responsibilities by organisations who wish to mobilise them for purposes that may or may not coincide with the communities' own perceptions of their needs. Superintendent Nigi, on the other hand, seeks practical solutions, talking with the people, at their level, throughout the Hela region. There is no doubt that the majority of Southern Highlanders want a peaceful province. We need to look at where they want the province to go. Educated Southern Highlanders, and successful sporting personalities, should be encouraged to rally together and appeal to their people for peaceful change.

Radio Southern Highlands should also be supported. The station manager, Andrew Meles, believes that Radio Southern Highlands can assist by promoting positive news. He says information is crucial, and it is important that leaders use radio to communicate with the masses. Southern Highlands who can, regularly tune in to Radio Southern Highlands, and the station receives requests and messages from across the province. Meles observes that the station was involved in the Mendi peace ceremony, communicating with the two warring tribes through public radio. Such initiatives can work well on the ground.

Once the people are on side, the next challenge is to educate and inform them. The situation in the eastern end of the province is progressing steadily. However the central and western parts of the province (Tari and Koroba districts) are badly affected by the social tensions. Banks and trade stores remain closed and government offices remain empty.

On a positive note, Southern Highlanders will rally together, as is evident in the Inter-City Rugby Competition when the Mendi Muruks are playing. We need to identify other measures to unite the province. Efforts by Peace Foundation Melanesia and Youth Ambassadors for Peace, largely driven by the churches, should be supported by government and donor agencies. Government should take heed of the various peace ceremonies and arms surrender ceremonies.

The challenges which the province faces are mostly a result of hasty transition, which has consumed people unable to deal with its impact. But people are tired of violence and lawlessness and want to get on with their lives. They know what violence can do to them, and many are committed to a better and safer society. They need initiatives that are meaningful and sustainable. There is still hope that these can be found and that the situation in the province turned around.

References

Chao, M. J. P. 1984 'Leadership', in D. Whiteman (ed.), *An Introduction to Melanesian Cultures: A Handbook for Church Workers*. Point No.5. Goroka: Melanesian Institute, pp.127-148.

Clarke, R. 1982 *Education in the Southern Highlands*. Five year Plan 1982-1986.

Cleland, R. 1985 *Pathways to Independence: Story of Official and Family Life in Papua New Guinea from 1951 to 1975*. Cottesloe, WA: R. Cleland.

Crocombe, R. 1983 *The South Pacific: An Introduction*. Auckland: Longman Paul.

Dinnen, S. 1998 'In weakness and strength — state, societies and order in Papua New Guinea', in P. Dauvergne (ed.), *Weak and Strong States in Asia-Pacific Societies*. Canberra, A.C.T : Allen & Unwin in association with the Dept. of International Relations, Research School of Pacific and Asian Studies, The Australian National University, pp.38-59.

Marjen, B. 1981 'Aust army is what counts in Southern Highlands', *The Times of Papua New Guinea*, 11-17 December, p.13.

Mantovani, E. 1987 'Traditional values and ethics', in Susan Stratigos and Philip Hughes (eds), *The Ethics of Development. The Pacific in the 21st Century. Papers from the 17th Waigani Seminar, volume 1*. Port Moresby: University of Papua New Guinea, pp.188-201.

Somare, M. 1975 *Sana: An Autobiography of Michael Somare*. Port Moresby: Niugini Press.

Utting, P., et al. 1995 *States of Disarray: The Social Effects of Globalisation*. Geneva: United Nations Research Institute for Social Development.

Whiteman, D. (ed.) 1984 *An Introduction to Melanesian Cultures: A Handbook for Church Workers*. Point No. 5. Goroka: Melanesian Institute.

Wiessner, P. and Tumu, A. 1998 Historical Vines: Enga Networks of Exchange, Ritual and Warfare in Papua New Guinea. Washington DC: Smithsonian Institution Press.

ENDNOTES

[1] The 'eastern end' refers to the districts of Ialibu, Pangia, Kagua and Erave. Mendi and Nipa are generally accepted as the centre. Magarima, Tari, Komo, Lake Kopiago and Koroba constitute the 'western end'.

[2] The titles of *luluai* and *tutul* were generally given to outstanding men in communities. Their job was to represent the colonial administration by upholding law and order and promoting communal harmony.

[3] Dick Mune was educated up to year eight. He joined the Royal Papua New Guinea Constabulary and served as a police commander in Wapanemanda, Mendi and Ialibu. He contested the 1982 and 1987 general elections, and won the 1991 by-election when incumbent Wiwa Korowi resigned to become governor general. He was a backbencher in the Wingti-Chan government from 1992-94, but following a government change was given the Housing ministry. He resigned to become governor in 1995.

[4] Namatanai, in New Ireland Province, was Sir Julius Chan's own electorate.

[5] Mantovani (1987) describes such loyalty as a transference of values from supporters to their leaders. These values are embedded in the subconscious and expressed through customs. People feel strongly, but often do not know why.

Cosmology, Morality and Resource Development: SHP election outcomes and moves to establish a separate Hela Province

Nicole Haley

There have been calls for the establishment of a separate Hela province for the best part of three decades now, and although such a province has not come to fruition the Somare-led national government evidently is sympathetic to the needs and wishes of the Hela peoples. In May 2003, for instance, *The National* reported that the current government had promised the people of the Southern Highlands a separate Hela province by 2007 (*The National* 11 May 2003). More recently it has come to light that the national government, through the Boundaries Commission, will 'look into the possibility of a separate province for Hela in 2005' (*The National* 13 August 2004). This paper will comment on the push for the establishment of a Hela province and on the supplementary election results in the Southern Highlands Province (SHP). It is argued that in recent years the support for a Hela province has waned in many parts of the province and that formation of a Hela province may well exacerbate emergent ethnic conflicts.

Calls for a Hela province

Newspaper articles and letters to the editor since independence reveal that the Huli have long dreamed of a separate Huli province. Initially, the calls for a separate province simply focussed on the fact that SHP is a large province with a large population, and that, as such, it warranted being split into two or three separate provinces (*Post-Courier* 18 April 1978). However, within a very short time the calls for a separate province became synonymous with calls for a separate Huli province.

The early proponents of this movement argued that the formation of a separate Huli province would promote stability and the preservation of Huli culture (*Post-Courier* 3 May 1978). On 18 May 1978, the *Post-Courier* reported that local government councils in Koroba, Kopiago, Tari, Komo and Magarima were demonstrating to push for the formation of a separate province 'to be called the Hela Province'. These demonstrations were followed by formal local government council resolutions rejecting the introduction of provincial government (*Post-Courier* 3 August 1978),[1] and coincided with public announcements that local government councils in the west of the province were 'not ready for provincial government in the Southern Highlands Province' (*Post-Courier* 30 August 1978). Proponents of the Hela province officially opposed provincial government for the Southern Highlands, arguing that the Tari, Magarima, Koroba, Komo and Lake Kopiago districts lacked economic and educational development — which they did.[2] They sought a separate province and argued that provincial government should be postponed until such time as they had gained the 'necessary educational qualifications and experience' required to successfully run a provincial government (*Post-Courier* 30 August 1978).

Although the movement was not officially endorsed by the Southern Highlands Area Authority, the arguments employed tended to echo those which the Authority had itself employed when opposing self-government and independence several years earlier (see Haley and May, this volume). Individual members of the Authority were certainly sympathetic to the push. Andrew Andaija, the then president of the Southern Highlands Area Authority and later premier of SHP, for instance, was reported as saying that many of the movement's complaints were genuine (*Post-Courier* 18 May 1978). He did not, however, wish to see the province 'break into pieces', pushing instead for service provision.

By the mid 1980s the push for a Hela province had gained momentum, due in part to the ongoing neglect of the west. This same neglect "served as an essential basis for the development of [a Huli/Hela] social and political identity" (Ballard J.A. 1989:142). In 1986, Andrew Wabiria, the former member for Koroba-Lake Kopiago, presented the prime minister with a petition calling for the recognition of the Hela people across provincial boundaries. The petition was from the recently formed Hela Gimbu Association. It demanded a share of oil royalties, insisted that all labour for development projects be recruited in the Hela area, and called on the national government to provide goods and services 'or face serious trouble'. Specifically, the petition demanded a road between Tari and the Gulf Province, improved telecommunications, an upgrade of the Tari airstrip, and fully funded health and education services throughout the Hela region (*National Times* 12 April 1986).

In more recent times, Huli people have called on the national government to split the Southern Highlands in two, because of the continuous armed hold-ups on the Nipa road, frequent roadblocks at Poroma, Magarima and Nipa, and ongoing ethnic conflict between the peoples of the west and the east, which has meant that the peoples in the west of the province have been cut off from Mendi, their provincial headquarters (*PNG Gossip Newsletter* 6 September 2000). Several of the key candidates in the 2002-2003 national elections took up the call for a Hela province. James Marape, runner-up in the Tari-Pori open electorate, for instance, held a press conference in August 2002 in which he demanded a more equitable distribution of services within the province, noting that if the Hela people continued to be denied essential services then SHP would go the way of

Bougainville (*Independent* 28 August 2002). He and others, including Damien Arabagali, the current chairman of the Hela Gimbu Association, have continued the call for a separate Hela province.

Cosmology and the idea of a Hela province

The peoples occupying the western end of SHP, namely the Duna, Huli, and Bogaia, along with their Paiela neighbours, share the view that they descend from a common ancestor, known as Hela (Haley 2002b). Accordingly, they often refer to each other as brothers (Glasse 1965:33; Biersack 1995:14-16), considering themselves sons of the same father. On the basis of this connection there have been calls for many years for the formation of a Hela province, which would take in the resource-rich districts occupied by the Duna, Huli and Paiela, namely the Komo-Margarima, Tari-Pori, Koroba-Lake Kopiago, Nipa-Kutubu and Porgera-Lagaip districts (Vail 1995:360; Haley 2002b).[3] The project is for the most part Huli owned and driven, and lacks wider support, although it does have the support of many key political figures. What local-level support it has derives directly from discontent over the lack of services in the western end of the province and the lack of benefits accruing from present resource developments. It is this same discontent which led to the formation of the United Resources Party by Anderson Agiru.

These peoples also hold that the world is bound up in a process of loss, degradation and decline. This is expressed in the way they engage with their environment and in the ways they perceive and interpret environmental and social changes. Ethnographers of the Duna and Huli have repeatedly commented on this all-pervading theme (Frankel 1986; Goldman 1983; Ballard C. 1995; Strathern 1991; Stürzenhofecker 1993; Haley 2002b), which is common to the region more generally (see also Jorgensen 1981, 1985; Poole 1986; Biersack 1991, 1995). Myths found amongst these groups reveal a common belief that the world originally consisted of formless clay-like mud which was given shape and strengthened by ancestral spirits; that the cardinal elements of the universe were born of an original ancestress; and that the landscape as fashioned by the ancestors is held securely in place by a subterranean cane or cane-like python known as the 'root of the earth'. These myths also reveal that the way of the world is such that the fertile substance, which sustains the universe, by nature dissipates, and that the expenditure of this substance will bring about the world's end.

The peoples living in the western end of SHP similarly share the belief that they are part of a regional system deeply rooted in mythology and ritual, and that the fertility of their region is morally constituted. This means they must act and behave in certain ways for their world to be fertile. Such was the basis of their pre-colonial cosmologies. Indeed, in the past, Duna, Huli, Hewa, Bogaia and Paiela participated collaboratively in ground-seeding and ground-making rituals which sought to ensure the ongoing fertility of the region (Haley 2002b). These rituals, which involved the sacrifice of human substances and body parts in order to replenish the root of the earth, were enacted along ritual 'roads' which criss-crossed the region.

Specifically, there were at least five major ritual roads crossing the Duna region, these being *Kirau atia*, *Ambua atia*, *Hewari atia*, *Nona atia* and *Miliano atia*, and another, *Ukuam Sama*, traversing the Bogaia region. One thing these roads had in common is that they all terminated outside the Duna area. The most southerly road, *Kirau atia*, started in Bogaia country near Bulago and proceeded via Nogoli to Gelogili in Huli country (Gelote in the Huli literature. See Goldman 1979; Ballard C. 1995). *Ambua atia* started on the Oksapmin side of the Strickland Gorge and, it seems, originally terminated at Bebenite, south of Tari.[4] The third road, *Hewari atia*, commenced at the Duna parish of Angora in the mid Pori River area and travelled through the Logaiyu and Urei river valleys into the Ipili-speaking areas and thence to Mt Kare where it terminated. *Nona atia* commenced in the Strickland Gorge on Yokona ground, traversed the south Hewa area, and likewise terminates at Mt Kare. The final road, *Miliano atia*, commenced in Hewa country, traversed Duna country from north to south, and terminated in the Bogaia area. Ritual sites linked by these roads typically featured ground oil seeps and natural gas seeps, which became the focus of the rituals which sought to replenish fertile substance in order to restore and ensure the ongoing fertility of the region.

Even today, despite the almost complete absence of indigenous ritual practice, Duna hold to the belief that moral behaviour conserves fertile substance, and that immoral behaviour sees it depleted and will ultimately bring about the world's end. Ongoing fertility continues to be something Duna must negotiate through appropriate moral behaviour and proper social intercourse (Haley 2002b). Indeed it is their actions which render specific substances, particularly (but not exclusively) fluid substances, either inimical to growth or capable of inducing fertility. Linked to this is the notion that inappropriate moral behaviour can render a previously fertile substance infertile (see also Ballard C. 2000:210). Mineral resources are seen as examples of fertile substance which originate from deep within the root of the earth. As such they must be properly handled and engaged with in a morally appropriate manner. Duna hold that social intercourse in relation to mineral extraction must also be properly managed, and that the flow of resources elsewhere must be curtailed, lest the fertile substance sustaining the world be depleted at a rate which brings about the end of the world.

How is this relevant to a discussion of politics? For generations, Duna, Huli and Paiela and their more immediate neighbours performed cooperative rituals aimed at re-making and re-fashioning the ground so as to ensure the ongoing fertility of the entire region. Specifically, these involved replenishing the earth's fertile core. In the contemporary context, Duna claim the Huli and Paiela have forgotten this. They cite their exclusion from Mt Kare as a case in point. Indeed although many Duna clans in the upper Pori area directly descend from Ko-Yundikia (the spirit associated with Mt Kare) and several old men from these groups had sacrificed pork to Ko-Yundikia in their own lifetimes, Duna were chased away from Mt Kare during the height of the gold rush. Duna feel that their Huli and Paiela 'brothers' should have recognised and acknowledged their claims, especially as they had been cooperatively responsible for Ko-Yundikia's ritual propitiation for generations. Furthermore, Duna maintain that they continued observances at Mt Kare well into the early 1970s, long after the Huli had abandoned these practices.[5]

Duna, today, charge the Huli, in particular, with having forsaken both the regional ritual projects which they once strongly promoted (Ballard C. 1994; 2000:213) and the ties which made such cooperative performances possible. Instead of being concerned to preserve the fertile substance of the earth's core, Duna see the Huli and Ipili as pillaging it. They regard the gold, oil and gas being extracted at Porgera, Mt Kare, Nogoli, Moran, Kutubu and Gobe as examples of this fertile substance, and insist that the Huli are wantonly consuming fertile substance which should be conserved so as to sustain them and the world.

> This blood taken along *Kirau atia* and *Ambua atia* was fertiliser for gardens, medicine for pigs and children. Those things started here. But where they stored them, that was at Nogoli [Hides Gas], on the Huli side. They have forgotten the true origins of *Kirau atia* and *Ambua atia*. We believe that there is something important here — mineral oil, gas or something. We don't know. Our ancestors told us not to dig the ground in the [Strickland] Gorge. They said, if we did, this thing would come out and burn us all ... Where those roads ended they are extracting gas. We too are responsible for that gas. Those things started here. (Andrew Makano 1997; Robinson Fieldnotes Notebook 4:129-130).

In the contemporary context, Duna feel that Huli have sold them out. They charge the Huli with monopolising for themselves the fruits born of their cooperative ritual efforts.

> The boy went that way and the girl went this way. She went with a female pig. That pig didn't take a walk by itself. The people here took it up that way. They would call the name of each group. One group would bring it and give it to the next, all the way to Gelogili ... Before we [Huli and Duna] stayed together like a married couple. Our union bore fruit. Our union bore the oil and gas ... Those things are as much ours. But they [the Huli] are using it, expending it. They have forgotten us (Sane Noma 1994; Haley Fieldnotes Notebook 3:48; 54).

The Duna likewise charge the Huli with having forgotten that they are brothers who trace descent from a common ancestor, Hela. Almost without exception, Duna now preface conversations and statements about mining and other large-scale development projects with statements to the effect that the Duna, Ipili and Huli are brothers — *Hela ingini* — sons of the same father. Such appeals to common descent also form the basis of an anti-Huli sentiment which now permeates all aspects of Duna discourse.

Despite espousing the rhetoric of Duna, Huli and Paiela as brothers, Duna have not embraced the growing calls for a Hela province (Biersack 1995; Vail 1995; Goldman n.d.). They vehemently oppose such a project, seeing it as a Huli owned and driven project which will bring them no benefits (cf. Goldman n.d.:12). Some even view the calls for the formation of a Hela province as sinister in intent, fearing that if the province comes to pass they will lose both their land and their identity (Haley 2002b).

> The Southern Highlands is big. The Hela people are there. Duna people are underneath … Hela had Duna, Huli and Obena. True we are brothers. But we Dunas don't fight. If there is trouble we sit down and talk. We don't fight. Hulis fight first. They think only of vengeance. We are different to Hulis. We come underneath Hela, not underneath the Huli. About this talk of a Hela province — we don't support this kind of talk. If the Huli want a province, let them have their own province. We don't want to be part of it. Give us our own province — a Duna province. Don't cover us up with this talk of Hela. That is something belonging to the Huli — they are misusing the name of Hela. The leaders here, we don't support that, we want to promote our customs and our culture. We don't want photocopied customs being sprayed all over the place. We are Duna, and we must not diverge from this (Jospeh Henepia 2004; Haley Fieldnotes Notebook 40:21).

The 2002-2003 elections[6]

In the face of such concerns, the past decade has seen growing calls for Duna unity. Campaigning in the Lake Kopiago sub-district (that part of the Koroba-Lake Kopiago electorate which is ethnically Duna) in the lead-up to the 1997 and 2002 national elections focused on the urgent need for Duna political unity to secure national representation (Haley 2002a, 2002b, 2004). Both elections were promoted locally as the 'final election', the last chance to gain political representation before the world's end (Robinson 2002). In 1997, for instance, several of the candidates formulated a *Memorandum of Agreement for Duna Unity* (Haley 2002a), which in part read:

> D. All Parties realise that there has got to be only one person representing the Duna, Hewa and Bogaye people in Parliament.

E. All parties realise that for the last 23 years the people of Duna, Hewa and Bogaye have being used, manipulated and marginalised for the benefits of a few elite [Huli] from the Koroba area (*Memorandum of Agreement For Duna Unity*, June 1997).

The role played by cultural identity and ethnicity in campaigning during both the 1997 and 2002/2003 national elections was profound. Dance festivals and dance competitions, in which much energy was spent on articulating Duna identity, were held on a regular basis, and sponsored by the various Duna candidates. Men and women, young and old, participated in earnest, with all participants being encouraged to dress in 'pure' Duna fashion.

In the Koroba-Lake Kopiago electorate the past two elections have produced electoral contests based very much on ethnicity, and have been concerned with who, from a Duna perspective at least, might provide for and best facilitate the advancement and unity of the Duna people, since the Duna hold the Huli directly responsible for their disadvantage and lack of services. Indeed, when Duna complain about a lack of support from successive national governments, their complaints are invariably directed towards the Huli, for they see themselves as having been colonised and governed by the Huli, and charge the Huli with monopolising access to the state.

Duna today fear that they are at risk of losing their cultural identity, especially in the face of Huli calls for a Hela province. They feel they are under the control of the Huli, and seek to represent themselves politically, to preserve the sociality and morality upon which their collaborative ritual endeavours were predicated, to reclaim control over ancestral lands transformed by mining (cf. Jacka 2001), and to (re-)make and (re-)fashion the world for the benefit of future generations.

That Duna fears and desires dramatically influenced the outcome of the supplementary elections held in 2003 might be illustrated by some observations on the elections. The failed 2002 national election saw 19 men contest the Koroba-Lake Kopiago open electorate. Of these candidates 6 were Duna and 13 were Huli. By contrast the 2003 supplementary elections were contested by 10 Huli candidates and only 2 Duna candidates. This came about because four of the Duna candidates stood aside in favour of Petrus Thomas, a first-time campaigner. They publicly stated that they stood aside for the sake of Duna unity. Thomas, a well known Mendi Muruk and one-time Kumul (national) rugby league player, campaigned without money on the platform that Duna people were suffering. He promised not to play politics but instead to unite the Duna and improve their situation. Duna people were generally of the view that he did not support a Hela province. Such a project, they knew, would not improve their lot. The other Duna candidate, Ben Peri, endorsed by the United Resources Party, actively supported the Hela movement, as did several of the Huli candidates.

The Huli have a clear demographic advantage in the Koroba-Lake Kopiago open electorate. In 2002 it was home to some 43,500 Huli, Duna, Hewa and Bogaia speakers.[7] Of these, 24,850 (57 per cent) were Huli speakers, 16,055 (37 per cent) were Duna speakers, 2,310 (5.3 per cent) were Hewa speakers and 285 (0.7 per cent) were Bogaia speakers. In the light of this, the results are quite remarkable. First, the two Duna candidates between them picked up two thirds (66 per cent) of the votes cast, despite the fact that Duna make up only 37 per cent of the electorate.

An examination of the ballot box counts reveals that Thomas and Peri both picked up large numbers of Huli votes. In Peri's case this had much to do, I believe, with the fact that he was endorsed by the disgraced former SHP governor, Anderson Agiru,[8] and because he has backed the Hela province movement with its calls for a greater share of SHP's resource wealth. Thomas, however, picked up the votes of disgruntled and what I would call marginalised Hulis — perhaps what Goldman (this volume) has termed 'naturalised Hulis', people who are now choosing to emphasise their Duna connections over their Huli ones. Indeed Thomas picked up many votes in the bilingual census units, which strongly suggests that there is not as much support for the Hela province as its promulgators would have us believe.[9] Further evidence for this is the fact that the 2003 results saw Hami Yawari (from Kutubu) elected as governor, against the trend which has seen the regional seat held by a representative of one of the three big ethnic groups.

Whilst it is clear that the Huli continue to seek a separate province, it should not be assumed that all the Hela peoples support this movement; in fact they do not. For more than a decade now the Duna have been calling for a 'pure' Duna province and have been seeking to differentiate themselves from their Huli neighbours. Duna do not want to be part of a Hela province, and are angered when Huli spokesmen presume to speak on their behalf.

> There are 19 Council wards within Kopiago Basin and another 13 council wards within the Auwi/Logaiyu area ... These are all Duna census divisions. All of us within these census divisions are innocent. We are not supporting this Hela province. The people pushing for a Hela province are using our name, the Duna name, without our permission. They don't speak for us. The Hela name belongs to all of us, not just the Huli. They have appropriated it and now we are getting the blame. Our name, the Duna name is being spoiled and we too are being blamed when trouble comes up on the Tari side (David Lundape 2004; Haley Fieldnotes Notebook 40:33).

If it is indeed the Somare government's intention to split the Southern Highlands, then serious consideration should be given to the formation of a Huli province as opposed to a Hela province, for the formation of a Hela province may well exacerbate the emergent ethnic conflicts, which have been brewing for decades. Alternately, consideration should be given to the formation of electorates which map more closely the ethnic divisions within the province; this would ensure a political voice for groups such as the Duna who currently number more than 30,000. Such discussion may, however, be purely academic as in 2002-2003 the Huli went from holding four seats in the National Parliament to holding only two, and this may well mean that there is now far less likelihood of progress towards a Hela province during the 2002-2007 parliament.

Whatever the case, there is no doubt that the Huli will continue to press for services in their areas and will continue to push for their own province. Back in 1978, the late Andrew Andaija called for calm, urging people that what they needed was services and not necessarily a province of their own. If Papua New Guinea's leaders were to provide the basic services Andaija fought for, then much of the discontent in the western end of the province would be quelled and the ethnic conflicts which are brewing might also be averted. The creation of a Hela province will not solve the Southern Highlands' woes, rather it will merely serve to fuel ethnic conflicts of a different kind.

References

Ballard, C. 1994 'The centre cannot hold: trade networks and sacred geography in the Papua New Guinea highlands', *Archaeology in Oceania* 29(3):130-148.

——1995 'The Death of a Great Land: Ritual, History and Subsistence Revolution in the Southern Highlands of Papua New Guinea'. Unpublished Ph.D. thesis, The Australian National University.

——2000 'The fire next time: the conversion of the Huli apocalypse', *Ethnohistory* 47(1):205-225.

Ballard, J. A. 1983 'Shaping a political arena: The elections in the Southern Highlands'. In D. Hegarty (ed.), *Electoral Politics in Papua New Guinea: Studies on the 1977 National Elections*. Port Moresby: University of Papua New Guinea, pp.174-195.

——1989 'Polarisation of a Province: The 1982 Election in the Southern Highlands'. In P. King (ed.), *Pangu returns to power: the 1982 elections in Papua New Guinea*. Canberra: Australian National University, Department of Political and Social Change. Political and Social Change Monograph No. 9, pp139-162.

Biersack, A. 1991 'Prisoners in time: millenarian praxis in a Melanesian valley', in A. Biersack (ed.), *Clio in Oceania: Toward a Historical Anthropology*. Washington: Smithsonian Institution Press, pp. 231-296.

——1995 'Introduction: the Huli, Duna and Ipili peoples yesterday and today', in A. Biersack (ed.), *Papuan Borderlands: Huli, Duna, and Ipili Perspectives on the Papua New Guinea Highlands*. Ann Arbor: University of Michigan Press, pp. 1-54.

Frankel, S. 1986 *The Huli Response to Illness*. Cambridge: Cambridge University Press.

Glasse, R. M. 1965 'The Huli of the Southern Highlands', in P. Lawrence and M.J. Meggitt (eds), *Gods Ghosts and Men in Melanesia: Some Religions of Australian New Guinea and the New Hebrides*. Melbourne: Oxford University Press, pp. 27-49.

Goldman, L. R. 1979 'Kelote: an important Huli ritual ground', *Oral History* 7(4):14-18.

——1983 *Talk Never Dies: The Language of Huli Disputes*. London: Tavistock Publications.

——n.d. 'Decorated being in Huli - parleying with paint'. Unpublished paper.

Haley, N. C. 2002a 'Election fraud on a grand scale: the case of the Koroba-Kopiago open electorate', in R. J. May and R. Anere (eds), *Maintaining Democracy: The 1997 Elections in Papua New Guinea*. Port Moresby: University of Papua New Guinea Press in conjunction with State, Society and Governance in Melanesia project, The Australian National University, pp. 123-139.

——2002b 'Ipakana Yakaiya: Mapping Landscapes, Mapping Lives — Contemporary Land Politics Among the Duna'. Unpublished PhD thesis, The Australian National University.

——2004 'A failed election: the case of the Koroba-Lake Kopiago Open Electorate', in P. Gibbs, N. Haley and A. McLeod (eds), *Politicking and Voting in the Highlands: The 2002 Papua New Guinea National Elections. State, Society and Governance in Melanesia Discussion Paper 2004/1*. Canberra: State, Society and Governance in Melanesia Project, Research School of Pacific and Asian Studies, The Australian National University, pp. 16-26.

Jacka, J. 2001 'Coca-Cola and kolo: land, ancestors and development', *Anthropology Today* 17(4):3-8.

Jorgensen, D. 1981 'Taro and Arrows: Order Entropy and Religion among the Telefolmin'. Unpublished PhD thesis, University of British Columbia.

——1985 'Femsep's last garden: a Telefol response to mortality, in. D.E.A. Counts and D. Counts (eds), *Aging and Its Transformations: Moving Toward Death in Pacific Societies*. New York: University Press of America, pp. 207-26.

——1990 'Placing the past and moving the present: myth and contemporary history in Telefolmin', *Culture* 10(2):47-56.

——1997 'Who and what is a landowner? Mythology and marking the ground in a PNG mining project', *Anthropological Forum* 7(4):599-628.

Poole, F. J. P. 1986 'The erosion of a sacred landscape: European exploration and cultural ecology among the Bimin-Kuskusmin of Papua New Guinea', in M. Tobias (ed.), *Mountain People*. Norman: University of Oklahoma Press, pp.169-182.

Robinson, R. P. 2002 'The final election', in R.J. May and Ray Anere (eds), *Maintaining Democracy: The 1997 Elections in Papua New Guinea*. Port Moresby: University of Papua New Guinea Press in conjunction with State, Society and Governance in Melanesia project, The Australian National University, pp.141-148.

Strathern, A. J. 1991 '"Company" in Kopiago', in A. Pawley (ed.), *Man And a Half: Essays in Pacific Anthropology and Ethnobiology in Honour of Ralph Bulmer*. Auckland: Polynesian Society, pp. 612-615.

Stürzenhofecker, G. 1993 'Times Enmeshed: Gender, Space, and History Among the Duna'. Unpublished PhD thesis, University of Pittsburgh.

Vail, J. 1995 'All that glitters: the Mt. Kare gold rush and its aftermath', in A. Biersack (ed.), *Papuan Borderlands: Huli, Duna, and Ipili Perspectives on the New Guinea Highlands*. Ann Arbor: University of Michigan Press, pp. 343-374.

ENDNOTES

[1] In August 1978 the Koroba local government council for instance resolved that their area lacked economic and education development and that 'Provincial government should only come after people in the west and Magarima area had equal development with the rest of Papua New Guinea (*Post-Courier* 3 August 1978).

[2] The Tari-Magarima road was not opened until mid-1977. Prior to this the western end of the province was effectively isolated (see J.A. Ballard 1983). As a result it was the last part of the province to obtain services and remains to this day the least developed.

[3] The movement is reminiscent of the failed 1980s push by the 'Min' (Mountain Ok) peoples to establish a Min province (Jorgensen 1990; 1997:603), which would have incorporated those peoples who trace descent from Afek.

[4] According to Chris Ballard (pers. comm. 2001) Bebenite was for a long time the most important Huli *gebeanda* (ritual site). Some Duna accounts, especially those collected at the Kopiago end, suggest that *Ambua atia* terminated at Gelogili (Gelote). Whilst this may have been the case following Bebenite's demise as a ritual centre, my informants in the upper Pori Valley were also clear that this route went to Bebenite and indeed on to Ambua Mountain.

[5] Chris Ballard (2000:216) notes that conversion amongst the Huli was 'a speedy and wholesale occurrence' and that 'most rituals … ceased to be publicly or openly performed during the 1960s'. Conversion to Christianity took place amongst the Huli earlier than it did amongst the Duna. While Christian missionaries entered the Huli area in 1951, they did not enter the Duna area until 1964. It is therefore plausible, as Duna claim, that they were maintaining sites such as *Ko-Yundikia kini* into the 1970s. Their claims are certainly consistent with those of other ritual specialists who had maintained remote sites elsewhere in the region.

[6] In 2002, elections in six of nine Southern Highlands electorates were declared null and void. Supplementary elections for these six seats were held successfully in April/May 2003.

[7] This figure and those that follow have been calculated from the 1990 census figures and the 1980-1990 population growth rate of 1.9 per cent per annum. They bear little resemblance to the most recent PNG census figures or the number of people listed on the Common Roll, which are both grossly inflated (see Haley 2002a).

[8] Agiru remains extremely popular in the western end of the province — as evidenced by the fact that Jacob Sekewa, endorsed by Agiru for the provincial seat, ran second to Hami Yawari, despite the fact he was a first time contestant and relatively unknown in the province.

[9] It is interesting to note that a recent letter to the editor, signed 'Hela elite, Tari, SHP' asserts that 'Thomas does not represent the bulk of the people of Hela' (*The National* 8 September 2004).

'Hoo-Ha in Huli': Considerations on commotion and community in the Southern Highlands

Laurence Goldman

Conflict — What problem? Whose problem?

Even for the most sensitive of post-colonial consciences, a 'community without conflict' is neither a destination objective, nor a socially imaginable outcome, desired by any stakeholder constituency (indigene, government or developer) in Papua New Guinea. Anthropologists, in particular, have long argued that disputes per se are not symptomatic of anomie. Social equilibriums are thus not perturbed by, but rather predicated on, cyclic patterns of grievance management. Notwithstanding its historical roots in comparative jurisprudence, the legacy of anthropological research then is that all cultures possess, or become endowed with, a spectrum of social control mechanisms for processing and settling their disputes.[1] Conflict and conflict resolution characterise all social organisations irrespective of their locale or level of development.[2]

These are salutary lessons for observers of dissension, where attitudes towards emotionally and physically scarred landscapes might otherwise compel us to read 'friction' as 'failure' — a lack of, or willingness to abide by, rules sanctioned by judicial institutions. Without engaging complex issues of 'false consciousness' and the local rhetoric about declining law and order (see Gordon and Meggitt 1985:3), we should remain mindful that in the traditional stateless and acephalous societies of Papua New Guinea, injunctions were rarely encoded in a formal *corpus juris*. Behavioural precepts were part of an undifferentiated class of 'correct ways of interacting' that were not further dissected into discrete categories of legal, social, religious or moral maxims. More often than not, norms were informally expressed through figurative genres of proverb or adage, frequently implicit in consensually arrived at resolutions, and rarely objects of explicit litigation. This does not thereby allow us to infer that rules were 'weakly' held, applied or understood. There are, then, no a-regulatory cultures,[3] just as there are no cultures that do not rely on 'talk' to express disagreement. The paradox of these universal truths is that while all languages have extensive vocabularies for wrangling, they reference such ubiquitous activity in 'negative' terms. Conflict is normal, but, equally, undesirable. Highlanders are agents of order but also disorder ('Everyone fights but no one wants to' (Gordon and Meggitt 1985:13)).

More disturbing perhaps (in the context of this volume) is the bystander apathy observers experience when confronted with the cultural truism that for many Papua New Guinea societies fighting is both a recurrent and legitimate means of prosecuting claims or seeking restitution.[4] That is, in what is loosely referred to as the 'cultural logics' (Strathern 1993:244) of indigenous conflict systems, fighting forms part of a sequenced set of behavioural responses that may itself constitute a coda, or precipitate closure. Attempting to gloss such commotion as realising an opposition between 'war' versus 'law' has long ago been rejected as ethnocentric and over-simplistic. More usefully, we need to focus on understanding the differential resort to various recourse options, and the prevalent sequential relationships between physical and verbal conflict (Roberts 1979). We might thus pose two immediate questions: first, what are the politico-economic and risk management strategies for *talking* and *fighting*? Secondly, what is the relative efficacy, cost and desirability of recourse to state judicial processes as opposed to, or in tandem with, exercises of power governed by 'custom'? In formulating these questions we seek to clarify the range of ground conditions and drivers that underpin perceptions of compliance or non-compliance behaviour when individuals operate within the pluralistic normative regimes of court and custom. Most often, such co-existent constraint systems are juxtaposed as an adjudicatory and hierarchical appellate system versus egalitarian self-help regulation.

We know that both the rule of law and custom continue to write the interactional scripts of disputants in the Southern Highlands Province (SHP). What we know less clearly is precisely why their underpinning cultural rationales continue to be in, and produce, conflict; that is, why cannot such formal and informal resolution regimes be mutually reinforcing agencies for stability in the Papua New Guinea highlands context? After more than three decades of concerted think-tank activity, problems of 'law and order' in Papua New Guinea continue to present as intractable.

Importantly, our understanding of commotion in SHP communities seems not to be anchored to, or informed by, reliable statistical data for the urban or rural environments.[5] Longitudinal research on conflict occurrence rates and the scale or nature of conflict across the SHP is scarce. The resurgence of tribal fighting is taken as an index of such conditions, but it remains unclear just how far down increased violence percolates through the layers of the social structure. Rather, what passes as 'conventional wisdom' is a *gestalt*, the triangulation of findings, drawn from the related experiences of visitors and workers, from feedback of local inhabitants,[6] from the discourse of Papua New Guinea 'law and order' analysts,[7] and from impressions given by national and international media broadcasts of world-wide trends and concerns in the Third World. These voices invariably foreground the plight of Papua New Guinea in terms of the prevalence of violence 'out of control'. From one vantage point, there may be nothing specious about advocating a position that says, 'What's *your* problem? Conflict is custom'.

Such a position appears untenable for two reasons. First, the nature, place and impact of conflict within the rapidly changing social environment of SHP differs from those circumstances which obtained in the pre-colonial era. Secondly, the now proclaimed and desired goals of development and sustainability appear to all stakeholders as unachievable without changes in the current regimes of conflict management and resolution.

The case, then, for 'intervention and prevention' is not easily rebutted by modernist academic arguments concerning the hegemony of Western knowledge, the cultural relativity of 'conflict paradigms', or the constrictive problem-solution prisms of applied science. In the SHP context, *intervention therapy* is very much a collaboratively constructed dialogue between indigenes and concerned outsiders to mitigate adverse risks posed by changing scenarios in dispute practices. Perception is 'reality', and interventionism constitutes a key policy objective in contemporary indigenous knowledge frameworks.[8]

This paper explores these contours of social change with respect to the Huli people of the Southern Highlands Province. In the following sections I address some of the key catalysts for 'violence' in the context both of the history of transformation in the region, and the options for settlement-directed activity discussed for other provinces, such as Enga. Few analysts who have observed conflict in the highlands over the last three decades would claim that finding magic-bullet solutions is easy. Not only might it be the case that a one-model-fits-all answer will likely drown in the sea of culture-specific conditions, but also the implementation and subsequent monitoring of solutions would likely tax the resources of responsible stakeholders. Progress will thus be pedestrian, but it will also be critically dependent, as we argue below, on achieving real change in the culture of mistrust, antipathy and opposition to government agencies, authority and legitimacy. Unlock the mysteries of fostering 'community' social responsibility and participation — i.e. establishing community agency — and you begin to scaffold an effective interventionist system for conflict management.

Customary dispute mechanisms in Huli

The Huli represent one of the major ethnic groups within the SHP, and indeed a microcosm of the endemic factionalism[9] that characterises both the region and the nation-state of Papua New Guinea. The Huli population of approximately 100,000 speakers is socially divided into some 300-400 named patrilineal clan units, each of which is segmented into lower-order descent units of sub-clans and lineages. Satellite descent units of any clan may be dispersed across Huli territory, though most usually each clan has a traditionally recognised locus of ritual and resource interests.

The Huli population now, as in the past, was formed by successive waves of in- and out-migration. Social mapping findings and genealogical data (see Goldman works 1997-2002 cited in the references) have consistently shown that the margins of this population are inhabited by 'naturalised' Huli clans whose origins can be clearly traced to neighbouring cultures such as the Duna, Etolo, Kaluli, and Onabasulu from the Papuan Plateau (collectively referenced as Dugube by Huli), the lowland lake peoples such as the Foe and Fasu, and highland groups such as the Ipili and Wola. Importantly, even in the pre-colonial era Huli retained a heightened self-consciousness about their own tribal identity, and divisions along 'ethnic origins' bases (even for naturalised clans of several generations standing) were and remain well entrenched.[10]

As elsewhere in the highlands, there was no pre-colonial overarching system of governance. Each clan and clan section had a 'headman' who was a repository of clan history and who led groups in feuding, ritual and warfare. They 'held the talk' and intervened in disputes only as one voice amongst many. Descent unit names were used to frame a dispute as between clan/sub-clan x and y, though rarely did such units act in concert. Fight parties were usually an *ad hoc* conglomerate of allies drawn through personal networks of a principal fight 'owner'. Apart from the resort to physical violence, disputes were also prosecuted in public moots — informal gatherings of people to 'share the talk' on some issue. Agreements could be reached by consensus and through mediation. Lacking institutionalised authorities with vetted power to impose judgements, it was not uncommon for claims to be aired in moots over a period of several months or even years.

To those unversed in the Huli cultural logic of revenge and redress (Glasse 1959) — the 'pay-back' system — the cycle of killing and counter-killing that can ramify from any breach of rights may appear indiscriminate. But this would be to ignore the calculus of segmentary descent principles whereby named clan sections that 'owned' a fight were held corporately responsible for the actions of any of its members. Any descent unit member, kin or affine became legitimate targets for retributive homicides. Such actions were underwritten by certain mores: beliefs that the spirit of a slain person would visit sickness on relatives who did not avenge a death;[11] anger of relatives against a fight 'owner' who did not both avenge and compensate the death of an ally; and descent unit pride at war prowess and the need to avoid public opprobrium and shame. The selection of particular individuals as pay-back targets might be fortuitous — they came, they saw, they killed — or combine a number of rationales based on the previous litigious history between perpetrator and victim or victim's group. Such opaque motivations allowed for multiple 'readings' of deaths depending on the social circumstances of the reader. Warfare always involved temporary cessation of movements between people over territory, and often if large-scale in nature there would be migration of women and children to other parishes.

Where disputes developed into cyclic patterns of violence, this was followed by a prolonged period of inactivity during which third-party intervention might occur to broker a settlement between the units. If the scale of the conflict was small, *wergild* might be offered by one group to another. Equally, the conflicting groups might nominate a day to settle scores, after which no claims for compensation would be pursued against the opposing fight owners. Most compensation payments were made to factions considered as allies. Internal dissension within a fight unit often followed as claims for injury and death compensation were laid at the fight owner's door. These structural strains might then result in new and more ramified patterns of pay-back in the area.

The local understanding of conflict and conflict settlement is one expressed in the language of 'sickness' and 'healing': disputes are like medical pathologies to which one applies compensation[12] as a form of folk medicine. *'Talk Never Dies'* (Goldman 1983) precisely because between potential litigants there was always a number of issues that simply remained unprosecuted, or unresolved after talking or fighting. That is, many claims would lie dormant until a strategically significant later occasion of dispute in which claimants could and would 'activate' these past unresolved disputes in a sequenced set of claims. Disputes were thus always 'multiple-claim' affairs. It was never the case that a 'conflictless' set of conditions prevailed within any Huli community.

There are two important corollaries arising out of the above discussion. First, conflict generation was more than simply an immediate reaction to some perpetrated breach of a person's rights or person. Litigants whose wealth stocks were substantially depleted by some compensation exchange might trigger any of a host of unresolved claims with other litigants to redress their depleted finances. Disputes then were a structurally inherent and consequential by-product of a system of 'talk-directed settlement' unconstrained by the dictates of time. Secondly, the onus for action and reaction was not delegated to or usurped by nominated agencies charged with monitoring adherence to rules, which might then intervene to restore 'order'. This critical lack of centralisation meant resolution by consensus and mediation occurred through individual discretion, and self-regulatory mechanisms. Dialogue not closure (Henton 2000:586) was the essence of the process of this system.

Huli fought about 'land, women and pigs'.[13] They fought with bows and arrows, and with their beliefs in the efficacy of toxic substances and sorcery. Importantly, the conflict system presented as uniform across the region in the precise sense that irrespective of locale, the types of disputes and the modes of management and resolution appeared equally represented from Margarima to

Mogra-Fugua. As is indicated below, resource development projects in the region became catalysts for non-uniform locale-specific disputes and claims on exogenous benefit streams.

The drivers behind traditional dispute resolution in part resided in the tacitly understood political and social-economic benefits of peaceful coexistence with resident others. Wars were most often fought with close neighbours between whom intermarriage rates were high. Because one fought against those with whom one exchanged, third-party intervention through cross-cutting loyalties occurred. Moreover, personal reputations could be made and enhanced within these conflict cauldrons by speakers employing rhetorical skills as 'middle-men' to achieve consensus on dispute outcomes.

Equally, however, there were drivers more specifically associated with 'compensation' still neglected in what passes for commonsense knowledge about Huli dispute processes.

Notwithstanding impressions of lawlessness in Huli over the last decade, there is no persuasive evidence that cultural mores regarding compensation are simply being ignored or rejected. The continuing incidence and importance of compensatory exchange behaviour indicates the resilient vitality of 'custom' governing inter-personal and inter-group relationships.[14]

Succinctly stated, paying compensation remains *the* conventionally-oriented coda to conflict; it symbolises more than merely a rationale for pig husbandry or accumulation of wealth. Paying compensation:

- demonstrates both individual and corporate pride, as well as power, to acquit corporate social responsibility in a public forum;
- addresses the risk of 'shame' (Epstein 1984) which might otherwise ensue, and which remains a forceful sanction in Melanesian culture;
- allows for other complex economic relationships of credit and debt — e.g. bridewealth, loans, land payments etc. — to be segued into and acquitted by these dispute resolution channels;
- provides closure on specific sets of issues that were the basis for compensatory calculation;
- symbolically invokes and reaffirms both the continuing memberships of people to personal networks and social group statuses through exchange and consumption, and the acceptance of norms of interaction that constitute the 'cultural identity and ethnicity' of the litigants;
- realises obligations and responsibilities of people towards the 'health' — both physical and psychological — of others 'injured' by their behaviour.

Western enculturation often compels us to oppose *talking* and *fighting* — we express this in phrases such as 'the time for talking is over', 'action not words', or 'walk the talk'. In Huli *bi* (talk) and *ba* (fight) are not similarly opposed in this way, but rather form analogous and continuous modes of dispute interaction; equally, they do not therefore attract opposed moral valences (Goldman 1983; Brison 1989). The pursuance of claims through fighting rests on comparable drivers of group reputation, group machismo, and religious ideology as wars conducted throughout Western history. Arrows and argy-bargy are but prosecution modalities in a continuum of options for dispute prosecution. Fighting and compensation are here ceremonial events in which consciousness of the 'system' rules is heightened and reaffirmed by participants. These are the cultural scripts about how and why people exist as they do. Such public attestation of power and status — what they get out of fighting and compensating in the manner they do — has yet to be radically transformed by any social change movement. Huli fight and compensate as a ritual of deference to collective norms and societal values. Opting out is not an option unless one's name and membership status is of no value. Power may flow from the barrel of a gun, but peace is financed from the banter of the garrulous.

There is nothing gratuitous about providing the above overview of customary Huli conflict. Historically informed and succinct understandings of these local systems of dispute are needed precisely because at this juncture in time they remain vital and operational. Notwithstanding the changes to governance structures chronicled below, the transformations wrought on dispute settlement were not so much *ideological* in nature — fundamental transformations in beliefs and rationales, as *idiomatic* — doing the same things for the same reasons but through different channels, auspices or practices. In the move towards modernity, Huli communities became subject to the implementation of new organisational and representational structures related to land, resources and judiciary. Change meant an exponential growth in the overlapping organisational entities to which an individual belonged, but traditional patterns of cultural identity based on kinship and descent were not thereby expunged. This made for an uneasy coexistence of *custom* and *court*, at the very juncture in history when central government began, in the eyes of landowners, to lose its core authority and legitimacy.

Changing social conditions

1940s-1980s

Following first contact in the 1930s, the traditional system of conflict management was impacted by all the administrative trappings conventionally associated with colonial mechanistic bureaucracies. These included the establishment of district and regional governance, and local government councils (LGCs); and imposition of a multi-tiered system of state-constituted courts following the 1962 Derham Report — land mediators, land courts, local and district, national and supreme courts (see Figure 6.1); the introduction of village courts, following the *Village*

Courts Act, 1973, and other administrative agencies such as the village councillor system. In addition to this forensic edifice, disputes were also taken to, settled by, or sought to involve, mission workers, administrative agents such as *kiaps*, or police contingents in Koroba, Tari or Komo.

The fundamental impact of this period was the erosion of the localised insularity of a people who had for millennia relied on indigenous, grassroots-generated, institutions of grievance management. This trajectory of increasing exposure to outside agencies, imported technologies, political representation structures, and non-traditional lifestyles was buttressed by an increase in tourism-related activities in the SHP; provincial management of district policy and public works programs in health, education and communications; assimilation and accommodation of knowledge of, and use and reliance upon, cash and cash economy goods; and the incremental impacts of a newly-educated youth dissatisfied with a subsistence-agriculture-based lifestyle, and which sought employment opportunities in Mount Hagen, Lae, Port Moresby and elsewhere.

There is good evidence to suggest that in this first-wave period of consolidated colonial presence, the various 'court' systems imposed a quantum of fines and penalties quite at odds with traditional custom. The cumulative impact in the short term was thus to actually increase the general level of litigation as disputants relied on the activation of pending claims latent in the customary conflict system to redress wealth imbalances. Elsewhere, non-customary impositions of homicidal compensation as 'penalties' merely exacerbated levels of inter-group conflict.

The cautionary warning one takes from this period of response to 'law and order' is that interventionist activities can often themselves be a catalyst for increased levels of the very activity they attempt to address. Importantly, the whole *kot* system became a larger referral network for dispute processing as an alternative avenue of recourse when customary *talking* failed to produce a desired outcome. Risk management strategies weighed up distance, time, cost, and effort considerations. Equally, levels of frustration were building with 'courts' because of two quite alien administrative conventions: first, the distinction courts maintained between civil and criminal cases often confused litigants, and secondly, interrogative procedures were aimed at disentangling claim issues to produce a single definition of a wrong/breach against which to apply a reparation calculus or penalty. This was quite foreign to 'custom' in which litigants sought to 'entangle' issues in sequential chains of causation to reveal the 'source/base/bone/root' event, and where compensation might subsume multiple issues between the litigants. For Huli, case prosecution became an alienating experience, often resulting in frustration that parts of the multiple-claim web not dealt with in the courts would then have to be pursued as separate, rather than aggregated, issues. Under these conditions state 'law' began to lose social acceptance.

In these decades of assimilation, accommodation and adaptation to change, inter-group behaviour was impacted upon by profoundly politicised agendas associated with national governance. Politics was viewed as a new theatre of competition for acquiring benefit streams. This was politics as patronage. This world-view was not impregnated with any embedded concept of 'the community good'. Rather, politics was subjected to localised maximising strategies: to secure a position (for oneself or related other) as a member; to ensure one had a '*wantok*' as an elected representative; and to invoke and rework regional myths of origins to create new provinces as smaller self-interested distributional pies. Fuelled by the belief — underscored by continual revelations and rumours — that national government was corrupt and inefficient, governance became burdened with a credibility gap problem for grass-roots populaces in the highlands. Equally, it has to be acknowledged that there were no predisposing cultural conditions for landowners to become 'team players' in nation building. Simply expressed, there was no community agency for social advancement. Succinctly expressed, politico-legal infrastructures and agencies were never welcomed as integral parts of people's lives; engendered without collaborative debate, imposed without full awareness and education campaigns, they induced apathy and antipathy. These were conveniences of and for an alienated cabal of decision-makers.

What precipitated a downward spiral in social order, after some initial development successes in the 1960s-1970s, was a conjunction of factors that laid the ground conditions for inequality, frustration, and pedestrian progress. On the one hand, there were unfilled, but equally exaggerated, expectations by landowners; on the other hand, they could rightly point to their disappointments with unsustainable agricultural and small business (e.g. trade store) projects. We witnessed the 'declining effectiveness of courts, the police, and other law-enforcement agencies of the central government; a useful point of departure is to regard them as otiose, if not obsolete' (Gordon and Meggitt 1985:247). What emerged was a newfound fervour for reparation streams through new claim types — road, vehicle and work related injuries — and even larger war compensation demands resulting from increased inter-ethnic communication and contact. Government infrastructure like schools, aid-posts, hospitals, and district offices became legitimate targets of vandalism in conflict or politically-related disenchantment. Penalties of imprisonment failed to stem the tide of disorder largely because incarceration lacks the stigmatic deterrent value found in Western cultures.

Figure 6.1. National judicial system (Chalmers and Paliwala 1977:94)

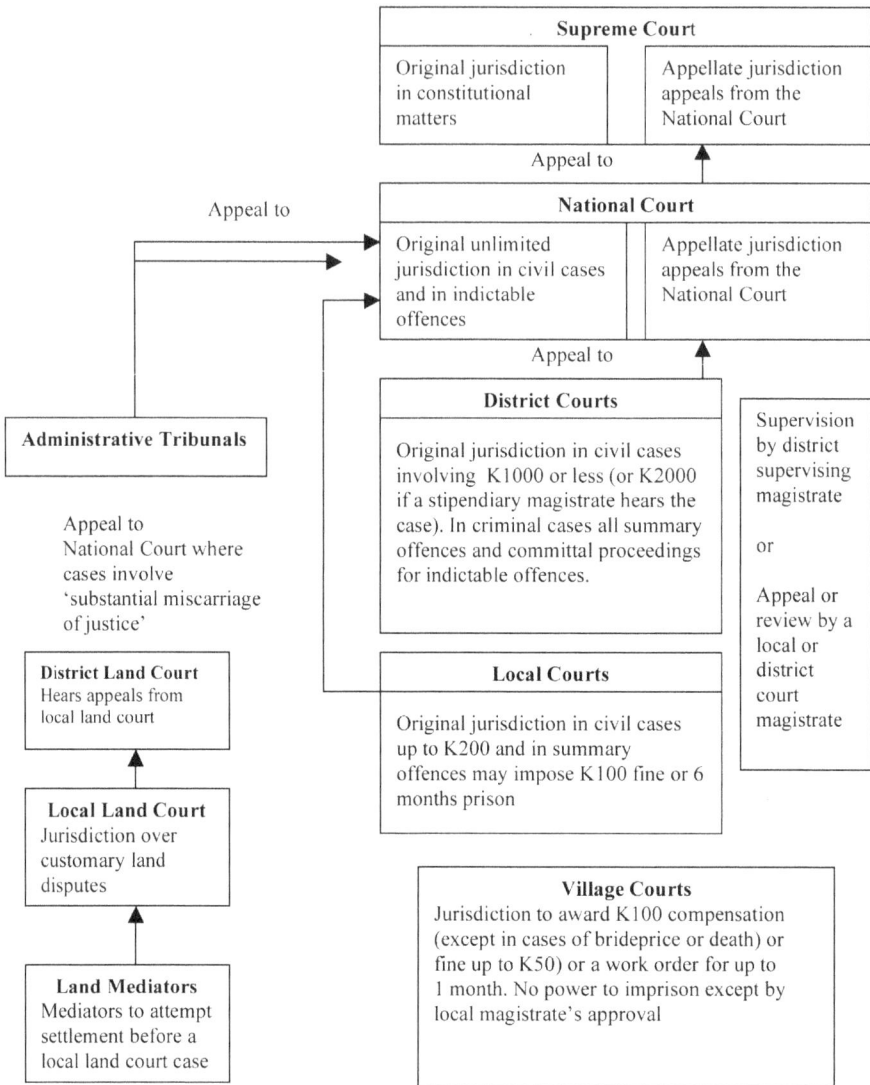

Supreme Court	
Original jurisdiction in constitutional matters	Appellate jurisdiction appeals from the National Court

Appeal to

Appeal to

National Court	
Original unlimited jurisdiction in civil cases and in indictable offences	Appellate jurisdiction appeals from the National Court

Appeal to

Administrative Tribunals

Appeal to
National Court where cases involve 'substantial miscarriage of justice'

District Land Court
Hears appeals from local land court

Local Land Court
Jurisdiction over customary land disputes

Land Mediators
Mediators to attempt settlement before a local land court case

District Courts

Original jurisdiction in civil cases involving K1000 or less (or K2000 if a stipendiary magistrate hears the case). In criminal cases all summary offences and committal proceedings for indictable offences.

Supervision by district supervising magistrate

or

Appeal or review by a local or district court magistrate

Local Courts

Original jurisdiction in civil cases up to K200 and in summary offences may impose K100 fine or 6 months prison

Village Courts
Jurisdiction to award K100 compensation (except in cases of brideprice or death) or fine up to K50) or a work order for up to 1 month. No power to imprison except by local magistrate's approval

There were, and remain, some systemic environmental (both social and physical) conditions that constrain development progress in Huli, which might be identified as follows.

- The residential settlement pattern of the Huli is one of scattered households, not nucleated village settlements. For a population of 100,000 people distributed over often inhospitable territory, the reticulation of water, electricity and sanitation is no more feasible than it is for, say, outlying 1 hectare properties in Brisbane. With wholesale settlement change unlikely in the short term, development confronts the twin tyrannies of distance and distribution.

- With the exception of those roads close to resource developments, only the main trunk highways have sealed surfaces and remain accessible and useable most of the time. In times of conflict, these arterial links may be closed by warring factions, or used by local landowners in roadblocks to extort money.
- Business ventures — cattle, coffee, cash crops, silkworms, etc. — have proved unsustainable over the decade due to many factors, including transport and communication problems alluded to above; lack of understanding about investment and replenishment strategies; competition by start-up trade stores which attract customers on a 'same descent unit' basis; and profit erosion through funnelling into customary exchange activities or debit-credit relationships.
- Virtually no local business employment other than small trade activities in Tari, Koroba and Komo. This remains particularly marked in non-project areas. Project benefits attained by the new 'Huli haves' rankled with the relatively disadvantaged 'have-nots'.
- Patterns of expenditure reveal an inexorable and inexhaustible consumerism. Disposable incomes are dissipated on consumables that lack any supporting repair and maintenance infrastructure. Goods bought quickly become unserviceable and deteriorate, driving the need for replacement expenditure.
- For that small percentage of Huli who bucked these trends, their options were very limited. Accumulation of wealth for its own sake could not yet be valued over traditional patterns and expectations of distribution forcing many skilled migrants to remain 'outsiders' for extended periods.

In effect the vast majority of the rural population saw themselves as impaled on the horns of a dilemma: trapped between their inability to extricate themselves from dependence on subsistence horticulture to simply survive, and the drive to acquire money to purchase cash economy goods and satisfy other needs. Income windfalls were transient in effect, making little substantial or sustainable difference to their lives. In the context of an increasingly alienated political and governance machinery, the rule of 'conflict custom' remained the viable anchor for redress of grievances.

1980s-2000

Until the late 1980s the geometry of social group formation and custom, the infrastructure of ties between descent groups and land, remained largely intact and to a degree impervious to these sweeping transformations. But this was now a system whose ethical underpinnings and familial control mechanisms had long dissipated. Elsewhere, the waning men's longhouse tradition and increased rates of male-female coresidence were having similar impacts.

The contexts (e.g. magic, ritual, warfare) in which traditional leaders operated no longer obtained, or had been dramatically altered. Many of the older incumbents of 'headman' status lacked education in or knowledge of Tok Pisin/English. Where their representative functions were needed, most especially in resource development areas, they were usurped by, or powers were devolved to, younger literate males. With large contingents of Huli now semi-permanently resident in Port Moresby, discontinuities in the voices of representation began to emerge between grassroots and migrant community members.

Cessation of most religious fertility cults, and indeed the bachelor cult, during the 1960s meant that the institutionalised inculcation of conventional Huli mores was now left solely to religious, school or family agencies. But these belief systems were long challenged by imported ideologies, producing a society with coexistent but plural moral codes. This non-uniformity and breakdown in low-level family control produced fertile ground conditions for a more nucleated outlook on strategies to maximise income streams. These became sedimented well before the onset of resource development. Importantly, policing order became impossible outside the restricted zones of influence adjacent to the small contingent forces in Tari, Koroba and Komo. Resources were simply inadequate for both the size of population and its dispersed settlement. In this respect, consider the comparative police: populace ratios of Australia, 1: 439; New Zealand 1: 692; and Papua New Guinea 1: 1,000. For Huli, it is likely that the ratio exceeded 1: 1000. Irrespective of these resource statistics, this was a rapidly transformed theatre of conflict:

- there was widespread importation of firearms and firearm technology that meant the sanction of force was not easily applied in this stone-to-steel landscape where most adult males over 18 boasted their own shotgun;
- new forms of injury were being perpetrated that included maiming and rape, as well as adopted practices such as kidnapping for ransom (as in the Koroba-Kopiago election of 2002);[15]
- inter-tribal conflicts escalated in number, frequency, and death counts, rendering police impotent much of the time;
- the phenomenon of '*raskol* gangs' that were mobile, armed, and transient in formation, posed insurmountable problems for policing in the area.

By the 1990s the true ineffectiveness of the court system had become apparent. There were staggering rates of acquittal, dismissed cases, adjournments, and not-guilty verdicts. The appeals system within the context of an under-resourced judiciary only strengthened public opinion that litigation was a form of gamesmanship, another arena for 'talking' that bred contempt. Huli became adept at marshalling their own 'evidence' including government reports that fell off the back of proverbial PMVs, using Huli lawyers and legal students, and even attempting to co-opt anthropologists.

The resource development cauldron

The developments of Kare, Porgera, Hides, Kutubu, Mananda and Moran established SHP as a resource-rich province. For many Huli, this fulfilled traditional cargo-cult prophecies and their understandings of sacred landscapes. But the accelerated pace of transformation with respect to infrastructure development, business training and development, roads, and general wealth creation were seen as unevenly spread.

Localised distribution of resource benefit streams was a source of frustration and division at both intra- and inter-ethnic levels. Outsiders saw themselves as rural spokes to advantaged hubs of 'elite' village bases that garnered newfound reputations as enduring symbols of inequity. In-migration to these mini-centres of wealth occurred with consequential increased levels of crime. Local governments were viewed as lining their own pockets by negotiating favourable landowner deals.

To accommodate modernity, project impact communities have been subject to the implementation of a raft of new organisational and representational structures. These include membership to agencies, incorporated land groups (ILGs), landowner companies (LANCOs), landowners' associations, petroleum prospecting licence (PPL) and petroleum development licence (PDL) status, village development committees, and local-level government wards following the 1995 Organic Law on Provincial Governments and Local-Level Governments (OLPGLLG). Precisely because many of these schemes have localised implementation only (i.e. often facilitated by developers in specific project areas) non-participant communities feel disadvantaged. Equally, the newly established entities are bedevilled by the same problems that afflict all governance institutions: inadequate resources, insufficiently trained personnel, and a constituency of 'members' lacking acceptance or appreciation of the concept of 'for the good of the community'. It is not simply that such entities become unsustainable, or unworkable under their guiding mandates, but that their constituencies treat them as new fora for pursuing politico-economic strategies. They become colonised by Huli custom.

Within the project areas, decision-making was often concentrated in the hands of a few individuals or organisations that were frequently less than transparent in their communications with grassroots members. This allowed certain individuals to amass and manipulate large amounts of wealth and political control, inducing divisiveness within communities.

Landowners continued to regard themselves as competitors with government for benefit streams through control of and access to their sub-surface resources. Equity, royalties, roads and infrastructure became the new battlegrounds. In this enterprise, politics was the means whereby they could influence outcomes by ensuring 'one of us' was in the Mendi lodge.

The argument put forward here is that there was a conjuncture of predisposing social and economic conditions which contributed to the deterioration in 'law and order' across the SHP. Whilst custom and court continue to operate in a coterminous fashion across the region, the efflorescence and vitality of custom is in direct proportion to the waning efficacy of state judicature. This finding addresses in some part our initial question about the relative recourse to state as opposed to locally engendered dispute resolution mechanisms. The efficiency with which Huli continue to colonise assimilated institutional arrangements renders them little more than theatres for political strategists. In the context of those environmental conditions described above, it was little surprise that the village court system also fell prey to suspicions of corruption, manipulation, and failure of magistrates to adequately supervise their administration.

From whence will solutions emerge?

It is pertinent to remind ourselves that despite numerous commissions of enquiry since the early 1970s, the introduction of village courts, states of emergency, and various development-oriented governance initiatives and reforms, few inroads have been made into the continuing deterioration in law and order conditions. Even the most cursory of reviews of the burgeoning literature on highlands 'law and order' problems can yield an intimidating set of 'I know why and we ought to' recommendations. Causal analyses have proposed the resurgence of violence as linked to the concomitants of globalisation, ethnicity and identity movements, dependency and inequality, and social frustration. Anthropologists have contributed their musings about conflict in acephalous cultures with floating hierarchies of prestige.[16] Proposed solutions have variously included some of the following: the removal of state law, with sole reliance on custom; a 'glass windows' approach with unprecedented levels of support for court institutions and imposition of group fines (see the 'Paney report', Papua New Guinea 1973); and reintroduction of the *kiap* system.[17]

The top-down options

National

Few would disagree that the Papua New Guinea nation-state presents as unstable, with impoverished infrastructure and lacking capacity to adequately service its constituencies. This fuels widespread perceptions of inefficiency and corruption. At the very least, there has been unmitigated erosion of partnership ideals, and little appreciation that the state is a 'nurturing' organisation. Such inculcation and embedding of a 'theory of social formation and responsibilities' can only realistically evolve over the long term, given present circumstances.

Provincial

Devolution of control and decision making to provinces, and more recently to local-level governments, was an attempt to address the tyrannies of distance and distribution alluded to previously. The scheme suffers from the hangover of general administrative decline:

- successive incumbent administrations find the infrastructure left by previous incumbents continually weakened by theft or destruction of computers, vehicles, and office equipment;
- suspicion and accusations of large-scale misappropriation of funds, and irregularities in contract regulation and tendering processes are rife;
- provincial planners do not get support through lack of a research culture whereby 'needs'-based project inputs are part of decision-making processes;
- infrastructure development since the 1990s reveals high levels of provincial resource project dependency through tax credit schemes, etc. For 1993-2000, Chevron NiuGuini Limited (CNGL), as operators for the joint venture partners, expended $US20 million in the SHP alone. Oil revenue for SHP in 1997 contributed 41 per cent of the total provincial budget. Both SHP and Gulf Province are dependent on national government grants and oil revenues to cover recurrent and development expenditures.
- Official statistics indicate that in the very years SHP income was at its highest level, the provision of health and education services actually declined. National health statistics for Nipa-Kutubu District indicate that by comparison with other provinces, or indeed Papua New Guinea median rates, Kutubuans have low numbers of health extension officers (HEOs), and poor communications and family planning. Immunisation levels dropped significantly in the period 1995-1998, to less than 30 per cent of the levels reported in 1995.

The 2002 Social and Economic Impact Statement for Kutubu-Gobe (Goldman, Kameata and Brooksbank 2002), identifies six health service indicators: clinical visits (25 in 1995 and none in 1998), community health workers (CHWs) and aid post orderlies (APOs) (53 in 1995 and 37 in 1998), communications (25 in 1995 and 11 in 1998), number of refrigerators (86 in 1995 and 78 in 1998), triple antigen cover rates (100 in 1995 and 35 in 1998), and monthly reporting rates (46 in 1995 and 73 in 1998), over a three-year period. The same scenarios are applicable across the region. Clearly, the problems of governance and administration of social services are not necessarily related to the presence or absence of resource development in and of itself.

Barriers and bridges

Given that in this paper we can provide no more than an opening onto the kinds of 'interventionist therapies' required to address problems outlined above, we offer the following set of recommendations:

- micro-management at new community levels to foster community agency and self-management in the process of development;
- institutional strengthening of the present 'court' system by wider distribution of judicial functions to provide greater accessibility, presence, and effective intervention;
- increased police presence with specific interventionist agendas at the outbreak of violence, and more effective policing of gun use and possession through implementation of group fines;
- increased business training in non-project areas focused on the development of small-scale business initiatives in maintenance and repair work.

It is our contention that, for all the reasons given above, custom will offer attractive avenues for conflict management while state legal institutions and administration continue to be weakened and undermined by 'image' issues. In the short-to-medium term what is needed is an accommodation and balance between court and custom by establishing firewalls to uncontrolled fighting. Triadic conflict settlement based on tradition is effective, is indulged in by the populace, and is continuous with established mores of social behaviour. Wholesale reinvention of indigenous grievance management processes for Huli is rather akin to showing Greg Norman how to hold a golf club. What is required is control at the margins of the system.

The reliance on custom is in part attributable to the success of Huli in their indigenisation of state legal control (cf. Weisbrot *et al* 1982). Village courts and other institutions manifest this upward colonisation, even though, paradoxically, in the initial periods the courts aped the style and penalties of district and local court magistrates. There would need to be a uniform, widespread and simultaneous change in the clan descent system, use of wealth patterns, and economic subsistence bases, to make any change in the recourse strategies of litigants. Transformation will most likely and most successfully evolve in the absence of any forceful imposition of conflict resolution regimes. Without unilateral disarmament, any increased use of legitimate violence by the state will meet forceful rebuff and antipathy by the populace.

Institutional strengthening of the court system is required but in a guise much changed from what has previously obtained. It may be that the new local-level government wards can service the needs for development of 'community agencies'. But whatever demarcation of social units is deemed appropriate, there needs to be deployment of supporting legal and executive functions: more courts and more police. As we have noted previously, changes to the residential settlement pattern will not occur in the short-to-medium term precisely because the land tenure system will not itself undergo dramatic transformation. For Huli, then, one has to select an appropriate level of administrative zone to develop corporate approaches to community wellbeing.

Micro-management in community development will most successfully occur in the short term within the resource project areas. In effect, these will provide the kinds of modelling and scaffolding precedents that can be adopted by the rest of the region if only because resources are available for such initiatives. The significance of establishing 'model' communities as incentives to others for change cannot be underestimated. At the same time, the success of engendering community agency will depend on how far one is able to educate landowners on the responsibilities of self-empowerment and control. Drawing again from the recent Kutubu Social and Economic Impact Statement (SEIS), when asked about the provision of better services in the area, 74 per cent of respondents indicated that they felt this was the duty of the developer, with only 26 per cent identifying their community as having any responsibility for development priorities.

While there are no magic bullets for sustainable development, most especially where the infrastructure to support a market economy is still underdeveloped, more can be done to encourage minor training and business ventures in non-project areas, such as repair and maintenance. Extension of training opportunities to non-project areas will go some way towards alleviating impressions of relative deprivation.

Perhaps hardest of all will be the challenge to unravel the skein of distrust and disrespect for all forms of state governance perceived as a cannibal of landowner protein. The baggage of the *wantok* system and endemic factionalism cannot be overridden by minor successes on the front of social progress. This is why any faith placed in the judiciary as the font for all control is misplaced and ill conceived. Furthermore, no amount of good intentioned psychotherapy via the medium of managed development will in and of itself halt the upward colonising tendencies of Huli. Whilst politics is perceived as a patronage rather than a participatory endeavour, the court system will continue to be subverted. Top-down role models may be one answer to these 'image' problems.

References

Brison, K. 1989 'Talk and no action? How "saying is doing" in Kwanga meetings', *Ethnology* 28:97-115.

Chalmers, D. and Paliwala, A. 1977 *An Introduction to the Law of Papua New Guinea*. Sydney: The Law Book Company.

Epstein, A. 1984 *The Experience of Shame in Melanesia*. Royal Anthropological Institute of Great Britain & Ireland. Occasional Paper No.40.

Feil, D. 1979 'From negotiability to responsibility: A change in Tombema-Enga homicide compensation', *Human Organisation* 38(4):356-65.

Fitzpatrick, P. 1980 *Law and State in Papua New Guinea*. New York: Academic Press.

——1982 'The political economy of dispute settlement in Papua New Guinea', in C. Sumner (ed.) *Crime, Justice and Underdevelopment*. London: Heinemann, pp.228-47.

Glasse, R. 1959 'Revenge and redress amongst the Huli', *Mankind* 5:273-289.

Goldman, L. R. 1983 *Talk Never Dies. The Language of Huli Disputes*. London: Tavistock.

——1997a *Chevron Social Mapping Consultancy. Final Report 11th February 1997*. Moro: CNGL.

——1997b *NW Moran Social Mapping Report*. Moro: CNGL.

——1998a *Social and Economic Impact Study for PNG—Queensland Gas Project. Report for inclusion in EIS submitted to PNG and Australian Governments*.Vols 1-3. Moro: CNGL.

——1998b *Social Mapping of the Omati Basin*. Moro: CNGL.

——1999a *Social Mapping Report on Western Province and Torres Strait for PNG—Queensland Gas Project*. Moro: CNGL.

——1999b *Preliminary Social Mapping for Oil Search in Hides PDL1 — PNG*. Hides: Oil Search.

——2000a *Preliminary Social Mapping of Mananda PPL 161/219*. Moro: CNGL.

——2000b *Preliminary Social Mapping of PPL194*. CUE Energy Resources. Melbourne: CUE.

——2001 *Preliminary Social Mapping Report on Hides-Kutubu Gas Pipeline*. Moro: Chevron.

Goldman, L. R., Kameata, R. and Brooksbank, J. 2002 *Kutubu-Gobe Petroleum Project Social and Economic Impact Statement*. Moro:CDI.

Gordon, R., and Meggitt, M. 1985 *Law and Order in the New Guinea Highlands*. Hanover: University Press New England.

Henton, D. 2000 'Singing songs of expectation', in P. Buchanan, A. Grainge and R. Thornton (eds), *Proceedings of the Fourth PNG Petroleum Convention*, Port Moresby, pp.585-593.

MacIndoe, T. 1981 'Tribal fighting and compensation in the Simbu Province', in R. Scaglion (ed.), *Homicide Compensation in Papua New Guinea*. Law Reform Commission Monograph No.1. Port Moresby, pp.25-36.

Paliwala, A. 1982 'Law and order in the village: Papua New Guinea's village courts', in C. Sumner (ed.), *Crime, Justice and Underdevelopment*. London: Heinemann, pp.192-227.

Papua New Guinea. 1973 *Report of the Committee Investigating Tribal Fighting in the Highlands (Paney Report)*. Port Moresby.

Roberts, S. 1979 *Order and Dispute: An Introduction to Legal Anthropology*. Harmondsworth: Penguin.

Sillitoe, P. 1981 'Some more on war: a Wola perspective', in R. Scaglion (ed.), *Homicide Compensation in Papua New Guinea*. Law Reform Commission Monograph No.1. Port Moresby, pp.69-81.

Strathern, A. 1977 'Contemporary warfare in the New Guinea highlands. Revival or breakdown?', *Yagl-Ambu* 4(3):135-46.

——1993 *Voices of Conflict*. Ethnology Monograph No 14. University of Pittsburgh.

Weisbrot, D., Paliwala, A. and Sawyerr, A. 1982 *Law and Social Change in Papua New Guinea*. Sydney: Butterworths.

ENDNOTES

[1] Most typically in Papua New Guinea, these span the gamut of (a) informal moots to court-like institutions; (b) the competitive channeling of opposition through forms of exchange; (c) retributive practices including physical violence, witchcraft and sorcery; (d) the diffuse sanctions of shame, and public opprobrium through harangue or public/private announcement protocols; (e) withdrawal and avoidance; (f) compensation.

[2] These understandings are implicit in much of the literature on 'law and order' in Papua New Guinea (cf. Fitzpatrick 1980, 1982; Paliwala 1982; Strathern 1993).

[3] That is, there are no cultures bereft of conventionally understood, attested and expressed behavioural mores governing interaction.

[4] See MacIndoe (1981) for similar sentiments about Simbu.

[5] Gordon and Meggitt (1985:19-24) alluded to similar problems in Enga in their sub-section title 'The problem in and of statistics'. See also findings of the *Report of the Committee to Investigate Tribal Fighting in the Highlands* [Paney Report] (1973).

[6] The Social and Economic Impact Statement (SEIS) for Kutubu-Gobe (Goldman, Kameata and Brooksbank 2002) noted that 79.5 per cent of respondents felt that 'law and order' problems had increased in the project-impacted areas. 44 per cent of interviewed subjects stated they thought it was resource-project-related, but 56 per cent felt that it was only partially or not at all related to the inception of the resource project — that in effect other drivers and social conditions were responsible for deterioration in 'law and order'.

[7] The phrase is understood to refer to levels of conformity to criminal law prescriptions about violence, theft, disturbance of peace, and the firm administration of penalties for breach.

[8] While this may not be reflected in any developed critical indigenous scholarship, it does subsist at the level of commonly agreed world-views.

[9] This phrase glosses the conditions of widespread and embedded fears, mistrust and security concerns within and between groups.

[10] In the Hides area, this manifested itself during the 1990s in a major land dispute between Huli and Dugube, even though, paradoxically, the Dugube in question were all long-term naturalised and resident Huli. Similar 'ethno-theories of ethnicity' are reflected in the mythical and ideological foundations of the Hela political movement which seeks to create a new province from 'common origin' landowners (see Haley, this volume).

[11] Similar findings have been made by Sillitoe (1981) for the Wola of the SHP.

[12] I have argued elsewhere (Goldman 1983) that the Huli nomenclature for compensation pigs encodes a folk medicine, just as the term 'compensation' in Huli is etymologically derived from the term 'to make/get well'.

[13] Claims most typically included pig damage, illicit sex, homicide, debts, theft, compensation, land, insult, poisoning, trespass, bridewealth, custody, and sorcery.

[14] There appear major differences here between Huli, and Melpa or Engan practices as described by Feil (1979) and Gordon and Meggitt (1985). Engans manipulated stereotyped ideas of compensation to exploit *baim bodi* homicide compensations. In Huli, to the contrary, there is no evidence of traditional payment categories having been subverted by new exigencies in the social environment.

[15] However, the rules of fighting and engagement appear, as in Enga (see Gordon and Meggitt 1985:154), to have remained much the same.

[16] Strathern (1977) identifies as structural conditions for warfare in the region the combination of (a) high population density; (b) large political units; (c) avid response to economic development; and (d) aspects to group dynamics.

[17] See Gordon and Meggitt (1985) for an overview of these suggestions.

Issues of Stability in the Southern Highlands Province

Laurie Bragge[1]

> ... there is no such thing as the 'balance of nature' ... It is a myth; an offshoot of the desire for stability — of an attempt to reduce the world to a tidy static, and therefore comprehensible and predictable place ... The search for stability is the most constant — and the most fruitless, quest of all (Wyndham 1980:63-64).

There was a time of order in the Southern Highlands

The author was assistant district commissioner in charge of the Koroba District from 1974 to 1976, a period spanning self-government in Papua New Guinea under the Australian administration (the era of the *kiap* or patrol officer) and independence under a Papua New Guinea government. At that time my family and I could safely travel anywhere in the Huli and Duna tribal areas without protection and be welcomed by the people.

Rural Papua New Guinea often harks back to the peace, stability and service delivery of the *kiap* era and calls for a return to it. But as this paper will show, the *kiap* system did not survive the changing post-independence social environment, and there can be no wholesale return to it. There are, however, guiding principles of the system that could be successfully applied in the Southern Highlands today.

Guiding principles and procedures under the *kiap* system

- *Authority and responsibility rested with kiaps to maintain the peace, order and good governance of a district or province.* In the 1970s the typical *kiap* in charge of a district such as Koroba concurrently held a number powers: he was a commissioned officer of police, district court magistrate, local court magistrate, coroner, gaoler, manager of the Commonwealth Bank agency, postmaster, meteorologist and acting departmental head of every government department not represented in the district — typically including Works, Transport and Finance. In short, to the local people the kiap personified gavman (the government).
- *Kiaps* generally achieved their objectives through cultural empathy, cooperation and understanding, rather than the use of authority and force. The key to successful administration was a 'hearts and minds' approach.
- *The rule of law — consistency and certainty*. The rule of law was fundamental to everything the *kiap* did. The establishment and maintenance of peace and

order were fundamental tasks that took priority ahead of everything else. Fundamental to this, the *kiap* system was loosely based on a military system. The approach to conflict situations was first of all to achieve the objective and, secondly, to do it as safely as possible.

- The inherent potential for accusations of conflict of interest in the *kiaps'* overlapping authorities made consistency in decision making a fundamental virtue. For the rural people, this provided certainty and left little doubt about perceptions of right and wrong. Very often, the first contact rural people had with the *gavman* was when the *kiap* and his police turned up to arrest them for wilful murder of a person or people already under government influence. This provided an ongoing dilemma: these new people did not know the new rules — they had always killed their enemies, why punish them? The answer was 'consistency'. In such cases the *kiap* would give the evidence necessary to get the conviction in the Supreme Court and then provide antecedent reports to ensure the judge was fully informed of the circumstances of these particular people and was thus in a position to provide an appropriate sentence. Generally the *kiap* wanted those convicted to be in gaol just long enough to see the 'outside world' and learn Tok Pisin, and then return to their area to be his ambassadors. Most Telefomin interpreters in the 1960s, for example, were convicted killers.

- *The concept of 'custom' as common law.* Under the provisions of the *Native Custom Recognition Act*, the customary law of every culture in Papua New Guinea was recognised more or less as the common law of the region, except where a custom was repugnant to statute law — headhunting, for example, contravened section 301 of the *Criminal Code* (wilful murder).

- A very important aspect of the *kiap* system was that it recognised, reinforced and relied upon the traditional leadership system. In matters of cultural complexity, such as land disputes among the Huli at Koroba, the *kiap* typically identified a cultural expert arbitrator (or arbitrators) acceptable to both sides and sent him to hear the matter on the *kiap's* behalf. After the matter was decided, the decision, and any associated compensation, would be recorded in the land dispute register and signed off by both parties.

- 'Cultural' common law often saw *kiaps* at odds with missionaries. In Ambunti in 1971-72, for example, the Seventh Day Adventist (SDA) Church insisted on ringing its bell during a three-week period of silence required for a yam fertility ceremony among the Kwoma people. A riot between the SDA and traditionalists saw the SDA missionary offered the alternative of stopping the bell ringing voluntarily or in response to a district court order. He did so voluntarily, noting, 'It is the Christian lot to be persecuted'.

- *The law as an agent of social change.* The *Native Administration Regulations* in New Guinea and the *Native Regulation Ordinance* in Papua made adultery a criminal offence (the imposition of a six-month gaol term offered a face-saving mechanism that often prevented the killing of the offender).

- The rule of law was well accepted and widely understood. Attempts were even made through spells to influence court decisions: an anthropologist at Yenchan (Middle Sepik) indicated the drums at the enemy village of Parembei had been beating for many days since a riot between the two villages; a spell was invoked on the *kiap* pending his visit to the village to resolve the issue — 'Three months is OK, six months is too much'. The *kiap* sentenced the rioters to three months, to the satisfaction of all parties.

- *Constant contact and communication. Kiaps* were noted for going on patrol. Every village in Papua New Guinea was to be visited at least once per year for annual census. So it was that the *kiaps* and medical staff saw more or less every person in Papua New Guinea at least once per year. The census was rural Papua New Guinea's registry of births marriages and deaths. Time and again the *kiaps* were made aware of how much the people appreciated the annual census revision.

- Typically, following the census the *kiap* would arbitrate a spectrum of disputes, ranging from compensation for pigs damaging gardens to lovers' quarrels. Perhaps 5 per cent of these would become local or district court cases. The *kiap* typically remained in the village until all the issues had been discussed and 'resolved'. While not every decision gave the people what they wanted, at least they received a decision.

- *Information management.* Ideally *kiaps* sought to know the district rural community well enough to identify specific triggers and be able to defuse potential problems before they became major issues.

- For example, until 1970 *kiaps* in the Western Highlands monitored traffic in and out of the Jimi Valley, the best source of black palm for the Minj/Hagen area. Black palm is used to make bows and arrow heads and its collection indicates a probable preparation for war. As soon as black palm was observed being trucked, the destination was noted and *kiaps* visited the villages involved. They then sought to defuse any issue likely to cause trouble.

- The tribal warfare that occurred in the Western Highlands between 1970-74 serves as an example of what happened when *kiap* intelligence and preventive measurers were withdrawn. In 1970 the Western Highlands was declared a police zone and was taken away from the field constabulary and placed under control of the regular constabulary, who only investigated matters after the event. In the absence of the *kiap's* intelligence gathering and 'preventive justice', warfare in the Western Highlands was seriously out of control by 1974. In December 1974 the *kiap* system was reintroduced, experimentally, and the author was seconded from Koroba for a month. The key concern was that intelligence had been received that firearms were about to be used in Papua New Guinea tribal warfare for the first time. The outcomes of this exercise were that tribal warfare in the Western Highlands Province abated for some time and the introduction of firearms was delayed (Andrew Strathern pers. comm., Basel 1984). Groups who had been involved in the fighting welcomed the return to normalcy, in as much that they now had identified limits beyond which they could not push without consequence. They particularly welcomed the reintroduction of the *kiap* census and of medical service delivery, tools used during the *kiap* law and order patrols of December 1974.

- *Service delivery*. Apart from the medical, census and arbitration services delivered on patrol, free health and education services were highly valued by the people. Facilities were provided both at government stations and at strategic locations throughout the community. These services were sustainable because the *kiap's* cash office ensured that the public servants manning them were paid on time and that necessary supplies were delivered.
- *There was always something happening that involved the local populace*. Rural populations were always involved, directly or indirectly, with their *kiaps* in a range of activities that kept them occupied, and diverted them from such activities as warfare. Such activities typically included road building, cash cropping, and infrastructure construction such as village schools and aid posts.
- The highlands highway and feeder roads were originally constructed and maintained by manual labour under *kiap* direction. Apart from the need for roads, this sustained activity and perceived progress was keenly supported by the local people, who usually worked without payment but got to keep the shovels for use in their gardens. It was a viable alternative to warfare.

Signs of the decline of the *kiap* system.

- *Direct administration gave way to indirect administration*. The *kiap* system worked most efficiently during the period of direct administration, that is prior to the introduction of the local government system and political education campaigns associated with national elections, self-government and independence. These awareness campaigns contributed to the inevitable downfall of the *kiap* system, which was criticised as an autocratic institution rife with conflict of interest — an easy target for aspiring politicians and political science students.
- At the same time, Deputy Administrator Gunther and others set about dismantling the authority structure behind the *kiap* system. Magisterial, police and corrective institutions powers were taken away and eventually assistant district commissioners became known as district managers or district coordinators.

- The fact was that the social environment had changed since the heyday of the *kiap*, so the institution itself was adjusted to match the needs of the times. Not all national policies were well suited to the changes.

- After the initial introduction of local-level government in the 1950s, there was a drive in the 1960s and 1970s to establish local government councils throughout Papua New Guinea. Senior local government council officers throughout the country had maps on their walls that they were desperately trying to have shaded in red to indicate the presence of local government councils. There were two problems with this for the ultimate efficiency of the institution of local government. First, the success of local government varied. The New Guinea Islands region, for example, adapted to local government better than elsewhere, perhaps because it was a better fit for the traditional leadership systems of the cultures involved. Local government was not as successful in the highlands, perhaps because it was an ill fit for the clan-based big-man culture. Secondly, a council *kiap* could very often appear to have an extremely effective local government council by doing all the work himself in his role as adviser, rather than allowing the democratic processes to take root in the often infertile ground of the elected representatives.

- *The localisation process.* The author has always supported fast-tracking of citizen staff (both *kiap* and petroleum industry staff) to higher positions, but also believes that there were three areas in which the localisation of *kiap* positions from Australian to citizen officers contributed to the decline of the *kiap* system.

- First, while some extremely capable citizen staff replaced senior expatriate officers, as former district commissioner Ted Hicks pointed out, on average it took an expatriate *kiap* thirty-two years of field experience and the maturity of middle age to gain appointment as district commissioner; at independence district commissioners were being replaced by much younger citizens usually with around five years experience. There is no substitute for experience. Secondly, citizen staff all over the country are regarded as being subject to sorcery, whereas expatriates are not. Citizen *kiaps* were naturally reluctant to take a firm stand in an arbitration or court case where the loser might get even through sorcery. Thirdly, until the average expatriate *kiap* proved himself to be in some way inept, he was generally credited, on the basis of his nationality, with being a fully capable *kiap*. This did not apply to citizen staff, who were typically told, 'we do not take orders from our own kind'. Fate and bad management in 1973 saw a *kiap* of Sepik Plains origin placed in charge of the Iatmul population of the Middle Sepik. Gewertz (1983) explains that the Iatmul have maintained a state of hegemony over the Sepik Plains people from headhunting days down to the present. After a riot, Middle Sepik men resisted arrest, leaving the *kiap* no safe option but to walk away. The expatriate assistant district commissioner then went to the village with one policeman, and arrested two dozen rioters, and brought them back for trial without incident.

Kiaps in resource industry community affairs organisations — some elements of adaptation

Given that resource project managers who understand the issues realise that the greatest threat they face comes from the land-owning community, most drew upon the ranks of the former kiaps for management of community affairs (CA). Ex-kiaps combined a number of essential skills: field experience; the ability to speak Tok Pisin or Hiri Motu or both; an inherent respect from the rural population; a willingness to work in Papua New Guinea; and a referral system that identified available personnel with the experience and these capabilities.

Most such CA managers recognised that they had to adapt to the new role in a number of areas, as discussed below.

- *A chain of command headed by a non-CA expert*. Most former-*kiap* CA managers have difficulties answering to a manager who does not intuitively understand the problems being faced. Cultural awareness work is multiplied as the CA manager not only has to interpret multinational corporate culture to Papua New Guinean rural populations, but has also to interpret Papua New Guinea culture to the project management. The latter is especially difficult because the project manager has the authority to approve or not approve CA solutions proposed to address identified problems. Closely related to this is the fact that the ex-*kiap* CA manager is a generalist manager who is used to thinking laterally and taking responsibility for the outcomes of his plans. In the resource industry he tends to find his duty statement somewhat narrower than he would be prefer.

- For example, one resource project in Papua New Guinea decided to divide CA functions into 'core' and 'non-core' according to whether or not the functions were central to drilling requirements. The non-core functions — community health, education support, women's affairs, and agriculture support — were discarded. For the landowners, however, the so-called non-core functions were core. CA staff consequently saw their relationship with their community slipping away on two counts: they were not meeting the community needs, and since they were not required to spend time in the field, they were less able to gather and assess information that allowed management of project risks.

- *The separation of security from CA functions*. As officer in charge of a district or province, the *kiap* was responsible for managing the community through appeal to hearts and minds and, on the rare occasion, through the use of force. It was a fine balancing act for the *kiap* in charge.

- Resource developments typically separate security and CA into departments. It takes coordination, therefore, to ensure that CA and security initiatives are properly aligned, even though both security and CA are dealing with the same project area community.
- *The role of health and safety.* International resource companies hold health, safety, environment and security (HSES) to be of the absolute top priority in their operations. If a task is not safe, it is not to be done until it can be made safe. This perceived reluctance or hesitancy to act is seen by landowners as a sign of weakness. Landowners tend to step into the void and empower themselves by making threats or actually breaking the law. The ex-*kiap* CA manager's military-style background, 'gut feelings' and lateral thinking make him immediately aware of what he can achieve and how it might be done. Unfortunately, any strategy he is likely to develop will get in the way of either HSES policy or the project manager's view that he needs to be a good neighbour to the community and as such is prepared to overlook minor breaches of the law.
- *The issue of becoming the de facto government of the area.* Given the lack of service delivery from the three levels of government in Papua New Guinea, resource developers find themselves relied upon to provide medical and health services, and to build and maintain infrastructure, particularly roads. Management typically takes the position that the project must not become the *de facto* government of the project area, whereas CA managers tend to take the view that, like it or not, they *are* the *de facto* government. There are benefits in recognising this as an opportunity rather than as a problem. Governments sometimes in fact encourage the concept of *de facto* government. In the late 1990s, for example, the Southern Highlands provincial government declined to provide medical supplies to the Kutubu area, telling the people that they should rely on the developer to supply them and that the provincial government would spend its limited resources in other parts of the province.

What are the key problems now facing resource developers in SHP?

- *Lack of governance 1 — service delivery.* The state has insufficient money for the provision of services, especially if large amounts of resources are being diverted to fictitious names on the pay role. Even those who remain at their posts have no supplies with which to do their job. A frequent occurrence is that a teacher or health official leaves his or her post to take a cheque to the bank to be cashed and does not return, there being no point in being at the post without the supplies with which to function — unless the developer provides them.
- *Lack of governance 2 — law and order and the whole judicial system.* There is an almost complete breakdown in the SHP judicial system (including police

and the magisterial system and corrective institution system). This makes enforcing the rule of law very difficult indeed.

- For example, people arrested at Kutubu on serious charges have been sent to Mendi by helicopter at great expense, only to be released on bail of K1 each. The developer is therefore not only subject to the expensive indignity of flying them back to the site, but also to enduring increased unlawful acts by offenders in the knowledge that the state will not punish them.

- The police no longer believe they have responsibility for tribal warfare. It is regarded as a 'traditional' activity rather than a crime, even when someone is killed or when a related payback takes place. Taking this a step further, when a company man is killed in a 'traditional' conflict and the company insists upon police intervention, the company and the police are accused of taking sides — the implication being that the police should not involve themselves. (Compare this with the concept of the rule of law under the *kiap* system, discussed above.)

- *Lack of governance 3 — regulatory functionality and unkept state promises.* A serious destabilising factor among the project area communities is the failure of the regulatory department to adequately do its job. Two related examples illustrate this.

- Substantially following Australian legislation, the petroleum resource is seen legally as the property of the state. Naturally, the landowners will never accept that anything that comes from their land can belong to anyone but them. The legislation thus provides for negotiation with landowners for access to extract petroleum resources from their land. The level of benefits to landowners is capped at 20 per cent of the state's take from the petroleum extracted from the resource area (*Oil and Gas Act*, Section 174). Unfortunately no realistic attempt is made to enforce the 20 per cent cap.

- As a result, promises running into hundreds of millions of kina have been made by the state to the project area landowners for infrastructure development in exchange for access to their land and the right to extract petroleum from it. Although these promises are signed off by the minister and /or the secretary of the Department of Petroleum and Energy, they are not referred to the Department of Finance or the attorney general, and as such have no legal standing and cannot be kept. The outcome is that landowners, while apologising to the developer, claim that to get the state's attention they must to shut the project down. This has happened on several occasions.

- *Corruption* is endemic in Papua New Guinea and particularly in relation to the distribution of landowner benefits. It is understandable that when genuine landowners are deprived of their project benefits by individuals who steal their money, they will respond by destabilising the industry and the peace of the SHP by threatening to shut down the project. There have been a dozen such threats since 1999 and two actual shut-downs of a pipeline valve station. Despite this, the benefits in question continue to be stolen from the landowners with the authentic claim.

- *Hela 'nationalism'*. Since before independence there have been calls for Hela unity and a separate Hela province. The Hela movement is discussed elsewhere in this volume. Evidence indicates that serious preparations are under way to create a Hela Province by 2007. The potential for destabilisation of the SHP by removing most if not all the resource projects into a new Hela Province is serious, particularly with a 'non-Hela' governor.

- *The rapidly changing social environment and gun culture*. The capacity of CA staff to foresee outcomes and defuse potentially volatile situations has been severely diminished by the rapidly changing social environment. For example, guns are now killing more people than were killed with arrows in the days of tribal warfare. Fighting in Mendi from 1999-2002 saw over 100 people killed. The traditional mechanism of paying compensation in pigs must fail; there are simply not enough pigs. Tribal warfare traditionally had clear rules about who was a valid payback. Now, given that there is sometimes a huge disparity in the numbers of dead between the antagonists, the rules have been altered in parts of the SHP, and geographic features such as rivers have become the determining factor in which side an individual is on and his/her status in a payback killing.

There are several 'givens' in the SHP situation. First, guns are there to stay. Indeed a 'Cold War' logic has developed: 'The enemy has automatic weapons, so we must have automatic weapons — as long as they know we have them they will not attack'. Secondly, issues of governance will not be quickly addressed, due to Papua New Guinea's economic crisis. Thirdly, if resource developers wish to see change in the social environment in which they operate, it will be primarily up to them to make the change happen. Fourthly, if the rule of law is again to become a guiding principle there will need to be significant developer input into infrastructure and relationships.

The vast majority of Southern Highlanders want a return to 'normalcy'. The common people are prepared to protect and support what they see as beneficial to them. For example, during the Nipa blockade of 1999/2000, the Hides people established roadblocks and turned armed thugs away from Hides, stating 'this is our garden'.

How can the *'kiap* system' address these problems?

The answer comes in two parts: how it might be done — that is, the performance dimensions — and what needs to be done — that is, the key responsibilities.

How it might be done

The *kiap* approach would involve spending time in the field, exercising cultural sensitivity and empathy in communications with the community to identify the key elements of their desire for a return to normalcy. The contact with the community needs to be ongoing to allow monitoring and adjustment. Key elements include:

- an end to corruption in the distribution of landowner benefits;
- involvement in money-making ventures;
- involvement and recognition in the petroleum industry;
- maintenance of a 'hearts and minds' empathy between CA and the community;
- service delivery, particularly delivery of medical services;
- sound leadership to achieve all these elements.

What needs to be done

To achieve the program outlined below, several preliminary tasks need to be undertaken:

- identification of programs in which the people could participate (see below);
- liaison between senior developer management and state representatives;
- planning of a capacity-building exercise for district administration staff and local-level government to promote proper coordination.

A possible development program to meet the six key elements

The developer should take over the management of benefits distribution. As is already done in the mining industry, the developer could do all the preparatory work to enable the regulatory department to make payments directly to the appropriate landowners on site. This could be done publicly and in cash if there were no local banking facilities. Such benefits distribution would satisfy the first key element and would be a hugely popular public relations exercise. The CA department, in conjunction with the district administrator, could also conduct annual patrols to conduct a *kiap*-style census, as was done in Kutubu in 1994. This would create the capacity to monitor the demographic and general statistical basis for all community socio-economic programs, and the benefits distribution program. It would also facilitate communication with the community and allow a monitoring of hearts and minds (the fourth key element). In conjunction with the provincial government, medical services could be provided during census patrols (the fifth element).

In the *kiap* tradition of involving the people in developments such as road construction and maintenance, CA could promote money-making ventures that could be undertaken at least in part by large teams of casual labour, rather than machines (satisfying the second key element). This would also provide an active sense of industry involvement (the third key element). Another possible area for community involvement is cash cropping. Despite the fact that SHP is less environmentally favoured for coffee growing than Western and Eastern Highlands, coffee does grow there. It is claimed in Chimbu and Eastern Highlands that the time and effort people spend on coffee, and the cash it earns them, are key factors in the relative peace and social stability of those provinces. As is already happening at Hides, there could be a serious drive by CA to re-establish the SHP coffee industry.

The leadership provided by the *kiaps* of the colonial and post-colonial era could be re-activated through liaison between the CA manager and the local district coordinator. As already stated, the developer does not want to become the *de facto* government of the area, so the leadership issue needs careful management. But someone needs to take the lead — the best ideas in the world are useless unless someone is passionately promoting them.

The people of the Southern Highlands in their current quest for a return to normalcy will respond with great enthusiasm to good leadership of well planned programs that meet their needs.

References

Wyndham, John. 1980 *Web*. Harmondsworth: Penguin.

Gewertz, Deborah. 1983 *Sepik River Societies: A Historical Ethnography of the Chambri and their Neighbours*. New Haven: Yale University Press.

ENDNOTES

[1] This paper is written from the personal perspective of an employee of a petroleum company, conducting business in an often unstable and sometimes unsafe working environment in the Southern Highlands. The views expressed do not necessarily reflect the views of my employer.

The Future of Resource Development in the Southern Highlands

Chris Warrilow

The need for contact and communication

During my 44 years in Papua New Guinea, and especially during the last decade, I have often said that the key to success in dealing with rural people involves contact, contact, and more contact. The government in Papua New Guinea has lost contact with its rural people. In resource-rich areas the vacuum has, to a large extent, been filled by resource developers through their community affairs staff.

One of the greatest assets of the latter days of the Australian administration, retained briefly after independence, was the Department of Information and Extension Services. Using its network of rural workers (*kiap, didiman, doktaboi,* school teacher, etc.) the government was able to widely disseminate information and conduct activities in the rural areas.

After all the lessons that could have been learnt — but were not — it annoyed me to read, for example, press reports, in early 2003, of Kagua people travelling to Lae in order to press claims of ownership to land upon which one of InterOil's exploration bores was to be drilled. The company hyped up the 'prospect' in the press, which got people from Kerema to Mendi excited as yet again a company, trying to mine the stock exchange floors in Calgary or Sydney,[1] created unrealistic expectations amongst those in whose province some speculative exploration work was to take place. A few days later another report stated that Baimuru people had called for a mass meeting of 'landowners' to press their claims to the same 'new oil field'. The unsuccessful bore was drilled nearer to Wabo than Baimuru and certainly a long way from Kagua. But lack of meaningful contact and communication by both government and company left two groups of people, living over 100 kilometres apart, in a state of confusion and high expectation. Had there been an unlikely discovery the scene was already set for chaos.

Unrealistic expectations are often raised by both the press and some companies. The press overuses the words 'huge' and 'rich' when reporting, whilst some explorers like to 'talk up' their shares. This leads to inflated demands from members of the landowning clans. Even when a prospect matures to a discovery and from a discovery to a project, it is not necessarily huge or rich. Hides, for instance, with its 7 trillion cubic feet (tcf) of proven reserves, is small in comparison to the Australian Northwest Shelf or recent discoveries in West

Papua's 'Bird's Head' region where discoveries of 15 tcf to 30 tcf have been made.

Leadership qualities

Joe Kanekane compares MPs who have represented SHP as its regional/provincial electorate member. He spoke of Ron Neville, SHP's first member (MHA) and of later representatives and their increasingly parochial attitudes (see Kanekane, this volume). This has been particularly evident in the feud between supporters of Dick Mune and Anderson Agiru (the Nipa and the Huli) (see Haley, this volume).

Neville was a former *kiap* who had served in various parts of Papua New Guinea before becoming a businessman and politician. He had 'opened up' Tari, been OIC at Erave and subsequently set up business in both the latter and Mendi. His first term in the House of Assembly was as regional member for the Western Papua electorate which included the present Western, Gulf and Southern Highlands provinces and half of the Central Province. He thus had a broad view and no 'tribal' loyalties, with the accompanying baggage of wantokism and its inherent obligations.

What SHP needs is a true nationalist as its provincial member governor, who can set an example to the open members and inspire civic and national pride — pride of the kind evoked at rugby matches when the Kumuls meet a foreign opponent. Even so, any elected governor will most likely still have two thirds of the province 'against' him — two of the three divisions of west (Huli-Duna), central (Mendi-Nipa), and east (Pangia-Ialibu-Kagua). A true nationalist from a minority area (Erave or Kutubu) could possibly provide the stability needed — though we have not seen this to date. The present situation is likely to exacerbate continued demands for a split to create a new (Hela) province, for which the current government has indicated its sympathy.

It is the negative aspects of developments in SHP which have dominated news reports and discussion. The province has its positive aspects that need to be identified and built upon. One positive element is the people themselves. A huge majority (in fact near unanimity in the case of women and children) want the re-establishment of law and order, and the return of services that will bring about. This in turn will bring back the goods and services to those who can afford them, and the means to afford them. More importantly it will enable the next generation to obtain the education so essential if the SHP is to progress to a brighter future.

With law and order established by a strong, competent, honest and disciplined police force, supported by a functioning court system and CIS which keeps convicted thieves, thugs, murderers and rapists behind bars, we might be able to re-establish an effective public service capable of implementing district administration. Only then will sustainable postal and communications services, banks, trade stores, and so on reopen, and schools, hospitals and aid posts be staffed again and the goods and supplies required to run and maintain them start flowing again. The limited surplus agriculture and cash crops which are produced may then find a market.

Before building up local institutions which can be run in a sustainable way there are state matters to be attended to by the national government. The SHP has been at the mercy of thieving, gun-running gangsters. The national government must use whatever force is necessary to restore its authority and do it in a way that will see its authority respected and therefore accepted. After that is achieved there can be devolution of powers and capacity-building of local institutions (such as village courts) which can run matters in a more appropriate fashion, taking into consideration traditional norms and values.

In light of the many years of increasing anarchy, measures to achieve the above may, initially, have to be somewhat draconian (at least that is the perception of some Australians). But it is essential that police be handpicked for such an operation and have strong, disciplined leadership.

Political 'leaders' (I prefer to call them the people's elected representatives and law makers) need to be less hands-on and leave the day-to-day administration of the SHP (enforcing laws, implementing policy, and providing services) to a strengthened, competent public service, recruited for the most part from outside the province.

Much has been said about the law and order situation. We have, for example, been told about the blatant stealing and destruction of public property in full view of the Tari police station (see Walters, this volume). Such petty crime seems to go unchecked. Some speakers exhort us to not look back but to look to the future. I believe that we must look back to some extent. How can we expect police to act to deter, arrest, and prosecute petty offenders when so many 'white collar' criminals go so blatantly free?

Resources and the breakdown of law and order

Elsewhere in this volume, Goldman and Bragge examine possible solutions for the problems they have identified, especially in the context of Huli tradition. However, I do not believe that it is entirely possible to achieve acculturation in a rapidly changing society, thrust into the modern world of resource extraction.

Whereas the 'general' law and order problems resulted in, for example, Oil Search Ltd. (OSL) changing its staff rotation travel arrangements, it was land and royalty issues which resulted in Chevron's many ongoing trials and tribulations at Kutubu/Gobe over the years. OSL felt it had to abandon Tari airstrip (a few road kilometres from its Hides project) and instead, initially, used Hagen airport, from whence it flew its staff by helicopter to and from Hides

(Moro airstrip is now used). This is an additional cost to what is a marginal project. Chevron, because of the fierce land disputes which seriously delayed development of the Gobe oilfields, had to contend with assaults on its staff, hostage taking, and even aircraft hijacking. So far as I know, few arrests were made and fewer still prosecutions launched. Chevron usually did not seek police intervention when it experienced similar woes later in the life of both Gobe and Kutubu.

Chevron's 'lead and manage, not rule' approach does not seem to have worked. Indeed it was not only physical violence that Chevron quietly tolerated, they also capitulated to verbal threats. Several times, as operator, Chevron has closed down operations because of such threats. They have not only suffered at the hands of 'landowners'; in 2002 the Moro camp was 'shot up' by angry police. Incidents such as this are not conducive to investor confidence. Chevron boasts of its 'landowner' management successes as much as it does of its environmental friendliness. It claims that oil production has never been interrupted because of 'landowner hostilities'. This is not quite true. Oil exports have never been interrupted, but production has been affected because of threats by a few so-called spokesmen of the people to forcibly close the valve at one or more of the pipeline valve stations. However, because Chevron has 600,000 barrels of oil in tanks at Kutubu, another 600,000 barrels in the pipeline itself, and a couple of hundred thousand barrels stored at the Gobe production facility, there has been enough oil to ensure that all export tankers have sailed with a full cargo. By the time the next tanker has tied up to the Kumul offshore loading facility, the dispute has been settled and the threats withdrawn.

The future of petroleum development in the Southern Highlands

It is well known that the proven Hides gas reserves are sufficient to support a major gas export project. BP pursued the liquid natural gas (LNG) option and before the Southeast Asian crisis of the late 1990s had carried out a number of studies which suggested the preferred option of a pipeline to the north coast, to an export loading facility onshore near Wewak. It then left Papua New Guinea.

Chevron took over as operator of the proposed project and pursued the gas-to-Queensland (GTQ) option. Chevron was not a party to the Hides project, but had realised that its gas reserves in the Kutubu and Gobe fields were insufficient to sustain delivery of the amounts required in the timeframe (30 plus years) to make the proposal economically feasible.

Export of LNG would most likely be more profitable than GTQ, but there is sufficient gas for both projects to go ahead, and the latter seems more likely to proceed in the short term. If GTQ does proceed, it will give Papua New Guinea good returns, especially from the liquids that would be stripped from the gas to be sold to the domestic LNG market and exported separately. Also, the infrastructure that would have to be put in place would put Papua New Guinea closer to being able to pursue domestic utilisation of its gas reserves. At the top of Papua New Guinea's 'wish list' is a pipeline to Port Moresby for power generation.

However, to maximise recovery from the fields they operate and presently have interests in, Chevron would have to produce ('blow down') the gas, either by flaring or exporting (they currently reinject the gas). Flaring is perceived to be not environmentally friendly, and in any case would be a waste of Papua New Guinea's resources. But is gas in the ground, at the expense of tens of millions of barrels of oil also left in the ground, of any benefit to Papua New Guinea in the light of its ongoing financial difficulties? A decision, if required in a few years time on these options, will be difficult for the government and the licensees, but the green-sensitive Chevron will no longer be part of the decision making.

The potential market for gas in Queensland was not initially realised by Chevron. Just as Kutubu and Gobe oil was discovered by others, so was the GTQ option first explored by another company, IPC, which had discovered a large gas reserve (Pandora) in the Gulf of Papua in the 1980s.

Of major concern to would-be purchasers of GTQ must be security and continuity of supply. Unlike coffee, tea, cocoa, copra, timber and even oil, gas supplies have to be guaranteed by the one supplier. There is always an oil tanker on the high seas with a cargo which may be diverted for the right price, at any time, to an alternative port where demand is greatest. In any case, countries and companies usually have relatively large reserves of oil stored to meet most short-term shortfalls in deliveries. Gas cannot be stored and moved around so freely. (One only has to look at what happened in Victoria in 1998 when gas deliveries ceased due to an explosion and fire at Esso's Longford plant, where gas from the Bass Strait is processed for delivery to the market.)

Meanwhile, however, one may ask, what about oil? The Kutubu fields (Kutubu, Agogo and Hedinia) are being rapidly depleted. Maximum oil production peaked at around 150,000 barrels per day (bblspd) and it is now less than a third of that. Gobe never reached anticipated production of 50,000 bblspd and is currently declining, at perhaps less than 20,000. Moran is now coming up to full production (maybe 30,000 bblspd), some six years after discovery. With perhaps 80,000,000 barrels of reserves the field will be exhausted in less than ten years.

What is going to replace this production? It seems nothing. There have been no new commercial discoveries and there seems to be no will to explore, with the cost of drilling wells now up to $US35 million each (the cost of Esso's recent Bakari well — which proved to be a dry hole). Cheaper wells have recently been drilled close to existing infrastructure, but even so, such wells seldom come in at less than $US8 million (the cost of Santos's Bilip, which discovered oil but seems to lack commercial reserves, despite its proximity to the Gobe facility). The main incentive for drilling at present, it seems, is compliance with licence conditions.

The main disincentive to future development is the failure to date of the GTQ project to proceed to front end engineering and design (FEED), due to lack of confidence in securing the required markets in Queensland. The success rate of drilling is about one well in ten being a 'discovery'; but that one well may not be a commercial discovery, especially if it is gas, which is mainly what has been discovered over the ninety years of drilling in Papua New Guinea. The argument thus goes, if we can't sell the gas we already have, why drill for more?

The only possible commercial discovery still undeveloped is that at South East Mananda, on the opposite side of the Hegigio Gorge from the Agogo facility (which also processes the output of Moran). To get oil from Southeast Manada to Agogo will be, to say the least, an engineering challenge.

There is still some potential at Juha and Hides, in so far as the three wells drilled on the former anticline and the four on the latter have yet to establish a liquid contact (that is, reach the lowest depth of the gas, where it sits on either water or oil). There are additional new 'plays' in the existing fields where the sub-thrust zones have yet to be tested by drilling into the footwalls of Hides, Mananda, Hedinia, Gobe and even Kutubu. Such wells would be expensive, despite being close to roads and other infrastructure, and the drilling fraught with the difficulties of penetrating deep down into the fold belt with its many geological faults creating a drilling engineer's nightmare.

Maybe, if the rule of law were re-established and government took back more of the responsibilities of governing and providing for its people, explorers might drill these wells. Perhaps some of the old players, who have tried and left after lack of success, might return to try new ideas and plays. Even so, as witnessed in the time gap between discovery and development at Moran, if there were a new commercial discovery tomorrow, it could well be that production would not commence until after all other oil reserves had been depleted some years earlier.

The province has not revealed any mineral wealth to date and there is currently no hard rock exploration taking place. Mount Kare, in Enga, if developed, would have spin-off benefits for SHP. However, I believe the Canadian operator, Madison Resources, is intent on attracting a buyer to take over its exploration licence.

ENDNOTES

[1] The prospect was named Moose — to promote the sale of shares in North America.

Community-Based Development in Tari — Present and Prospects

John Vail

The current situation in Tari is very poor, following a long period of decline. The restoration of law and order, services, and infrastructure is a basic need. But this will not be adequate in itself. A community-based development approach, in which people participate in the improvement of their own living standards, is required if the rural stagnation underlying the current malady is to be overcome. The experience of the Family Health and Rural Improvement Program (FHRIP) and Community Based Health Care (CBHC) in Tari over the past eight years provides a model for development that can provide shared benefits and participation for all those involved.

However, considerable support is required if such initiatives are to grow and flourish. The Melanesian Farmer First Network, an innovative attempt to bring together a network of community organisations to assist one another, is one such source of support, but commitment to community-based development on the part of government and aid agencies is essential.

The situation in Tari

There has been a period of decline since the 1980s in the distribution and quality of services, and the state of law and order in Tari district. By September 2000, communications were not functioning, the road to Mendi was impassable except to police-escorted convoys, the bank and post office were closed, and the town power supply was not working (Family Health and Rural Improvement Program 2000). There was no doctor at the hospital, and several health centres and many rural aid posts were closed. Immunisation patrols had all but ceased. Several community schools had been destroyed or were closed, and most others were short of teachers. Agricultural extension services had long ceased functioning. Few public servants were at their posts in town. Almost no aspect of the administration was functioning properly.

In early 2003 things were no better. The last major retail/wholesale store in town had closed following the violence accompanying the 2002 election. The College of Distance Education centre had been razed. Widespread fighting had caused loss of life and destruction in the west and north of Tari.

Background

Three interrelated problems characterise the situation in Tari: law and order breakdown, failure of service delivery, and rural stagnation. They have arisen over the past two decades from a complex of factors which are discussed below.

Fighting and crime

Inter-group warfare has increased both in scale and firepower over the past 15 years. Large-scale fighting re-erupted in the Tari basin in late 1986 after many years of relative peace. Since then battles involving many hundreds of warriors, some drawn from areas quite remote to the battleground, have become almost commonplace. In the mid 1990s firearms became widely used, increasing the number of fatalities and serious injuries in battles. The resulting, often inflated, compensation demands made conflicts harder to settle and fed into subsequent battles. In time, and in the absence of a suitable response by the authorities, recourse to arms reasserted itself as an acceptable way of dealing with disputes.

Criminal activity, especially roadblocks and robbery, has likewise increased in scale and violence, seriously affecting service delivery in many parts of Tari and Southern Highlands Province (SHP) generally. This activity is linked to tribal fighting, which creates an environment in which lawless activities can proliferate, entrenches a gun culture, and glorifies criminals who become 'folk heroes' in times of warfare.

The fighting itself has many causes. Most fights still arise from local matters. Population growth and an increasingly degraded environment in the less fertile areas (Yamauchi and Ohtsuka 2002) have exacerbated pressures on land and put people in closer proximity to each other, raising the number of everyday disputes and incidents. The increasing monetisation of the local economy is another contributory cause to crime and fighting. Roadblocks have become more common within Tari district in recent years, sometimes directly related to resource company payments. The Mt Kare gold rush in 1988 led to battles both at Mt Kare and in the Tari basin.

The corruption of the political process has also worsened the situation. The winner-takes-all nature of political contests has greatly raised the stakes in getting particular candidates elected. Over the years elections have become marked by a wide range of illegal practices, ranging from vote buying, rigging of electoral rolls, multiple and underage voting, to intimidation, violence and the hijacking of ballot boxes. Physical confrontation between supporters of rival candidates has resulted in death and destruction, the fighting in Tari town following the 2002 election being the most recent example. Political rivalry has also raised warfare to a new plane. In August 1999, a virtual 'civil war' broke out between Tari and Nipa districts following the death of a former provincial governor in a road accident. For a short period there was near-anarchy in Tari town, in which vehicles were hijacked and police-escorted convoys of men armed with shotguns circled the town before heading to the 'front' two hours east. Although the fighting was brought to a halt by the intervention of the provincial governor, Tari district remained largely isolated thereafter.

It should be emphasised here that warfare is usually a last resort, after mediation has failed. Many fights probably could be halted before they escalated if law enforcement authorities were active. Some battles have been defused by the intervention of police and district officers, but they are the exception rather than the rule. In general, attempts at suppression have been confined to punitive raids after the fighting has already caused destruction and loss of life.

Warfare must also be seen in its social context. For males at least, it is a participatory, inclusive activity. In a rural development vacuum, where men and youths have no organised, productive outlet for their energies, fighting brings an element of excitement in an environment in which there seems relatively little to lose. Few in Tari want to see a return to the era of endemic warfare, but few too have a realistic vision for a productive, peaceable alternative.

Service delivery failure

In the mid 1980s, most services in Tari were functioning. The road was open and passable and the town well supplied with consumer goods. The bank, post office and government offices were open. Power and communications worked most of the time, and were repaired when they broke down. Aid posts and health centres serviced remote areas, giving rise to excellent vaccination coverage of under five-year-old children. Schools were open and reasonably well looked after. But even at this relative highpoint, things were far from perfect. The public service was under-resourced and public servants did not, for the most part, venture far from town. Services in remote parts were less reliable than those nearer to the town.

The effects of public service shrinkage became obvious in the 1990s. Many different reasons have been advanced for this recession — under funding, mismanagement, corruption, politicisation, nepotism, lack of accountability, and lack of enforcement. Wherever the truth may lie, during the 1990s services began to be withdrawn from Tari town, and public servants retreated to provincial headquarters or simply failed to turn up at their offices. Morale among previously effective officers declined as their budgets were cut, despite a growing provincial budget. Equipment broke down, and was not repaired. Services declined further in remote areas. Aid posts were not staffed, teachers could not be found for classes. Roads and bridges were no longer maintained, and vehicles were misused or broke down. The public service largely ceased serving the rural population, and became instead a paid, town-based, elite serving mainly itself.

Not all of this was due to internal problems in the public service. Crime and fighting damaged public infrastructure and made travel unsafe for public servants. Communications facilities on remote mountain tops were subject to compensation demands and pillaged or destroyed. However the decline in the effectiveness of the administration, police and village courts contributed to the general demise by allowing these lawless activities to continue unchecked.

By 2000 Tari had been denuded of almost all its functioning services, and even those most valued and resilient, health and education, had been reduced to a bare minimum due to a lack of supplies and personnel.

Rural stagnation

Stagnation rather than decline characterises the plight of rural areas in Tari. Away from the town, little change has occurred in material standards of living for many people over the years (Vail 2002b). Most families still live in bush materials dwellings with no water supply or sanitation. Few people have a range of nutritious crops in their garden, and most rely on sweet potato for their subsistence. Although the amount of money in the local economy has grown many-fold, due to the arrival of the highway in 1980, remittances from people working outside the district, and payments received directly or indirectly from the large resource projects surrounding Tari, the main result has been increased consumption of purchased goods, the price of which has risen steeply due to inflation and supply restrictions.

A number of reasons may be advanced as to why there has been so little rural development in Tari:

- Lack of productive economic activity. This in part arises from a lack of opportunity, due to unreliable prices for cash crops and distance to ports, but has been further undermined by crime, tribal fighting and the lack of maintenance of roads and public infrastructure.
- Lack of a suitable rural policy. In part this is due to a bureaucratic mentality that maintains a deep division between the lifestyles of paid public servants and subsistence villagers. More generally, there has been a failure to formulate practical policies allowing rural people to participate in development.
- An education system that is not geared to the majority who 'drop out' after six or ten years of school. Youths are educated in the expectation of paid work and ill-prepared for subsistence activities and community life.
- False expectations by rural people, who were led to believe that their role was a passive one in which goods and services were delivered by public servants and wealth handed out by those in power.

The result of the neglect of rural communities by the authorities has been disaffection and discontent. Failed expectations and income inequality are an oft-stated justification for the take-up of crime by youth. Likewise, few well-educated people are willing or prepared to work for and in their communities while rural conditions are so poor. Essentially, a vicious circle has been set up linking law and order problems, service delivery failure, and rural stagnation. Is there a circuit breaker?

Community-based development

While the restoration of government services and imposition of law and order are essential steps, alone they cannot solve the problems currently afflicting Tari and many parts of rural Papua New Guinea. A dynamic is needed that will involve people, especially youth, in constructive and fulfilling occupations. Their needs cannot be met through the formal sector and so an improvement in the quality of life for the rural majority must rely upon community-based development. In fact, the answer to many of Papua New Guinea's fundamental problems lies with making its rural communities attractive places to live.

First, what is community-based development? Simply put, it is a form of development that takes place within the community, emphasises maximum participation of community members in its design and implementation, is ongoing, meets real needs, and is basically self-reliant. To achieve this, the community needs to have a structure, and persons trained in appropriate methods of implementation. Usually, community-based development will be small-scale, low-cost, and use simple technologies. The model must be equally available to all communities, irrespective of their location, denomination or means, and provide for all members of the community according to their needs.

Much so-called development assistance is the antithesis of this. The predominant mode, service delivery, is in serious decline in rural areas. Even at its best it is expensive, non-participatory and inefficient. For example, community health workers, who are full-time public servants, rarely do more than dispense medicines for a few hours a day, and play no role in preventive health in the community they serve. An allied form of aid is the construction of objects, some useful, many not — for example, the council chambers built over five years ago in each sub-district of Tari, only to lie idle. Schemes may range from the political and grandiose — such as the proposed international airport for Tari — to the local and well-intentioned, such as village water tank installations; but most are expensive, rely on outside contractors, and lack sustainability. Another popular form of assistance is grants, often for small, local activities such as grass cutting along roads, or village livestock projects. The results are usually ephemeral and there is little or no accountability. The common thread in all such assistance is a lack of community involvement in the design, implementation and maintenance phases.

Community-based development offers a way to improve on this, but not a simple or quick way. Communities in Tari are loose associations of people bound by kinship who live in proximity to each other. People come together for traditional purposes such as warfare, brideprice payments and compensation, but otherwise pursue fairly private lives. To organise them into functional bodies capable of understanding community needs and able to pursue the means to satisfy them takes considerable time and effort. For community-based development to occur people must adopt a new attitude, in which they become actors rather than recipients, and embrace small incremental change generated internally rather than expect large infusions of external wealth and technology.

The issue of water supply in Tari may be used to illustrate the different approaches. Often community water supply is taken to mean a large tank built in a central location such as the local aid post. However there are problems with this approach. First, while people may be able to obtain adequate quantities of drinking water from the tank, there is also a need for water for cleaning, cooking and washing. Most families will be too far away to benefit for these purposes. Secondly, if the tap is damaged, there may be no one prepared to take responsibility for repairing it. The tank is left idle while people argue about who was to blame and send requests to the donor to come and fix it. Hence costs may be high, benefits low and needs left unmet. A better solution for people living in scattered homesteads is likely to be small low cost units that are owned by individual families, and supply water on their doorsteps for all their domestic needs. To choose this mode of water supply, the community must obtain materials, train volunteers, and prioritise among families in terms of need. Families in turn must invest some of their own money, materials and labour in obtaining a water supply unit, and maintain their own units. By this method needs are better met, there is more participation, and more ownership. But the community must be organised and able to weigh the costs and benefits, not passively allow the choice to be made for it.

Hence community-based development encompasses forms of development as well as the structures needed to achieve them: it is biased in favour of participatory, community-controlled methods. The Family Health and Rural Improvement Program (FHRIP) was one initiative designed to address key community needs at the lowest level using simple low-cost methods and technologies, and training local people to run and implement the program. It hoped not only to improve the quality of life for families but also engage communities in constructive enterprise, making them less likely to be drawn into the self-destructive activities witnessed in Tari and many parts of the highlands over the past decade.

The Family Health and Rural Improvement Program

FHRIP started life in 1995 as the Nutritional Garden and Household Improvement Program, using the resources of the Papua New Guinea Institute of Medical Research and funding from Porgera Joint Venture. The basic aims of the program were to improve family health, particularly through preventive means, and to stimulate small-scale rural enterprise. Initially the network of Institute of Medical Research demographic reporters was used as the interface with the community. As time went on, and a more community-oriented approach was adopted, voluntary groups replaced individuals.

The components of the program were water supply, sanitation, nutritional gardens, small livestock, and health education. Each element embodied a degree of innovation. Water supply units were designed to be cheap, portable and easily constructed. They were made chiefly of bush materials, using a plastic sheet for catchment and a 400 litre bag with snap-on tap as storage. The water supply was placed as close as possible to the house of the mother and children, who were the intended principal beneficiaries. The sanitation component consisted of a pit latrine with a tapered concrete block and a bucket, which together with the water supply unit enabled the latrine to be kept clean. The key aim of the nutritional garden was to provide a supply of protein and greens close to the family home and therefore readily available to be included in meals. To some extent it was an extension of the 'kitchen garden' that surrounds most village homes, with the inclusion of a range of protein-rich crops such as soybeans, peanuts, lablab beans and pigeon peas. To reinforce their use, cooking demonstrations were held at a community level to familiarise families with the crops and the best ways of cooking them.

Composting was encouraged as a means of sustaining yields. FHRIP also promoted mixed crop/livestock farming, which was run successfully at its agricultural resource farm at Koli for many years. Among the animals kept there were chickens, ducks, rabbits, sheep and goats. These animals were supplied to program families at subsidised prices according to certain conditions. For example, a pen was required before Australorps chickens could be purchased. Similarly, cages were constructed in the workshop and supplied with rabbits to new farmers. And as well as supplying lambs and kids, FHRIP co-coordinated the breeding program to ensure the quality of stock was maintained. By applying these conditions, and an ongoing program of extension, the chances of success in village livestock-keeping ventures were enhanced.

Under the health education component, female health extension workers visited families to explain the relationship between hygiene, nutrition and the prevention of disease, discuss family health problems, and train the family to properly use the small kit provided by the program. The kit contained buckets and a brush, to help the family make best use of their water supply, and swabs and antiseptic ointment so that mothers could treat their children's sores and cuts at home and prevent them from becoming clinical problems.

The program was both integrated and phased. In order to join the program, each family had to agree to implement the entire phase one, consisting of water supply, toilet and nutritional garden. Only when they had achieved satisfactory results with these components were they allowed to proceed to phase two, in which they could acquire small livestock or roofing iron for a 'permanent' water catchment.

In order to run the FHRIP program, a team of local workers was assembled and trained. They in turn trained community workers, either singly or in groups, as female local health promoters or male local assistants. These community workers then assisted families to construct program items, delivered preventive health kits, and made regular visits to check progress and discuss health matters. Over 60 community workers were trained between 1995 and 2000. Each participating community constructed a 'support station' at which tools were kept and seeds and livestock propagated. These support stations enabled local workers to take more responsibility for running their own program as time went on.

The Papua New Guinea Institute of Medical Research office in Tari was the administrative centre and workshop for the program, while Koli farm served the role of agricultural resource, training and demonstration centre. Innovations used in the program were developed at these sites. In addition to the major components such as the water supply unit and concrete blocks, seed storage cupboards and driers, cane brooms, chicken feeders, rabbit cages and many other items were designed and distributed to families and support stations.

The cost of running the program in 2000 was approximately K118 ($A60) per new family for the basic inputs of water supply, toilet and nutritional garden. Cost of livestock including fencing material or pens was around K150 per family. The phase one preventive health inputs were provided free of charge while livestock and roofing iron were provided in prescribed quantities at subsidised prices. A community support station, complete with tools and shed, cost around K1150. Other costs involved in running FHRIP (excluding capital items) amounted to about K60,000 per annum. Wages for FHRIP team members accounted for the majority of this, the remainder being divided between vehicle, administration, resource stations and training.

Results

A total of 312 families participated in the program between 1995 and 2000. This represents about 10 per cent of all target families in the Tebi, Tagari and Haeapugua sub-districts of Tari. Figure 9.2 shows the distribution of families in the program whose location was recorded by GPS (Vail 2002a).

Sixty-one families (20 per cent) left the program or were dropped, either for their own reasons or due to external circumstances such as fighting. Of those still in the program in April 2000, 195 families were ranked according to a point score that measured the number and condition of program components each family had acquired. By this measure, 143 families (73 per cent) were rated as doing well, while the progress of 23 families (12 per cent) was regarded as unsatisfactory.

While it is difficult to demonstrate that general health improved as a result of participation in FHRIP, it is fair to say that families with a supply of clean water, a well-kept toilet and nutritious crops in their garden are better able to meet their basic needs than those, the majority, who do not. There were many individual examples of families who became better off because of their participation in the program. Those who acquired small livestock took the first step towards the more diversified and productive local farming system that will be needed if the challenges of environmental degradation and population growth are to be met in the coming years. The additional labour input required also provides potential employment for underemployed youths and men.

Figure 9.1. Distribution of FHRIP families 1995-2000

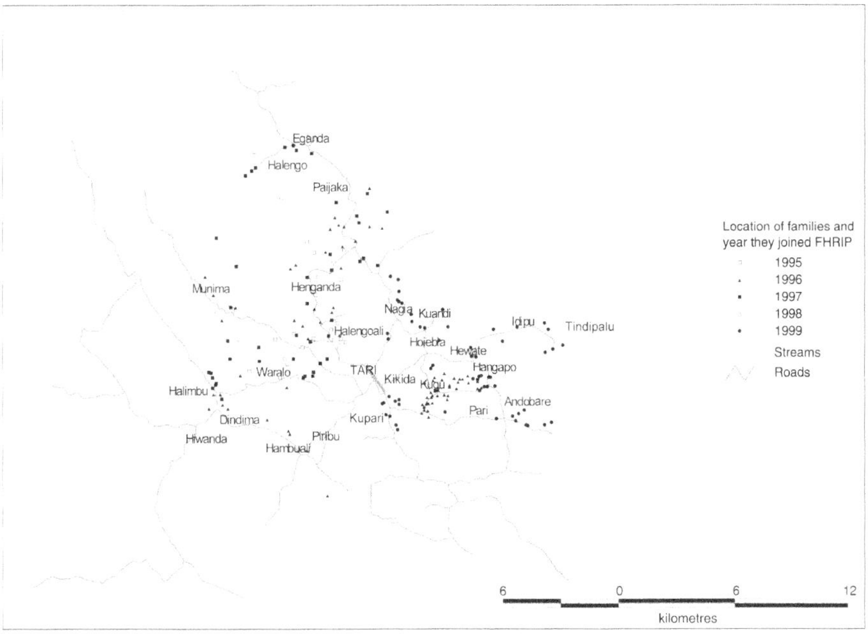

In terms of individual program components, the water supply unit proved to be fairly robust in a family setting. The main problem was the deterioration of the plastic sheet used as a catchment, which had to be replaced after about six months to one year. Rabbits were slow to be accepted, but became increasingly valued and popular among people in the program and outside it. By area, the best results were in the western parts of Tari, where excellent local program leadership provided an inspired role model for peers. On the other hand, nutritional gardens did poorly in the more remote, environmentally degraded areas to the north of Tari. In the east, local voluntary groups ran most programs, and results depended upon their organisation and commitment.

These mixed results illustrated a flaw that became increasingly evident as time went on. Because most communities lacked an internal structure capable of running a diverse and challenging set of activities, the burden was placed upon individuals, groups, and the FHRIP management team, rather than the community as a whole, to keep the program running. Hence FHRIP satisfied only in part the prerequisites of community-based development — it offered forms and inputs but lacked the capacity to build a structure in the community able to take advantage of them.

FHRIP survived the strains placed upon it by breakdowns in law and order, communications and transport, but the decision to close the Tari branch of the Institute of Medical Research in 2000 meant that a new operating arrangement would be required if the program were to continue. FHRIP had been cooperating with Community Based Health Care (CBHC) for some time, and in September 2000 a partnership was formed under which CBHC provided management and a new direction, based on their experience in Tari and other highlands provinces.

Community-Based Health Care

CBHC, a division of the Nazarene Health Ministries, commenced working with community groups in Western Highlands Province in 1995, and over the next five years expanded into neighbouring highlands provinces. Their principal aim is to provide holistic health care for communities through preventive, curative and health promotion activities. More generally, CBHC encourages communities to become self-reliant, self-regulating and productive. To do this CBHC embarks upon a comprehensive program of awareness raising, capacity building and training. Each community is assisted to establish a health and development committee, comprising local councilors, peace officers, and clan, youth and women leaders, to coordinate their development plans. These plans are then devolved to the clan level, at which volunteers implement the program activities and construct a focal meeting house at which local needs and issues are discussed for consideration by the committee. Communities must attain set minimum standards, in respect of family hygiene and community unity, to be accepted as a CBHC community and qualify for further assistance. The ultimate goal is the declaration of the community as a 'Healthy Village' after meeting all the set requirements.

The structure of a CBHC-trained community is as shown below (Nazarene Health Ministries 2002).

Figure 9.2. CBHC structure

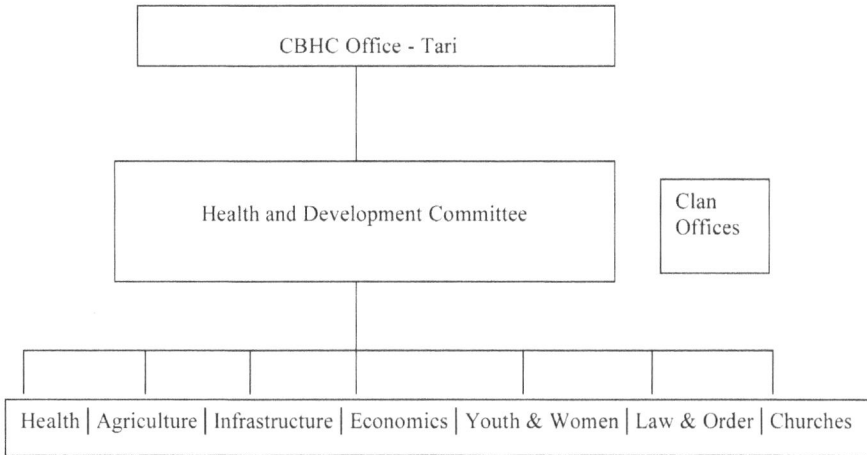

```
                    ┌─────────────────────────────┐
                    │      CBHC Office - Tari      │
                    └─────────────────────────────┘
                                  │
      ┌───────────────────────────────────────┐   ┌─────────┐
      │   Health and Development Committee     │   │  Clan   │
      │                                        │   │ Offices │
      └───────────────────────────────────────┘   └─────────┘
          │
  ┌───┬───┬───┬─────────┬───┬───┬───┐
  │   │   │   │         │   │   │   │
┌─────────────────────────────────────────────────────────────────┐
│ Health │ Agriculture │ Infrastructure │ Economics │ Youth & Women │ Law & Order │ Churches │
└─────────────────────────────────────────────────────────────────┘
```

In late 1999 CBHC started working with the Pari-Andoware community in the east basin of Tari. Many of the activities shown in Figure 9.2 have been set in action since. Under the key health component, CBHC trained village health volunteers to dispense first aid drugs, and village birth attendants to perform deliveries. Arrangements are made with the Maternal and Child Health program nurses to visit communities so that the target of over 80 per cent vaccine coverage for women and children is attained. Under the law and order activity, two village police officers were trained to work in cooperation with the law enforcement authorities. The infrastructure program covers repairs to local roads and bridges through community participation. Among the agricultural activities were the procurement of coffee seedlings, arrangements with coffee buyers to visit communities, and the import of fingerlings for family fish ponds. There is also a small-scale project facility which provides seed money for projects on a 40/60 ratio of CBHC to the local community. At the household level a community cooperative credit scheme has been established to promote savings and loans for basic household needs.

By April 2003 CBHC was supporting six communities in different areas of the Tari basin. Each new community inducted into the CBHC program is regarded as a role model for others to follow. CBHC trains 'trainers of community health volunteers' from among these communities so that there is the capacity to induct new communities that have expressed peer interest in becoming part of the program.

In order to introduce a more community-oriented approach into the national and provincial health departments, CBHC runs training courses for government health workers at its headquarters in Western Highlands Province. Some CBHC training positions are funded by the Health Department. CBHC involves itself closely in district management committees and seeks partnerships with government departments, missions and other organisations assisting community development.

CBHC/FHRIP partnership

Since the merger of CBHC and FHRIP in September 2000, FHRIP has been integrated into its partner's management structure. FHRIP no longer pursues an independent program but works alongside CBHC communities, training local volunteers in water supply construction, seed propagation and small livestock management, and supplying the initial needs of communities in respect of these items from its resource station. FHRIP workers have also been instrumental in initiating new communities into the CBHC program. While the partnership has not been without its tensions, the pooling of resources and experience by these two highly complementary organisations has strengthened their capacity to support community-based development in Tari. The fact that six communities, comprising hundreds of families, are now part of the CBHC program, indicates both the commitment of the management and the desire for development among rural people.

However the relative success enjoyed by CBHC/FHRIP over the past eight years should not be taken to mean that such local organisations can run their programs without support or resources. On the contrary, appropriate assistance, financial, technical and managerial, strengthens their capacity to reach more communities sooner. The Melanesian Farmer First Network provides one means by which such assistance may be provided.

Melanesian Farmer First Network

The Melanesian Farmer First Network (MFFN) represents a coming together of community-based organisations in Papua New Guinea and elsewhere in the Pacific to share experience and expertise among themselves. It is predicated on the idea that organisations with similar goals and methods, working in culturally similar environments, should be able to exchange ideas and practices for their mutual benefit. It also represents an attempt to move away from undue reliance on costly Western-based advisors and methods as the primary source of development assistance.

The concept of MFFN was developed by Terra Circle, a group of persons with wide development experience at the community level in the Pacific, and is co-coordinated by the Kastom Gaden Association in Honiara, Solomon Islands. The initial MFFN partners are Kastom Gaden Association, Planting Material

Network (based in Solomon Islands), CBHC and Paruparu Education Development Centre (on Bougainville). An inaugural meeting of the partners was held in Tari in April 2003. Among the objectives of MFFN are:

- to strengthen the technical and management capacity of non-government and village organisations to implement their programs, particularly in respect of food security;
- to help local organisations meet their needs for information, education and communications through appropriate methods;
- to develop low cost networks linking government departments, regional and international organisations, NGOs, and farmers and village organisations (Kastom Gaden Association et al 2002).

In Tari, MFFN is supporting training, capacity building, and exchanges, using the resources and expertise it has within the network. As an example, a worker from Tari has recently visited the Kastom Garden Association and Planting Material Network in Solomon Islands to learn seed saving methods, which she will put in practice to assist CBHC communities to improve their seed multiplication and storage methods. To improve communications, MFFN is currently looking into acquiring an HF radio modem to provide an email link between CBHC, other partners in the network, and the wider world. Other exchanges are planned in which CBHC/FHRIP staff will play a training role, which will involve strengthening the management capacity of each of the organisations involved.

Program requirements

Although MFFN, which has limited start-up funding from Oxfam/Community Aid Abroad, can provide technical support, considerably more assistance is required, both financial and material, if the CBHC/FHRIP program is expanded to meet the needs of the many communities in Tari/Komo-Margarima and Koroba districts interested in joining. Priority areas are:

- Funding. The current funding cycle for the wages of FHRIP team workers, negotiated with New Zealand Overseas Development Agency in 2000, comes to an end in October 2003. Without a renewed commitment a dozen staff will have to be laid off, causing the loss of valuable skills and experience, and weakening the vital implementation end of the program. CBHC will also require funding for additional training positions as the program expands.
- Management capacity. Currently there is an over-reliance on key individuals in the program. More persons need to be trained in management techniques to reduce this burden.
- Communications. The unreliability of communications with the outside world has been a major obstacle to acquiring program inputs, networking with other organisations and keeping in touch with donors.

- Transport. The poor quality of the roads, dispersed nature of the communities, and lack of facilities for service mean that wear and tear on vehicles is high. As the program expands vehicle replacement and maintenance costs will rise.
- Improved monitoring and evaluation skills. Participatory appraisal methods together with better record-keeping will mean the program is better able to identify program strengths and weaknesses and act upon them.
- Upgrading of the resource station to enable it to fully meet its functions as supplier of seeds and livestock, training and demonstration centre. A volunteer is being sought to assist with the management of the resource centre.

Other needs also exist, in the areas of office space and equipment, and tools and materials for use in the communities.

Conclusion

Community-based development has been badly neglected in Southern Highlands Province and in Papua New Guinea generally over the past two decades. Greater inclusiveness and participation by communities in the development process may hold the key to the long-term solution of many of the problems besetting the rural areas of Papua New Guinea. More engagement by youth in their local community reduces the potential for frustration and discontent that underlies the law and order problem. Better functioning communities, meeting more of their own health, law and order and development needs, reduces the load on the public service, providing it with more space for reform and revitalisation. More productive communities also diminish the economic imperative to migrate to the towns and hence counteract the imbalance that will grow for as long as rural areas remain stagnant and neglected.

Such development is by its nature very management-intensive and must be nurtured; it cannot be 'delivered' by outside agents in large technical downloads. It need not be very costly in monetary terms but it does require adequate resources to grow and flourish. The worst outcome is to starve promising initiatives of the means they require to assist communities, as this demoralises local program workers and leaves communities ever more bewildered about what development actually means.

The government and aid organisations need to recognise the importance of community-based development and include organisations like CBHC/FHRIP with proven track records in district and national plans, not just to provide funding but also to secure the commitment of public servants to work innovatively alongside these organisations, in the community, to meet rural needs that are currently not being met.

More generally, there needs to be greater attention focused on the internal generation of wealth, through local markets, trading networks and exchange systems. While this does not preclude agricultural and extractive industries as sources of income, it should be recognised that export-led growth is but one means of development, and one which has not worked well in the past. In one sense, the future of the highlands of Papua New Guinea may lie in the past — a return to more self-reliant, more self-contained systems, but less insular than before, learning from each other's knowledge and experience, and based upon well-ordered and well-managed communities.

References

Family Health and Rural Improvement Program. 2000 *Combined Quarterly Reports for April-June & July-September 2000*. Tari: Papua New Guinea Institute of Medical Research.

Kastom Gaden Association, Planting Material Network, Family Health and Rural Improvement Program, Paruparu Education Development Centre and the Farm-Support Association. 2002 *Farmer First: A Pacific Food Security Network of Melanesian Community Organisations*. Solomon Islands: Kastom Gaden Association.

Nazarene Health Ministries. 2002 *Community Based Health Care Program Strategic Plan 2003-2005*. Kiam WHP: Community Based Health Care Program.

Vail, J. 2002a 'The Family Health and Rural Improvement Program', *Papua New Guinea Medical Journal* 45(1-2):147-162.

——2002b 'Social and economic conditions at Tari', *Papua New Guinea Medical Journal* 45(1-2): 113-127.

Yamauchi, T. and Ohtsuka, R. 2002 'Nutritional adaptation of women in contrasting agricultural environments in Tari, Papua New Guinea', *Papua New Guinea Medical Journal* 45(1-2): 99-105.

A Brief Overview of Government, Law and Order, and Social Matters in the Tari District

Noel H. Walters

The 2002 national election highlighted the extent of anarchy throughout the Tari District and greater Huli area — Koroba, Komo and Magarima. Similar situations exist in other regions of the Southern Highlands Province. Early indications of the now rampant situation were observable 15 years ago. What started as pockets of anarchy have now developed to cover the entire province.

Key factors

Some of the many factors contributing to the present situation in Tari will be briefly discussed; most also apply to other provincial locations.

Social evolution

Social evolution has always been apparent in Huli society, but this process increased in intensity 15 years ago and in rapidity during the last five years.

The younger generation, up to 35 years of age, has little or no regard for the norms and values in which their fathers and grandfathers were indoctrinated. These were tenets which regulated action and social behaviour within the clan and behaviour towards other clans. The traditional 'bigman' system operated in this social system. It has almost disappeared.

Often the clans and subclans no longer have unity of purpose. Positive behaviour among peers and towards elders is not practised by many of the younger generation. The authority of elders is constantly challenged and physical injury and sometimes death are the result.

Illegal gun culture

In recent years there has been a proliferation of illegal weapons throughout the highlands. Possession of weapons is now regarded as a right by an ever-increasing number of the younger Huli generation. It has become one of the means by which some aspects of the present social situation are regulated. Misery, deprivation, confusion, death, injury, stealing, destruction of property and road blocks are some of the results of the illegal gun culture.

People often live in fear at their residential locations and have to move out during uncontrollable clashes; this equates to being refugees in their rightful areas. The right to pass safely along public roads is often endangered by gun-toting thugs.

Such illegal acts are assisted by poor road conditions. Gang rapes of women are frequent occurrences.

Compensation

Traditional compensation generally aimed to right wrongs within the group and restore equanimity between groups. Strict rules and regulations were observed in the implementation of compensation arrangements.

The traditional compensation process cannot be satisfactorily applied to the present social situation. The use of automatic weapons often results in many deaths and much destruction of property in a short time span. There is not enough wealth, which comes mainly from the pig culture and cash, to compensate for what is occurring in the ever-changing social process. Excessive compensation demands are now used as a weapon to further suppress opponents.

Lack of government

At the time of writing (mid-2003) there was no effective government at Tari, at any level. This has been the situation for quite some time. Tari is a gazetted town. In fact it is a run down non-functioning district station with a few remaining relics of what used to operate in a bygone era. Such a situation occurs in many parts of the country. Some examples of the vandalisation of Tari, with no state action, are as follows:

- Encroachment on state land: people have made gardens on station land and graze their pigs at various locations.
- Police house previously occupied by OIC: windows taken, walls removed and some furniture stolen.
- Police house near police barracks: walls removed, hot water system taken.
- Single quarters, Tari Hospital: generally vandalised and parts of the building carted away.
- Bank building: doors broken, furniture (tables, chairs, washing machine, etc.) stolen.
- Main office building: flyscreens broken, louvers stolen.
- Airstrip: some fence wire and gates stolen, enabling people to walk across airstrip, thus causing a safety hazard.
- Education Centre (located about 200 metres from the police station): this is supposed to be the 'engine room' for Tari district education matters. There have been cuts in the perimeter fence, slashing of flyscreens, removal of louvers and frames, ransacking of filing cabinets, removal of electrical fittings and removal of the kitchen sink. Two buildings in the Centre were burnt after the recent election chaos.
- Tari rugby league field (located across a road from the police barracks): iron posts and wire fencing and a small grandstand were provided as a PJV tax

credit scheme project. The wire and posts were stolen and the grandstand dismantled and carted away.

The following is a list of serious crimes committed in the precincts of Tari station in recent years. No one has been brought to account for any of these incidents; no coordinated government control exists.

- Police station burnt down.
- An Air Niugini office security murdered; no successful prosecution.
- Bromley and Manton manager shot dead; no one successfully prosecuted.
- A PJV employee murdered.
- Purani man murdered.
- Bank robberies (two).
- Menduli store robbed twice.
- Fuel service station robbed.
- Public service payroll from Mendi stolen at airstrip.
- Hospital female staff attacked and raped.
- House burglaries.

These two lists cover illegal acts around Tari station. The mind boggles at the extent of serious crime which occurs continually in the Tari District's rural environs.

Police

Police is a national government function. Some police stationed at Tari have become compromised by the community, through alcohol, women and various dubious activities. This has been going on for some time. There is little or no ability to deal with crime emanating from rapid social change.

In October 2000 I had a brief but interesting meeting with the mobile squad's commander in Tari. During discussions he said that no functioning government system existed in Tari; that the police, alone, could not rectify the negative law and order situation; that there was no functioning local-level government system at Tari which could contribute to bettering the law and order situation. The commander was disappointed that no government officers attended a community meeting, at Paijaka, on law and order matters.

Courts

Courts are a national government function. Major court work has not functioned in Tari for several years. When people are arrested they are held in the police cell for days before being taken to Mendi and charged before a court.

Health

Health is a provincial government function. Tari Hospital is the major hospital for the greater Huli area. It is a district hospital under the relevant act. It used to have a compliment of four doctors a long time ago. The most recent appointment was stationed at Tari for several months in 2000, before he went to Mount Hagen in early 2001. I suspect that because of the run-down condition of the Tari Hospital it was deemed that the doctor's services could be better used in Mount Hagen.

Most aid posts are also in a run-down condition, and reasonable health services do not exist. No positive action has come from provincial headquarters, Mendi, to help rectify the unsatisfactory situation.

Education

Education is a provincial government function. Generally, the education system throughout Tari District is in a run-down state, and has been for a long time. In a ten-day working fortnight many schools operate only five days. Teachers use the other five days to try and access their pay from Mendi.

There is no local-level government system to help service teachers at their workplace. No effort has been made at provincial level to rectify the situation.

Provincial government personnel

Mendi divisional sectoral heads do not visit Tari or report on problems faced by their district counterparts in health, education and other matters. No remedial action is forthcoming from Mendi. The provincial level of government has no relevance to the majority of people in the greater Huli area. Over recent years there has been closure of government departments once represented at Tari. These include Works, Plant and Transport, CIS and the Welfare Office.

Local-level government and district administration

There are four local-level government councils within the Tari District. None of these operates as required by the relevant act. Local-level government is the one closest to the people and should be a focal point for rural people's attention. Unfortunately this is not the case.

District administration should provide the framework within which the district activities of all levels of government are coordinated. It does not.

Rural extension work is not done: neither rural health extension, agricultural extension, nor general face-to-face contact between government and the people. There is no continuous reporting on social developments or law and order matters in the district.

Well trained, motivated and disciplined officers, at all levels of government in the district, should act in a coordinated way to explain important government policies to the people, and to ensure that policies are implemented and reporting requirements met. Unfortunately the Tari District lacks any meaningful overall government presence.

Members of parliament

If there has ever been any representation of people within the Tari-Pori electorate it has been only for that group from which the member came. The larger population has been ignored. In many instances sections of the larger group are regarded as the enemy.

During the five years (1997-2002) of overall government neglect of the district electorate, the member did not seem to worry about matters of serious concern: the station was vandalised; people were not able to post letters or access banking facilities; law and order problems escalated; road conditions further deteriorated; medical and education services declined; and so on.

If the member was not concerned for the wellbeing and safety of the majority of people, and the provision of basic services to which they have a right, one can only wonder what motivated him to become a member. Obviously the concept of 'government of the people, by the people, for the people' is a foreign one.

Post-election activities

Developments since the 2002-2003 elections have included: the destruction of more bridges; looting of the Bromley and Manton store; vandalisation and looting of the Menduli store; burning of buildings at the education Centre; closure of the MAF office; closure of Sullivans; cancellation of Air Niugini flights; roaming armed gangs, increasingly frequent road blocks and hold-ups. Bashings and rape have also occurred.

Bromley and Manton brought supplies in from Mount Hagen by convoy. All shop plant and equipment, fittings and the like were loaded and taken back to Mount Hagen. Since then there have been reports that the vacant staff houses have been broken into and items stolen.

The Dauli Teachers College has been closed and students and staff evacuated to Mount Hagen. From there they will go to their home destinations. Prior to closure, it was reported that a lecturer's house was broken into and that a female coastal student was raped.

Group disputes before and during the election period will have some form of resolution, peaceful or otherwise, as time passes. The number of dead and wounded and the extent of destruction of property arising out of group warfare have not been reported for many years. An efficient administration would keep track of such things.

What to do

Huli society is changing and there is no operating government to help people get through what is often a chaotic, lawless and painful process. This has been the situation for a long time.

Recently there has been recurring damage to the Hides-Porgera electricity transmission line in rural Tari locations. Notes which have been left at locations where pylons have been felled express anger towards the various levels of government, references to political concerns, and demands for services and infrastructure to be restored throughout the Tari District.

Gold cannot be produced when power is cut to the Hides power station. Because of the worsening situation the PJV has been considering withdrawing. If this were to happen, the signal would be quickly picked up by would-be investors in the PNG-Queensland Gas Pipeline venture.

There has to be political will at the highest level of government in Port Moresby to rectify the existing unsatisfactory situation. This requires a step-by-step plan, with adequate resources — financial, technical, and human — to re-establish a sound base of law and order. At the same time, a coordinated and integrated framework must be developed for all levels of government in Tari District. This is prerequisite for delivery of services and for social and economic development.

What has to happen will take several years. However, an immediate start, with full political support, is necessary. The people have to see that something is happening. When this is achieved, measures will have to be taken to ensure sustainability of the restored government system.

Conclusion

Some people are of the opinion that what is happening in the Huli area, and other parts of the highlands, is what the people deserve — it is the 'highlands way'. Such an attitude is small-minded and irresponsible.

Most Southern Highlanders want a stable law and order situation that allows them to go about the daily requirements of life unimpeded and without fear. There should be health services for children and adults. Postal and banking services should be available. Education services at all levels should be operating at a national standard. Small and large business should be able to develop and run in a safe environment. Businesses should not be closed by pillage and plunder, roadblocks, and other illegal acts. Firm practical action should commence as soon as possible, and be supported by the necessary resources.

Porgera Joint Venture's Presence in the Southern Highlands Province

Kai Lavu

The Porgera Joint Venture (PJV) operates an open pit gold mine at Porgera, in Enga Province. The principal partner in the PJV is Placer (PNG) Pty Ltd, a subsidiary of Canadian mining company Placer Dome Inc. Mineral Resources Enga Pty Ltd, which represents the Enga provincial government and landholders, holds ten per cent equity in PJV. Although the Porgera mine is located in Enga Province, power lines to the mine cut across SHP, and disgruntled landowners in the SHP have on a number of occasions cut down pylons and damaged lines carrying electricity to the mine site, bringing mining operations to a standstill.

PJV has held talks with local communities and with the national government in attempts to address the problems associated with their grievances.

The PJV presence

The PJV has a high voltage electricity transmission line, 78 km in length, situated within a 60 metre wide legally-granted easement. Regrowth in the easement is generally cleared to a 30-metre width, on a regular basis using locally hired labour.

In the absence of available suitable government officers, PJV employees carried out the land investigation for the granting of the easement. This was done over a twelve-month period including field surveys.

The transmission line consists of overhead conductors supported as required by single-legged pylons with four stay-wires per pylon. There are some 228 pylons along the route.

Environmental impact

Where there was existing forest, this has been cleared to an average width of 30 metres. Additional areas were cleared as required for construction (helipads, camps, etc.). Compensation, as per the Papua New Guinea valuer general's schedule (approximately K13,000 per hectare at 2003 values) was paid to identified owners. The original construction would have been disruptive to local fauna but its present impact is minimal. In populated areas, subsistence gardens were affected and compensation paid to identified owners according to the valuer general's schedule (approximately K35,000 per hectare at 2003 values).

Pylons are secured on a concrete pad, as are the stay wires. These are within a 10 metre x 10 metre 'footprint' which is considered to be 'lost land' for the life of the transmission line. Overhead inspections of the line are made by helicopter on a monthly basis with some accompanying noise factor.

Community impact

Prior to the construction of the power line, the communities living along the route had established flexible arrangements regarding land usage, and while land issues did lead to violence from time to time, most conflicts could be resolved amicably. Construction meant that there was an inflow of cash for labour. This created some conflicts as people expected to be hired to work on their own land, and there were some disputes over boundaries and ownership. Similarly, there was an inflow of cash from compensation. Within the settled areas there were no immediate problems, as the money flowed to those who owned the improvements (gardens, houses, etc.) and such ownership was clearly established. Within the forested areas conflicts of ownership did arise as land usage in these areas is very complicated and there were no established boundaries. The cash flow was sufficient to appease most parties, as there was enough to go around and the disputes, while not settled, were put aside. The PJV took the boundaries established in the land investigation report as correct.

After construction was finalised the cash flow dried up. From then until today what cash enters the local economy comes from the payment of annual occupation fees (easement rent at about K40 per hectare) and *ad hoc* payments for labour to carry out underline clearing. This is a small amount in absolute terms but relative to per capita income in the Tari basin at present it is a significant sum, and has led to a very large number of disputes regarding land boundaries and who is entitled to payments. Where the people were able to resolve disputes amicably before, this has changed by virtue of money being involved. There is now antagonism amongst many of the communities that previously lived in relative harmony.

In the settled areas the people were encouraged to replant subsistence gardens within the easement so as to minimise the impact of the transmission line. The presence of a residential population also meant that there were large numbers of unpaid local security personnel who sought to prevent any untoward actions that may have led to the line being damaged.

In the forested areas local fauna returned very quickly after construction. In the lower reaches, the easement became a well-established foot track. This was not the case in the higher ground as the terrain is too rugged for direct line walking and the people used the traditionally established foot tracks.

What is required (from a resource developer's viewpoint)

Normal government services to be available to people

With access to government services, community development can take place. Education, health, agricultural extension, business development, and so on all lead to an improvement in living standards. Energy is directed towards constructive activities.

A resource developer can play a major role in this regard by being a good neighbour and providing assistance in many ways. The danger is that assistance can be taken for granted and government planners begin to assume that the developer will take over the responsibility for all community work in the area upon which it impacts. The expectation levels of the community can very quickly become excessive.

Access to a competent legal system

The process of developing a resource will inevitably lead to disputes, between the community and the developer, and within the community itself. Nearly all disputes begin as very minor, however if they are not addressed promptly they grow in magnitude. Village-based systems such as the village court work extremely well when proper training and adequate supervision are provided. The next pertinent level for most resource development disputes is the district land court, which takes care of nearly all cases that village courts cannot resolve. The requirement of a competent legal system includes a well trained, disciplined and equipped police presence. Once again the developer can be a good neighbour by offering suitable assistance, but the same caveats apply.

Without a competent legal system in place, the resource developer is left to try to work through issues with the people. This is a no win situation as nothing is binding and disaffected parties will ignore any resolution reached.

When disputes grow in magnitude serious repercussions can arise. The disruption of power supply to the Porgera mine by criminal activities in the Mt Be area during the three years after a dispute arose could well have been averted if a functioning legal service had been available to the disputants. That no legal action was taken against the perpetrators was a major factor in the developments that caused the mine to be closed for three months.

Institutions to function as expected

When members of a community go to a village aid post they expect to find the orderly present and medicines available. The same applies to other government services in the rural sector. The role of the public servant in maintaining the supply of goods and services is vital. For government services to function well, district and provincial public servants must be well trained, ethical, competent and responsible. Unfortunately, training and support is almost totally lacking in SHP and this leads to a collapse of the services in the rural areas.

Resource developers can aid and assist government offices at the local level in a number of ways but there is no way that a resource developer can undertake to retrain a public service.

District and local-level government plans to be established

For many reasons it is desirable for medium-term plans to be in place at district and council levels. A resource developer can tap into these plans, if they are available, and help maximise the benefits. All developers have a community assistance program of some kind. With a close relationship with the local administration, great achievements can be obtained in a collaborative manner; local ownership is created and greater care is taken of the asset.

The Office of Planning and Rural Development

The Office of Planning holds the authority to accept or veto proposals made under the Tax Credit Scheme (TCS). The TCS has been operating for many years and has been well accepted. There is commitment to the construction and maintenance of institutional buildings in both urban and rural areas. Developers gain much in the way of public goodwill from the TCS and it is an extremely efficient way of obtaining what become state-owned assets. The TCS is a vital tool in establishing rapport with affected communities. A difficulty has arisen, however, in that there appear to be no firm guidelines for developers to follow when preparing proposals. Lengthy delays are incurred obtaining approvals. Often communities are aware that proposals have been submitted and become impatient when projects do not proceed. There is an urgent need to have this situation examined. Clear and firm policies and guidelines must be established in order for the TCS to function.

Donor agencies to utilise resource developers' knowledge

Numerous donor agencies operate in Papua New Guinea. They usually operate at a high level of efficiency and deliver many essential services to the country. Resource developers are long-term residents and accumulate a profound knowledge of their impacted areas. Donor agencies should be encouraged to tap into this knowledge to maximise the affect of proposed projects and programs. This needs to be managed in such a way that the credit for the project is not hijacked by the developer.

These are only a few of the 'requirements' that a developer would like to have in place within a resource area. The most important of these are the first three points raised above. Without the availability of the basic services at community level, the developer becomes the target for unreasonable and unacceptable demands. Without the availability of a competent legal system, the developer is exposed to unreasonable demands followed by criminal activities to take what is wanted. Personal risk levels to employees become unacceptable. Without the availability of a competent government system in place at district level, the developer is expected to assume the role of the government, a position which is untenable.

The remaining points are not, of course, a necessary requirement for resource development. However, they are powerful tools in establishing a strong collaborative relationship with the impacted communities, providing the lynchpin that links developer and the community and greatly enhances the sustainability of the resource development.

Conclusion

At the present time, however, none of the above exists. The resource developers carry out their business virtually from crisis to crisis, using their own manpower to overcome the problems. Major road blockages, power line damage, and shutdowns are becoming more frequent. Most landowner groups causing these problems are simply reacting to a lack of government services and lack of government attention to dispute resolution. The resource developer supplies funds to the national government through taxes and royalties. By shutting down the resource, the cash flow is halted. Then the government is forced to act. However many commitments are made and never honoured. Agreements are reached but not carried out. Each time this occurs the frustration amongst the landowners grows. Unless positive, continuous, and sustainable steps are taken to re-establish good, solid ethical governance throughout the province, the maintenance of any long-term development of resources in the Southern Highlands Province will be doubtful.

The Huli people have expressed their viewpoint in a simple way: 'We are tolerant people and traditionally we count the number of times that we are given bad answers. We count them one, two, three, up to 14. When the count reaches 15 we must react and react with violence. That is our way'. The count is currently hovering around the 12/13 mark.

What if they don't want your kind of development? Reflections on the Southern Highlands

Maev O'Collins

In his entry for the Southern Highlands in the Encyclopaedia of Papua New Guinea, McAlpine (1972:1089) noted that:

> The bellicosity of precontact society was indicated by the fighting ditches and trenched roads lined with defensive gate barriers noted by early exploratory patrols....The District was the last to be brought into contact with European society and partly as a consequence is one of the least developed heavily populated areas....Isolation and the recency of pacification have delayed economic and social development.

After the major exploratory patrol by J.G. Hides and L.J. O'Malley in 1935, the Southern Highlands remained relatively undisturbed until after World War II, with increased Australian administrative contact gathering momentum only in the 1950s and early 1960s. McAlpine described the task as 'virtually completed by 1965' and considered that: 'Despite the penchant for intertribal warfare pacification was remarkably peaceful' (ibid). Nevertheless, as French and Walter reminded their readers (1984:20):

> It was not until the early 1970s, however, when the last isolated groups were located and the Hewa area north of Kopiago was derestricted (in 1973), that this phase was completed province-wide.

First contacts on the road to independence

When I commenced teaching at the University of Papua New Guinea in 1972, Southern Highland students in my classes provided vivid first-hand accounts of the first Australian patrols that had come to their scattered communities. Schools had been established and they had gone on to high school and now, in their mid 20s, they were to become the first university graduates from their areas. Self-government was a reality and independence was on the horizon. This was both an exciting and a daunting prospect, as it was expected that these new graduates would assist their people to 'catch up' with the more developed areas of Papua New Guinea.

At the same time, it was clear that the Australian colonial system of government and administration, which was now to be handed over to a national government, had not yet been fully understood or accepted. The inherent difficulties in taking on responsibility for economic and social development activities and projects were also appreciated, and students began to question the wisdom of imposing a preordained form of development on their people.

At a seminar in 1973 a group of students, who had spent several weeks in Wambip, a village in what is now the Karint sub-division of the Mendi District (see Bourke *et al* 1995), reported on their findings (Bais *et al* 1973). After a lively discussion as to whether silk worms, citrus, cattle, coffee or other projects could, or should, be established, one Southern Highlander challenged me as the only Australian present.

> What happens if they don't want your kind of development? What do we do if they want to go back to the way things were before you people came and disturbed their lives?

The students' field experience had been further enlivened by differences of historical record on what had happened in the early1950s when the first Australian-led patrol had come into the area. The older villagers recalled with great detail how the patrol had crossed their 'fight ground' so their group attacked, as they knew these were hostile enemies. But the patrol retaliated with gunfire and six or eight had died. The men pointed to the places on the nearby hillside where a father or uncle had fallen. Although they had heard about earlier patrols, this was the reality of the new system of administrative control.

On the other hand, the Australian administrative officers in Mendi were outraged that the students had reported this story so uncritically. The official patrol reports they held told a very different story. 'The patrol had been attacked when it was peacefully crossing an open area. The numbers of dead were greatly exaggerated. The villagers had wanted to impress the students with this story'. I had to work hard to gain official approval for further student fieldwork in the Southern Highlands. All involved in the debate seemed unaware or unable to accept that both stories could be true. The villagers felt they had indeed been 'pacified' and the patrol officer's record indicated that his men had come under unprovoked attack and that they had to defend themselves.

Similar questions were raised a few months later, when I taught a long-vacation 'Working with Communities' course for high school teachers and administrative officers. The opening community development theme was:

> Start where the people are. Go at their pace. Learn what they want and try to help them achieve these economic or social goals.

Nice sentiments but reality was a very different matter. One exasperated teacher responded:

> I am the first person from my area to be a teacher. They think I have become a woman as I am twenty-six and I have not killed anyone. A

strong man is someone who has killed a member of the enemy group. In the past a really strong man would have killed a policeman. What does your community development say to that?

The lessons from these stories are both in the time-scale and in the responses to external intrusion and control. My students were trying to consider the appropriate action to take to bring about effective development in some communities whose experiences of outside administrative control had begun less than twenty years earlier. I was again reminded of this in September 1975, when pictures appeared in the *Post-Courier* and on television of Australian patrol officers raising the Papua New Guinea flag in remote Southern Highlands patrol posts, while local community leaders looked on.

Achieving development may be a slow and painstaking process, which requires more than one generation from the first contact and many changes in strategies to achieve real and lasting success. Another question, which was frequently asked at this time, was: 'Development for whom?' One response was: 'If they don't want the suggested development, we should leave them alone.' But, as became even clearer over the next few years, it was not possible to leave them alone. In any case, most Southern Highlanders wanted to gain access to economic opportunities and the main problem was their unrealistic expectations of the overall benefits which they thought would be obtained from particular projects.

The new provincial administration: 1975-1984

In the first year or so after Papua New Guinea became an independent nation state, there was relatively little change in the administration of the Southern Highlands but a number of social development activities were initiated. The Papua New Guinea Institute of Medical Research had established a pneumonia research unit, based in Tari, and government-sponsored literacy and other non-formal education training programmes were initiated – often in cooperation with church groups, and staff and students from the University of Papua New Guinea.

At the same time, the debate over whether and when to introduce provincial government quickened, with arguments and counter-arguments as to whether this would make government more understandable and accessible, and encourage economic development (see May *et al* 1997). Unrealistic expectations that 'more power to the people' would automatically be achieved were countered by dire warnings that the dearth of administrative skills and experience at district and sub-district level would make it an unworkable and costly exercise. Noting these conflicting arguments, Conyers (1976:74) concluded:

The history of decentralisation in general, and the establishment of provincial government in particular, demonstrates very clearly the conflicting forces of centralisation and decentralisation which are in operation in the country… it is perhaps particularly evident in contemporary Papua New Guinea because of the contrast between the exceptionally decentralised traditional organisational structure and the relatively centralised system introduced by the Australian administration. This is not something that can be solved overnight by a single political or administrative reform and, although the decision to establish provincial governments has finally been made, the conflict will undoubtedly continue in Papua New Guinea for many years to come.

On one occasion, during this period of administrative confusion and transition, I visited Pangia to discuss a student fieldwork project with community leaders, administrative officers and the student involved. Heavy rain made it impossible for me to go out to the student's village, so I spent a few days with the district officer in his official residence until the vehicle from Mendi could get through.

Already the downturn in funds and qualified staff to undertake repairs and maintenance was in evidence. The indoor toilets had broken and there were no replacement valves so hastily built pit latrines were being used. The Milne Bay government officer who was my host had completed a course at the Administrative College in Port Moresby and remarked that his training had not prepared him for the experience of being held hostage by a secessionist group on Bougainville in 1975. He was suffering from a severe eye infection, which the aid post orderly was treating with very out-of-date ointment, but this did not and could not prevent him from continuing to carry out his role as the symbol of government authority in the area. Some young men had vandalised a government house. A local village woman was in a severely delusional state and had to be restrained to avoid violence to herself or her children. And, braving the muddy road, an intrepid researcher had dropped in a number of questionnaires on local contraceptive practices, with an urgent request that these be completed immediately.

I was very impressed by the imaginative and committed way in which this recently appointed district officer approached the problems and resource limitations he experienced on a daily basis. Discussions with community leaders were needed to try to resolve the incipient but worrying signs of a breakdown in traditional authority. Emergency transport had to be quickly found to take the village woman and her concerned relatives into the Mendi hospital. However, the request for him to carry out a survey of contraceptive methods was more problematic. He had just begun to feel accepted by the local leaders and did not want to do anything that would jeopardise their cooperation and trust. At the same time, his superiors expected that he would respond positively to requests from outsiders, particularly expatriate outsiders, as their favourable reports would be helpful when dealing with the central administration in Port Moresby.

Finally, he decided that, as he was confident he knew about traditional practices in the area, he would just complete all the questionnaires himself and send them back.

Returning to the University of Papua New Guinea, with a very favourable opinion of the way this officer approached different challenges and his overall responsibilities, I quickly discovered that my positive impression was not universal. Some researchers had felt that he had not taken sufficient time to assist them, that he was a bit 'sloppy' with required paper work, and that things were not nearly as efficient as in the 'good old days' before independence.

Clearly, some of the difficulties he encountered were related to diminished resources and back-up administrative support, and to a lack of clarity as to who had ultimate administrative responsibility. In 1978, after a World Bank team visited the Southern Highlands, it recommended that a massive injection of funds would be needed to address the reality that this was one of the poorest and least developed areas they had encountered (World Bank 1978). Following this report the Southern Highlands Rural Development Project (SHRDP) was initiated, with the aim of linking economic, social and infrastructural projects to achieve more rapid and sustainable development in the province. This was during the period when provincial government was being introduced, but Southern Highlands did not yet have full financial autonomy (Regan 1997). In hindsight at least, it is not surprising that confusion often arose as to which particular administrative functions or project activities were under the ultimate authority of provincial officials, and which functions were the responsibility of the SHRDP (see Hinchliffe and Ilave 1984:66-68).

At the same time, law and order problems associated with the lack of economic opportunities for young people had heightened a general feeling throughout Papua New Guinea that the perceived breakdown in family and community authority required more organised and measured government intervention. After lengthy consultations and some political and community indecision, a National Youth Movement Program (NYMP) was established in 1980. Although there was some misgiving that this was an artificial and 'foreign' solution to community tensions, it was clear that the programme would be attractive to Australia, New Zealand and other bilateral aid donors.

> An important element was that the gradual firming of government support for some kind of national youth activity took place at a time when many church and voluntary youth organisations were attempting to review their own involvement in order to reflect political and economic changes in the wider society. Whatever their own attitudes might have been, some politicians, or aspiring politicians, recognised that young people and older supporters were a political power base and supported demands for recognition by youth groups and community activists....

Fears that more extreme 'law and order' approaches would prevail if the National Youth Movement Program were defeated may also explain the rapidity of its final introduction (O'Collins 1984:19).

Youth and their communities in the Southern Highlands

In December 1980, the Southern Highlands was one of fifteen provinces with Provincial Youth Councils, which received initial grants of K10,000 to initiate the NYMP in the province. By May 1981, thirty-eight groups had been registered, and further government grants were received to enable recruitment of community youth coordinators.

By July 1983, 250 groups had been registered with the Provincial Youth Council and were involved with a wide variety of activities. These were a mix of economic, educational, social, sporting and religious activities, reflecting the life of young people and their communities. Nevertheless, the stated emphasis on, and the time spent undertaking, economic activities were particularly emphasised in reports sent to the National Office of the NYMP, and its international funding agencies (see O'Connell and Zarriga 1991 for an outline of the development and implementation of the NYMP).

In 1983/1984, as part of a sample survey of three provinces (Manus, Morobe and Southern Highlands), I coordinated a survey by students and youth workers on 'youth in groups' in the Southern Highlands. The purpose of this survey was to learn why groups were formed, and their sponsors, problems, activities and ways of raising finances. It quickly became apparent that the groups being surveyed had become very sophisticated in their approach to outside researchers, and that some earlier surveys had reported a much higher percentage of time spent on direct economic activities than we found to be the case. At the same time, it was unwise to disregard the economic impact and benefit of what might be categorised as 'social development' activities. This was because:

> A social event to raise funds for sports equipment or a church hall; house-building by a youth group for a village leader; sports days with cash prizes to be won, are complex activities which may involve all the community, not just youth or women's groups. But, if government intervention is seen only in terms of economic development, informants considered it inappropriate to emphasise other aspects of community life (O'Collins 1984:74).

It was also beginning to be of concern to the NYMP Headquarters officials that, after receiving a small 'seed grant', many youth groups seemed to flourish for a time and then ceased to function. However, the NYMP was now receiving major funding from Australia, and an extraordinarily complex system of reporting had been instituted, so most national or provincial youth officers were reluctant to question, or to report on, what was really happening. During this same period, the SHRDP was involved in parallel community activities, sometimes in cooperation, but often in competition with the NYMP and other national government services. There was also a feeling among many Southern Highlanders whom I met that the involvement of expatriates as expert development specialists in both projects seemed to be continuing the same style of benevolent colonial interaction that they had experienced before independence.

On one occasion, when the promised government transport was suddenly unavailable, the Mendi-based provincial youth officer suggested that, as I was an expatriate, the chances of 'borrowing' SHRDP transport was commensurately greater than if he were to make the approach. He was quite correct in this assessment, and we spent a very productive few days visiting more distant youth groups and gathering helpful hints from the government driver. On one occasion, when we were unable to locate a particular youth group, he remarked it had ceased operations under that name and was now known by another name, which was also on our list. With this new name and a slightly changed executive it had been able to obtain another start-up grant. It became obvious that these youth groups were often really community groups, and, in the same way as with earlier nutrition or informal education projects, they provided spin-off benefits to the wider community.

Older members of the community viewed with alarm the single-minded focus on 'youth', as there was a danger that the unequal benefits going to one section of the community would be divisive. One way of avoiding a concomitant breakdown in traditional authority was to rein in the power of local youth group 'leaders' and to ensure that older members of the community accompanied youth groups attending district or provincial meetings. At the same time, as was the case with other economic resources, all members of the community often benefited from the NYMP funding of 'youth' activities.

> Participation of older community members in youth group activities was noticeable in most of the rural communities which I visited in Mendi district. Older men were building community centres and constructing playing fields, younger men cleaned the roads as part of a council contract and women worked on garden projects. The Youth Office staff and local youth workers pointed out that these were activities where older people had control over the management of resources (O'Collins 1984:74).

By 1983, the Southern Highlands Provincial Youth council had funded fifty-one projects, with the majority (forty-two) categorised as economic projects. At the same time, there had been considerable criticism from NYMP Headquarters staff that there had been 'interference' from Non-Formal Education, as the aim was to amalgamate extension activities in a more orderly fashion. I had been impressed by the provincial youth officer's commitment and understanding of the needs of youth working within their own communities. Yet, he was clearly more comfortable in his role as an adviser and resource link for youth groups than when required to complete the lengthy formal quarterly reports required by NYMP Headquarters. So it came as no surprise to read a statement in the *Second NYMP Grants Scheme Implementation Report* (Office of Youth, Women, Religion and Recreation 1983:14) that the Southern Highlands Provincial Youth Office (presumably the provincial youth officer) needed to improve its general management of the NYMP. I was more surprised to read that 'transport was not a problem'.

Youth projects in the Southern Highlands: Success or failure?

By July 1983, when our survey commenced, approximately 250 youth groups were registered with the Provincial Youth Council, and although many success stories were reported other groups were inactive, or had collapsed after a period of intense and somewhat frenetic activity. An initial student fieldwork report suggested that a youth group at Umbimi (a village in the Kambiri Division of the Mendi District), was an example of the sustained economic and social benefits which could be achieved through external financial assistance (O'Collins 1984: 75-76).

This group was registered in 1982 with the Provincial Youth Council. It was described as having an initial membership of twenty, a savings bank passbook and a constitution (Kombeson 1983). Office bearers included employed members of the extended family, which was the basis of group membership. They planned to start with a number of small projects, obtain a substantial grant or loan, and establish a large chicken and piggery project (personal communication by group members).

When I visited Mendi in July 1983 the group was at a peak of successful activities. A volley ball court had been levelled and male and female teenagers participated in sports days. Plans were underway to build a church, a trade store was in operation, fully grown chickens were ready for sale, and ducks, pigeons, and a gardening project were other ongoing activities. The community youth worker (also a group member) and an older clan spokesman were confident that the group would succeed and spoke of obtaining further finance and expanding their level of economic activity. I revisited this youth group in April 1984 and found that most of the activities had ceased after the chickens had been sold. The K400 obtained from the sale had gone to purchase a second-hand truck which shortly afterwards broke down and was abandoned. There had been difficulties in finding markets for the ducks, the volley ball was destroyed in a dispute and, although a number of minor activities were being carried on, the level of enthusiasm and youth involvement had diminished. The president of the group was said to be in Port Moresby and there was a feeling of marking time, waiting for the next development project when perhaps enthusiasm would rekindle and activities would recommence.

In hindsight it is hard to decide whether this project had been a failure or whether the spin-off benefits for those who participated made it a success. It was clear that when the opportunity arose to gain external financial assistance, older members of the community were able to quickly mobilise the youth to meet the conditions of the NYMP Grants Scheme. But younger members of the community had also gained valuable experience, which would be useful in negotiations with external development agencies and in the management of future economic activities.

The very centralised youth-centric focus of the NYMP could also be seen as both its strength and its weakness. I had been concerned that there was a lack of flexibility; the 'one-size-fits-all' policies and implementation guidelines did not meet the different development needs, community relationships, and levels of management skill throughout the country. However, this was not the view of NYMP senior staff, who saw the subsequent decline of the NYMP as due mainly to pressures towards decentralisation and political interference:

> As the central directing and co-ordinating unit became weaker, the national and nationalistic themes running through the youth programs lost their impact. Provincial procedures and identities became stronger. By the end of 1989, the National Youth Movement was financially weakened and showed clear signs of fragmenting. Youth program operations were subject to ministerial intervention on a scale considered unacceptable by the designers of the NYMP and earlier governments (O'Connell and Zarriga 1991:240).

At the same time, they (ibid:241) concluded that:

> Centralised direction, quality control, and performance monitoring of accountability standards are not inconsistent with decentralised decision-making, locally negotiated working relations amongst legitimate but competing power structures, and responsiveness to grass roots needs. On the contrary, this mixture makes for a powerful and efficient development process, much more effective than the usual alternative models of constipatory centralism and dogmatic functionalism ('let the managers manage').

The Lake Kutubu Project: 'What sort of development is this?'

In June 1989, accompanied by my sister Dympna, and the wife of a UPNG colleague, I spent several days in the Lake Kutubu area. We flew from Port Moresby to Pimaga, and, after a night in the local guest house, walked along the track to Lake Kutubu. There a motorised canoe took us to the more established guest lodge, which had developed a programme for short-stay tourists. After a few days visiting nearby villages, we returned the same way. Apart from a young schoolboy who walked with us along the track, we had no other guides, relying upon advice from local villagers who warmly welcomed us along the way.

Large helicopters were constantly flying overhead, transporting heavy equipment to the site of the future Lake Kutubu Joint Venture oil pipeline development. The task of identifying villagers who would be impacted by the development was already well underway. We met several members of the community survey team who were engaged in recording groups with a possible claim for compensation or future royalties. The track from Pimaga to Lake Kutubu took us through Foi land. It was clear that many villagers were deeply suspicious of this impending development, while others had very unreal expectations of the financial windfalls they would receive.

Walking back towards Pimaga, we stopped at a small village near the Mubi River. After a long negotiation to persuade the owner to accept a few kina for this old and seemingly quite valueless item, Dympna acquired a 'working' canoe paddle from a village elder. During the discussions, it became clear that we had had several enjoyable and informative encounters throughout our journey, and this struck a chord with our audience. A spokesman who had completed some years at high school made a lengthy statement in Tok Pisin about how they saw the future, and the positive and negative impacts of the oil exploration, the planned pipeline developments, and the possible payment of royalties. He pointed out that once the track we had walked on was upgraded into a vehicular road, jobs would be available, money more plentiful, people would become greedy, and conflict would be inevitable:

> Everything will soon change. *Raskol*s will come and beer will be easier to get. It will not be possible for old white women like you to walk safely through our area without armed guards. We will have to fight outsiders to protect our communities and we may even begin fighting each other. People say that those helicopters will bring us development but what will it cost? What sort of development is this?

There were other clouds on the horizon. Both the small guesthouse at Pimaga and the larger and more substantial guesthouse on Lake Kutubu had been managed by volunteers. The aim was to train suitable locals to take over and to develop appropriate economic tourist activities. However, access to necessary supplies, and booking and banking facilities were needed to provide the level of food and accommodation needed to attract all but the most intrepid travellers. The planned road might make it easier to bring in supplies but for how long?

The answer to this question came in 1993, when I was engaged as an AusAID-funded consultant to the Royal Papua New Guinea Constabulary, working with women police and police-community relations. The trip had begun awkwardly when I spoke at the Mendi police station about the police commissioner's policy on domestic violence. The officer-in-charge clearly did not agree with any official attempts to modify his off-duty behaviour and it was a relief for my counterpart and myself to be able to travel to Tari the next morning, where we anticipated (and received) a much more positive and friendly reception.

Our driver and the armed police guards who accompanied us were happy to talk about the pressures and tensions they were increasingly experiencing since the gas pipeline had progressed, and the road to Kutubu had been opened up. As we passed the access road to our former walking track they remarked that armed holdups and confrontations were now commonplace. There had been an upsurge in tribal fighting in some areas and houses had recently been burnt down in a nearby village. In addition, there had been an increase in the operation of young *raskol* groups who wanted to get their share of the action. Closer to Lake Kutubu, demands for large compensation payments after inter-group fights were now the norm, and conflicts over anticipated royalties had increased (see Sagir 2001 for a discussion of conflicts in 1993/94 between the Fasu and Foi landowners, and between landowners and Chevron officials).

Demands were now frequently made for the police to take control and restore law and order. Life was clearly very fraught for these symbols of state authority and control, and I was reminded of that earlier patrol that had blundered onto the fight ground. Reports of police encounters with community groups and *raskol* gangs would vary widely, and all sides would feel that they were caught up in a situation that had somehow got 'out of control'.

Conclusion: Whose kind of development do they want?

Reflecting back on the development discussions I have shared since 1972, it seems as if nothing has really changed. Southern Highlanders were wary when the first patrol crossed onto their fight ground more than forty years ago. They had every right to be cautious, as since then most externally-planned large economic activities have mainly benefited the outsider while others have remained unaffected. Even where smaller, more manageable and socially acceptable, economic projects have been introduced, policy and implementation guidelines have already been approved, without their knowledge or input. It is usually only when the economic or social development 'patrols' arrive that they are really aware of what is happening. At this stage, it is too late to change the course of the project, so wary acceptance and manipulation to gain the greatest possible advantage may be the only possible response.

In recent years, it has been suggested that lessons have been learned from earlier mistakes, and that foreign investors and aid project managers are more sensitive to the importance of working with local stakeholders. Chevron's community development approach is cited by some observers as being the way forward, an approach that minimises conflict and resolves disputes before they threaten to seriously compromise the whole project. Others (for example, Brunton 1992; Kennedy 1996) see these initiatives as continuing, albeit under a more acceptable guise, the cycle of external manipulation and control. From their perspective, this does not address the fundamental differences between what the people want, and what outsiders consider is good for them, or stand to gain by using this 'softly, softly' approach.

But another, and perhaps more hopeful, conclusion is that Southern Highlanders have themselves become more adept and confident in their ability to benefit from the numerous economic initiatives to which they have been exposed. Describing his first encounter in 1980 with the complexities of cultural change, the late anthropologist Jeffrey Clarke recalled how he had been driven to Takuru in the Pangia District 'in a Toyota belonging to the Southern Highlands Rural Development Project (SHRDP) funded by the World Bank'. Revisiting the Wiru in 1992, he found that a type of 'cultural revival' was taking place but considered that this was really a way of seeking the economic tourist advantages of traditional culture (Clarke 2000: Preface). He concluded (ibid: 172) that:

> The cultural 'revival' was a quest to regain the lost autonomy denied by colonialism, and to withdraw to some extent from the control of the state.

Southern Highlanders may not wish to completely withdraw from the control of the state, and certainly not from the economic opportunities that foreign investment sanctioned by the state offers. Yet they remain ambivalent towards 'our kind of development'. In these circumstances, some conflict is inevitable and understandable, as it is an integral part of their ongoing quest to regain cultural autonomy and a sense of their own identity and place in the modern world.

References

Bais, T., *et al.* 1973 *'Wambip community study'. Report of a student field trip to the Southern Highlands.* University of Papua New Guinea, typescript.

Bourke, R. M., Allen, B. J., Hide, R. L, Fritsch, D., Grau, R., Hobshawn, P., Konabe, B., Levell, M.P., Lyon, S., and Varvaliu, A. 1995 'Southern Highlands Province, Text Summaries, Maps, Code Lists and Village Identification'. *Agricultural Systems of Papua New Guinea, Working Paper No.11,* Canberra: Department of Human Geography, The Australian National University.

Brunton, B. 1992 'The Struggle for the Oil Pipeline in Papua New Guinea'. *Discussion Paper Number 68*. Boroko: National Research Institute.

Clark, J. 2000 *Steel to Stone: A Chronicle of Colonialism in the Southern Highlands of Papua New Guinea*. Oxford: Oxford University Press.

Conyers, D., 1976. *The Provincial Government Debate*. Boroko: Institute of Applied Social and Economic Research, Monograph 2.

French, W. and Walter, M. A. H. B. 1984 'Background to the Southern Highlands Province', in W. French and M. A. H. B. Walter (eds), *What Worth Evaluation? Experiences with a World-Bank Aided Integrated Rural Development Project in the Southern Highlands Province of Papua New Guinea*. Boroko: Institute of Applied Social and Economic Research, Monograph 24, pp. 15-26.

Hinchliffe, K., with Ilave, H. 1984 'Project organisation and management', in W. French and M. A. H. B. Walter (eds), *What Worth Evaluation? Experiences with a World-Bank Aided Integrated Rural Development Project in the Southern Highlands Province of Papua New Guinea*. Boroko: Institute of Applied Social and Economic Research, Monograph 24, pp. 27-68.

Kennedy, D. 1996 'Development or sustainability at Kutubu, Papua New Guinea?' in Richard Howitt, with John Connell and Philip Hirsch (eds), *Resources, Nations and Indigenous Peoples, Case Studies from Australasia, Melanesia and Southeast Asia*. Melbourne: Oxford University Press, pp.236-250.

Kombeson, B. 1983 *'Umbimi Pentacostal Youth Group'*. Student fieldwork report, typescript.

May, R. J., Regan, A. J. and Ley, A. (eds) 1997 *Political Decentralisation in a New State. The Experience of Provincial Government in Papua New Guinea*. Bathurst: Crawford House Publishing.

McAlpine, J. 1972 'Southern Highlands District', in P. Ryan (ed.), *Encyclopaedia of Papua New Guinea*. Melbourne: Melbourne University Press (in association with University of Papua New Guinea), pp. 1085-1091.

O'Collins, M. 1984 *Youth in Papua New Guinea: With Reference to Fiji, Solomon Islands and Vanuatu*. Political and Social Change Monograph 3. Canberra: Research School of Pacific Studies, The Australian National University.

O'Connell, C. and Zarriga, R.I. 1991 'Papua New Guinea's National Youth Movement', in Sandra Sewell and Anthony Kelly (eds), *Social Problems in the Asia Pacific Region*. Brisbane: Boolarong Publications, pp. 210-243.

Office of Youth, Women, Religion and Recreation 1983 *'Second NYMP Grants Scheme Implementation Report'*. Port Moresby, mimeographed.

Regan, A. J. 1997 'The origins of the provincial government system in Papua New Guinea', in R.J. May and A.J. Regan with A. Ley (eds), *Political Decentralisation in a New State. The Experience of Provincial Government in Papua New Guinea*. Bathurst: Crawford House Publishing, pp. 9-20.

Sagir, B. F. 2001 'The politics of petroleum extraction and royalty distribution at Lake Kutubu', in A. Rumsey and J. Weiner (eds), *Mining and Indigenous Lifeworlds in Australia and Papua New Guinea*. Adelaide: Crawford House Publishing, pp. 145-156.

World Bank. 1978 *Papua New Guinea, its Economic Situation and Prospects for Development*. Washington DC: The World Bank.

Conflict Vulnerability Assessment of the Southern Highlands Province

Neryl Lewis

The Southern Highlands Province (SHP) is undoubtedly Papua New Guinea's worst performing province. It is abundant in natural resources and its provincial budget is one of Papua New Guinea's highest, yet services barely operate and human development indicators are amongst the lowest in Papua New Guinea. Whilst conflict has always been a part of life in SHP, since the late 1990s the incidence of violent conflict and crime has increased markedly. Correlating with this rise in violence has been a serious decline in governance standards and an associated deterioration in basic service delivery.

This chapter seeks to provide a Conflict Vulnerability Assessment of SHP.[1] As such its main objectives are to identify the key sources or drivers of conflict in SHP and to identify the issues that have the potential to further inflame conflict or promote peace and stability.

A modified version of the *Country Indicators for Foreign Policy (CIFP) Risk Assessment Template* [2] was utilised as a framework for this assessment. CIFP attempts to apply rigour to the process of conflict risk assessment by analysing a country's situation against internationally identified conflict risk indicators.

Specifically, this report is structured around seven of CIFP's leading conflict risk indicators, namely:

- historical factors;
- political/governance factors;
- security sector factors;
- social factors;
- economic factors;
- environment and natural resource factors; and
- international factors (see Table 13.1).

As peace-conflict dynamics are fluid, this vulnerability/risk assessment will be subject to ongoing review and refinement. It should therefore be considered as a *preliminary* diagnostic only, providing a foundation for ongoing analysis and monitoring of peace-conflict dynamics in SHP.

Historical factors

Assumption

Repeated episodes of violent conflict and lawlessness indicate propensity to resort to violence to air grievances/ resolve disputes.

Table 13.1. Summary of conflict risk indicators for Southern Highlands Province

Clustered Conflict Risk Indicators	Key issues in SHP	Level of Concern
1. Historical factors	• Tradition of tribal fighting • Effectiveness/applicability of traditional conflict resolution mechanisms diminished in contemporary nation-state	Medium
2. Political/governance factors	• Patronage model of governance and corruption • Volatile electoral processes with intense inter group rivalries for political and resource control • Service delivery breakdown • Moribund public service • Lack of national government intervention • Emergence of non-government service providers • Lack of information (media) • Separatist sentiment - Hela Province movement	High
3. Security sector factors	• Endemic lawlessness • Competency and size of police service • Proliferation of small arms	High

4. Social factors	• High level of language group (tribal) diversity
	  • Declining standards of living
	  • Poor human development indicators
	  • Lack of employment/income generating opportunities
	    • Youth bulge
	    • Violence against women
	    • High population growth rate
	    • 'Quick' development
	    • HIV/AIDs
		High

5. Economic factors	• Relatively large provincial cash flows from resource sector • Reliance on resource sector for provincial revenue (small agricultural sector) • Skewed income distribution • Criminal encroachment on the informal economy	High
6. Environmental and natural resource factors	• Land/resource ownership • Land pressure and growing food security issues	Low
7. International factors	• Lack of donor engagement in SHP • Proximity to instability/conflict in neighbouring provinces (Enga, Gulf, Western) • Illicit cross-border small arms /drugs trade	Low

Tradition of tribal fighting

- Fighting is viewed as a legitimate means of prosecuting claims and exacting retribution for 'wrongs'. However, traditional non-violent dispute resolution mechanisms exist and there is *not* typically an immediate recourse to violence.
- Probability of SHP-wide civil conflict low when a fight is triggered by localised dispute. This is because divergence in 'tribal identities' means that conflict in one part of SHP typically does not translate into conflict in other parts of SHP.
- Traditional disputes are, however, increasingly manipulated for political purposes (e.g. election campaigning), raising the potential for these conflicts to spread beyond localised areas. For example, it is possible that support for the creation of a Hela province in the 2007 elections could prove divisive if political leaders are successful in mobilising the public for or against the cause.
- Ready access to small arms has changed the character of contemporary tribal warfare and increased casualty rates (see security sector factors).
- SHP's Western regional administrator reports that there were 164 conflict-related deaths in the Tari area alone in 2003 and 40 such deaths between January and August 2004.

Effectiveness/applicability of traditional conflict resolution mechanisms diminished

- The transition to nation-state has diminished the influence of those traditional power structures that kept violent confrontation within certain limits, and has created a power vacuum in areas where the state's role is minimal and traditional authority has broken down.
- The Western justice system is about crime and punishment, whereas the Melanesian system is about crime and reparation (compensation). Disputes cannot be resolved and justice is not seen to have been done until compensation has been paid. For this reason, the magistrate in Mendi reports that awareness-raising is required to educate people about the legal system and the role of a magistrate (many think he 'makes up the law' rather than interprets it).
- Lack of state-consolidated power and capacity to intervene has meant that modern law and justice systems are a 'veneer, an overlay'.
- Tribal fights tend to be triggered by small disputes over 'pigs, land and women'. Village courts if they were functioning could most likely resolve these disputes before they escalate. Unfortunately village courts have largely ceased to function in SHP and those that are functioning have no power to enforce rulings.

- Traditionally conflict sprang from the community level or 'bottom-up', but now many conflicts are triggered from the 'top-down' (being politically motivated), rendering traditional conflict resolution methods less effective.
- During the 1980s traditional leadership structures began to change, with more senior leaders devolving responsibilities to younger 'Western educated' males with better ability to interact with foreign resource companies.

Trend

Resort to violence for dispute resolution is a longstanding feature of SHP society. While conflict is usually localised and non-violent dispute mechanisms continue to function, the declining influence of traditional mechanisms and weakening state justice institutions (combined with increased access to firearms) indicate that the incidence of violent conflict is likely to increase — particularly when manipulated by provincial leaders for political purposes.

Political/governance factors

Assumptions

Poor performing political institutions and governance systems aggravate conflict risks; unrepresentative government, corruption, poor transparency and accountability, inadequate service delivery and lack of information can lead to a strong sense of injustice. Furthermore the denial of civil and political liberties increases the likelihood dissenting views will be expressed through violence.

Patronage model of governance and corruption

- Political office tends to be seen as means to gain access to state resources for oneself and supporters ('*wantok*'), with parliamentary and electoral systems unable to transcend local loyalties.
- SHP was the last area of Papua New Guinea to be colonised, giving Southern Highlands less time than other areas of Papua New Guinea to adapt to the introduced political systems.
- There is a degree of acceptance of *bigman* corruption — perception that one's elected leader is not so much a politician looking after SHP, but a politician looking after constituents personally.
- However, there are also increasing levels of public dissatisfaction with lack of service provision and unmet expectations, with the potential for this dissatisfaction to be mobilised by political agitators for violent political change.

Volatile electoral processes with intense inter-group rivalry for political and resource control

- Stakes are high for political control of SHP's considerable resource wealth, fuelling inter-group rivalries particularly during election periods.
- The 2002 national elections led to violent conflict in SHP with the election results declared invalid in six of SHP's nine electorates due to widespread vote rigging, intimidation of voters, theft of ballot boxes and violence. These six electorates remained unrepresented in the parliament until supplementary elections were held in April 2003 (with 2,000 police deployed to uphold security).

Service delivery breakdown

- Provincial government funding for service delivery in SHP has decreased markedly in recent years. Many services are only operating on the basis of contributions from the national government, donors, church groups and resource companies.
- In the health sector continuing security problems threaten to close both Mendi and Tari hospitals. Mendi Hospital is operating but is overstretched, with surrounding aid posts not operating due to lack of funding or absent staff. Tari Hospital (serving about 250,000 people) is without a doctor and is operating as an outpatient clinic only.
- In education sector the provincial governor introduced a free education policy. Under this policy, a private firm (Treid Pacific) has been contracted to run all SHP schools. The policy has suffered from poor planning and insufficient funding, which has meant few schools have been able to operate effectively, and some not at all. There is also a shortage of teachers (though many are still on the payroll), with a generation of children in SHP's more remote areas having never attended school.
- In regard to policing, the national government has generally responded to increased conflict/crime in SHP with the short-term deployment of police mobile squads. These squads have generally been insufficiently resourced and reliant on assistance from the resource companies. RPNGC has 200 regular police (100 of these are Mendi-based). The provincial police commander (PPC) is not able to liaise with SHP's political leaders as most reside in Port Moresby (his only point of liaison is with churches and other community groups). Mobile squads are an unsustainable solution over the medium term.
- In the justice sector, SHP has insufficient magisterial services (one magistrate may still be Tari, but operating without provincial government support) — there should be 12 magistrates. Village courts have not operated effectively since 1995 (when the *Organic Law* shifted from the national government to provincial governments responsibility for funding village courts).

Moribund provincial public service

- Few of SHP's political leaders spend time in the province, instead residing in Port Moresby. As a result the public service lacks political direction and access to decision-makers.
- Many senior public servants are also absent from the province and it is claimed that all key decisions (e.g. the 2004 provincial budget) are made in Port Moresby.
- Public servants attempting to operate in the province are becoming increasingly agitated.
- Increasingly the public service is being politicised, with SHP MPs appointing supporters to positions within the SHP administration. This situation has led to multiple employees on the provincial payroll for single positions, rendering public administration of the province unmanageable. It is reported that political appointments have been made all the way down to the village court level. For example there are currently there are two provincial administrators occupying the single position — engaged by successive SHP governors. Also, there are disputes between the former and new politically-appointed district administrators in Ialibu and Tari.
- There are also claims that duly elected LLG presidents have also been replaced by political appointments.
- SHP public servants claim they fear losing their jobs if they are perceived to be critical of current SHP government practices, decisions and policies.

Lack of national government intervention

- The 2002 SHP audit, conducted by Pricewaterhouse Coopers, found that approximately K50 million had been misappropriated from provincial revenue by successive SHP governments over the audit period 1998-2002. There has been no effective follow-up by the national government on the report's findings.
- This lack of national government action following the audit report highlights serious capacity and commitment problems within Papua New Guinea central and prosecuting agencies, as well as complicity with SHP corruption. Several national government ministers and senior bureaucrats in Waigani were implicated in corrupt dealings with SHP's leaders.
- The *Organic Law* gives substantial power to provincial politicians, making it difficult for the national government to intervene in provincial affairs and suspend provincial governments without declaration of a state of emergency.
- Successive national governments have found it difficult to confront governance breakdown in SHP when the government has needed SHP MP support to retain power.

• Growing fatigue within the national government to deal with the problems in the SHP with public servants feeling increasingly despondent, seeing little returns for their efforts.

Emergence of non-government service providers

• Resource companies operating in SHP (Oil Search and the Porgera Joint Venture [PJV]) have become a 'surrogate state', funding schools, health care and roads through community programs and the tax credit scheme. Whilst this can certainly be positive where companies refuse to operate through patronage, thereby allowing less powerful groups such as women's organisations more chance of gaining resources, it is also the case that resource companies cannot possibly meet service delivery expectations and needs in their entirety.

• Mine closures which are expected within the next decade will increase pressure for state services at a time when the resource base will already be diminished.

• Churches (mainly Catholic and Uniting churches) also play an important service delivery role in SHP. However, the mainstream churches also rely on national and provincial government funding (salaries and equipment) to fully function.

• The churches currently manage a considerable number of schools, health clinics and aid posts and would be prepared to take over more if the provincial government allocated staff to these aid posts.

Lack of information (media)

• Most Southern Highlanders have no access to media sources such as newspapers or radio. People rely on 'word of mouth' — information that can easily become distorted and rumours spread unchecked.

Separatist sentiment — Hela Province movement

• The Huli are the dominant language group (with an estimated population of 250,000) in the north-western corner of SHP and are the main proponents for the establishment of a separate Hela province.

• The proposed province would encompass all of SHP's major resource projects (located mainly in the west) and benefit flows from Porgera in Enga Province — making Hela Papua New Guinea's wealthiest province. Other groups in SHP see Hela as a push by the Huli to control the province's resource wealth.

• Lack of perceived legitimacy of the state (undermined by its inability to provide an adequate level basic services and corruption) has increased the push for greater autonomy for the Hela region.

• Several Huli MPs have lobbied in Waigani for the establishment of a separate Hela province. In mid-2003 Prime Minister Somare announced that there would be a Hela Province by 2007 (with National Alliance campaigning to maintain SHP MP support).

• This issue has the potential to incite conflict not only between the Huli and language groups to the east, but also between the Huli and other groups within Hela region, such as the Duna. Although they believe that the Huli, Duna, Hewa and Bogia peoples descend from a common ancestor called 'Hela', the Duna charge the Huli with forgetting their common links and believe that the establishment of a Hela province will mean the Duna will loose their unique identity. In reaction, many Duna instead advocate the establishment of a Duna Province.

Trend

Given the high stakes for political office, elections will likely continue to be periods of increased tension and conflict, with MPs remaining under pressure to distribute the benefits of office to supporters. The increase in political appointments in the public service will further increase dysfunction within the provincial administration. Lack of national government action to address corrupt practices by SHP leaders will continue to create a permissive environment for greed-driven conflict, while further service delivery breakdown will fuel grievance-driven conflict. Moves to establish a separate Hela Province will likely trigger conflict between Huli and neighbouring groups cut off from SHP's resource wealth, as well as between Huli and other groups within Hela who do not want to be dominated by the Huli.

Security sector factors

Assumption

The intrinsic relationship between stability and development objectives has led to growing awareness within aid agencies of the importance of a functioning security sector that is fully accountable to civilian authority. Excessive militarisation not only reduces investment in social sectors but may also indicate mobilisation of state resources for repression of minority/dissident groups.

Endemic lawlessness

• Warlordism may not (yet) be applicable to SHP as *raskol* gangs are still predominantly based on tribal affiliations (*wantok*) rather than gravitating around a warlord. However, crime gangs (such as the late David Agini's) indicate that crime gangs are beginning to operate beyond clan lines. These groups operate as mercenaries or 'guns for hire', with warring parties hiring gangs (who possess high-powered weapons) to fight on their side.

• Criminal networks can become powerful in lieu of the state. They build upon existing networks e.g. traditional marriage and trading links.

- *Raskol*/criminal gangs have operated along the main trunk road (the only road connecting the west of the province to Mt Hagen in the east), particularly in the Nipa area. These road blocks have served both criminal purposes (to rob travellers, particularly those heading to or from Mt Hagen with cash) and warfare purposes between the Huli and the Nipa (with the Nipa blocking the Huli's access in and out of the province).

Competence and size of police service

- The current provincial police commander (PPC), Simon Nigi, has a good track record and is committed, but police service is overstretched and under-resourced. The population (over 500,000) to police (300 police) ratio is very low, making it impossible for the police to be effective.
- Police officers feel under-utilised and disaffected. Incidents of criminal gangs capturing police have further lowered morale and the police believe that they are 'outgunned' by these gangs.
- Low public confidence in police service — due mainly to poor police discipline (including incidence of police and criminal collusion) and an unwillingness by communities to cooperate and provide information to police out of fear of retribution from criminals.
- PNGDF deployment if state of emergency was declared in SHP could trigger further conflict if under-resourced and not well-managed (particularly considering the negative impact the PNGDF's deployment had on the Bougainville conflict).

Proliferation of small arms

- Most commercially-manufactured firearms in SHP have been leaked/stolen from PNGDF and RPNGC armouries, with many purchased by local MPs for supporters.
- Some evidence of illicit gun/drug trade operating in/through SHP, though views differ on the scale of this problem.
- Potential for increased cross-border small arms trafficking and further arms build-up, particularly given the growing demand for firearms in SHP.
- It is claimed that most adult males in SHP own home-made shotguns.

Trend

Heavy demands on finite police resources and the proliferation of small arms is overwhelming the capacity of the state to provide stability. However, the police service is probably better placed to deal with SHP's law and order problems than the PNGDF. The growing demand for firearms may lead to increased weapons and ammunition trafficking.

Social factors

Assumption

Ethnic and religious divisions within society represent cleavages around which dissent may be mobilised, particularly where one identity group exercises its dominance to accumulate economic and political benefits. High population density and growth rates can also accentuate the risk of conflict by heightening competition for physical and social resources. Young, unemployed populations can be politically volatile and prone to violence, placing less trust in political institutions and traditional patterns of authority. A decline in living standards can fuel grievance and competition for development benefits, with a lack of confidence in the state's ability to provide essential services correlating with political instability and civil unrest.

High level of language group (tribal) diversity

- SHP is highly socially and linguistically diverse (with at least 16 distinct language groups in SHP). Such social diversity can inhibit widespread conflict as no one social group has the numbers to gain political monopoly.
- However, ethnic affiliation also acts as a conflict mobiliser — particularly where there is perceived inequality between neighbouring groups.

Declining standards of living

- Service delivery breakdown is a major source of tension. Coupled with this, perceptions of 'needs' have changed such that hospital care now widely considered a right. It is felt that people who have become accustomed to accessing services may be more likely to react to their withdrawal than those people who have only had sporadic access to services.
- Postal, banking, trade stores and telecommunications are not available having closed down across much of the province. This is largely due to increasing security concerns.

Poor human development indicators

- SHP has some of the lowest human development indicators for Papua New Guinea. For instance, literacy levels in SHP are estimated at 50 per cent for men and 30 per cent for women, while children are shorter and on average weigh 300g less at birth than those in Papua New Guinea's other provinces. The 2000 national census found that child malnourishment was a serious and widespread problem in SHP.

Lack of employment/income generating opportunities

- There are few employment opportunities in formal sector. The mining sector, for instance, generates little employment and there are few agricultural employment opportunities beyond subsistence farming.
- Household income levels in SHP are rated low to very low — on average household income is estimated to be K20 per annum.
- Youth unemployment is an increasing problem in SHP, as it is throughout Papua New Guinea.
- Frustration over lack of opportunity and poverty is a potential trigger for violence particularly amongst young men.
- It is difficult for many Southern Highlands to access markets — over 100,000 live in areas reachable by air and foot only. The residential pattern for most groups in SHP is one of scattered households, not nucleated village settlements, inhibiting conventional economic development.
- SHP has the lowest levels of agricultural cash-cropping income in the country (in 2002 SHP produced 830 tonnes of coffee worth K3.6 million and in 2003 produced 1,020 tonnes worth K4.61 million).

Youth bulge

- SHP exhibits many familiar demographic characteristics of developing countries around the world — high population growth rate with associated 'youth bulge'.
- A 'youth bulge' typically leads to high youth unemployment with an associated increase in criminality and other social maladies. It also puts pressure on traditional support mechanisms.
- Growing up without traditional clan support mechanisms but surrounded by trappings of modernity can lead to growing dissatisfaction and resentment. Youth alienated from traditional mechanisms for addressing grievances tend to be more likely to resort to spontaneous violence or criminality.
- Intergenerational conflict over royalty payments is of increasing concern in SHP, with the sons of landowners agitating for access to the benefits their fathers receive as the officially registered landowners (similar in this regard to the Bougainville conflict).

Violence against women

- Traditional attitudes of male dominance have been accentuated by lack of income-generating opportunities, leading to disenchantment and increased propensity to resort to violence against women.
- Belief in sorcery (*sanguma*) is common throughout SHP. Women are most often the victims of sorcery allegations and violent retribution.

High population growth rate

- SHP's annual average population growth rate is estimated at 3.5 per cent — higher than Papua New Guinea's average.

'Quick' development

- Rapid resource development has created enclaves — with sharp economic and social difference between the 'haves' and the 'have-nots' (including intergenerational conflict between benefiting landowners and their sons).
- Anthropologists have also noted incidents where groups have started fights after receiving royalty payments in order to offer generous compensation and demonstrate their group's wealth.

HIV/AIDS

- The incidence of HIV/AIDS in SHP appears to be rising dramatically. This will inevitably have major economic and social implications for SHP.
- HIV/AIDS is little understood by general population in SHP.
- There are seemingly links between an increase in sorcery-related killings and a rise in HIV/AIDS incidence in SHP, with women predominantly being blamed for unexplained illnesses suffered by an increasing number of men.
- Mendi and Tari hospitals are equipped to conduct HIV testing but often lack the chemicals needed to conduct these tests. Smaller aid posts are not equipped to do such testing.
- SHP's Provincial Aids Council has performed poorly.

Trend

The rise in HIV/AIDS is of serious concern with far-reaching social and economic implications. Continued service delivery breakdown is also of humanitarian concern, with many Southern Highlanders unable to access basic medical care. Growing levels of dissatisfaction and agitation in SHP can render the population increasingly vulnerable to political manipulation — particularly with a large youth population.

Economic factors

Assumption

Economic decline and poor economic performance (including high debt burdens and inequities) reduce the capacity of the state to meet its obligations to citizenry, fuelling popular unrest and other preconditions for violent conflict, in particular scapegoating of economically privileged minorities.

Relatively large provincial cash flows

- SHP has the largest provincial budget in Papua New Guinea. The provincial budget for 2004 totalled K96.5 million. Of this K40 million was allocated for salaries (including teachers), K24 million provided through the Tax Credit Scheme for development projects, leaving over K30 million for goods and services — substantially more than most other provinces.
- The national government, provincial government and incorporated landowner groups have all received large cash flows from the resource sector. From 1992 to 2003, Papua New Guinea's national government received an estimated $US3 billion from SHP's resource companies. During the same period SHP's provincial government received over $US282 million while landowner groups received over $US1 billion.

Reliance on mining sector for provincial revenue

- SHP is highly dependent on the mineral resource sector, with little investment in the agricultural sector. Indeed agriculture in SHP remains largely subsistence based with negligible commercial outcomes. Compounding this there are few incentives for economic activity. The deterioration of the road network and the law and order situation are key constraints to production.
- Business ventures such as cattle, coffee, silkworms, etc. have proved unsustainable over the past decade in SHP due to: (i) transport and communication problems; (ii) lack of understanding about investment and replenishment strategies; (iii) trade stores attracting customers on a 'same descent' or *wantok* basis; and (iv) profit erosion through funnelling into customary exchange activities or debt-credit relationships.
- On the other hand, it can be argued that communities are resourceful and have an ability to survive when cut off from the country's formal economy, and that with declining revenue there is less to fight over.
- The national government and SHP provincial government are both reliant on SHP's resource wealth. It is currently estimated that 8 per cent of annual national revenue is derived from SHP's resource sector.
- This dependence on SHP's resource sector leaves both governments vulnerable to sharp economic deterioration if the resource companies withdraw suddenly or unexpectedly from SHP due to security concerns. With this is mind it is worth noting that Oil Search continues to face ongoing security problems in maintaining infrastructure, such as the pylons providing power to the Porgera gold mine. The cutting down of these pylons is typically a form of protest directed at the Papua New Guinea government over lack of service delivery and perceived inequality in distribution of resource benefits, rather than a protest directed against the company.
- The PJV and Oil Search maintain an active program of community engagement along the powerline route, so as to minimise disruptions. Felled

power pylons give rise to lost production costs which are estimated to be in the order of $US1.2 million per day. As it often takes several days to restore a felled pylon, regular felling of the power lines would most likely see the mine shut down.

Skewed income distribution

- The inequitable distribution of wealth has given rise to polarisation within the SHP community — the 'haves' being those who receive royalties and benefit from the Tax Credit Scheme and the 'have nots' being those outside the immediate project areas and therefore unable to access any benefits.
- Southern Highlanders living outside the resource project areas have some of the lowest income levels in Papua New Guinea as well as very poor access to basic services. The Koroba-Kopiago district in northwest of the province, for instance, is repeatedly rated as one of the poorest areas in Papua New Guinea.
- Those benefiting from SHP's resource wealth tend to invest their money outside the province (e.g. in Port Moresby real estate), leaving little money to circulate within the province. This means that there is little if any 'trickledown' effect.
- A lack of banking facilities in SHP also encourages quick consumer spending rather than re-investment within the province.

Criminal encroachment on the informal economy

- Informal market networks (and criminal networks) can become powerful in lieu of the state, with an increase in illicit commodities e.g. guns, drugs.
- Aspiration for cash is now universal with traditional barter systems breaking down (e.g. in 1971 bride-price payments typically equalled fewer than seven bride wealth items — mother of pearl shells, cowrie shell ropes or several pigs. In 2003, however, the going rate in some areas was around K10-20,000 plus pigs.)
- In some cases people are resorting to criminal activity to access cash for these payments.

Trend

SHP does not suffer from a lack of money, but from the inequitable distribution and reinvestment of that money. Unless the Papua New Guinea government takes action to prosecute egregious acts of corruption and set standards for provincial economic governance (together with increased SHP civil society demand for reform) there will be little incentive at the leadership level in SHP for change — resulting in continued conflict over economic inequality.

Environment and natural resource factors

Assumption

Environmental degradation and depletion of renewable resources constrains economic productivity and growth; Natural resource ownership, particularly customary land ownership (and inheritance thereof), is vigorously defended in Melanesian societies.

Land/resource ownership issues

- Disputes over land tenure and natural resource ownership are pervasive.
- Land ownership can be a fluid concept. Formal land registration systems demand final adjudication on settlement, but indigenous systems require ongoing renegotiation.

Land pressure and growing food security issues

- Approximately 50 per cent of SHP is unoccupied due to difficult terrain. The most fertile land in SHP is found around Mendi, Tari and Ialibu, with the rest of the province being difficult to cultivate due to steep slopes, high altitude and increased cloud cover.
- Its been estimated that women in SHP produce 20 per cent less sweet potato for the same labour as women in more fertile areas.
- Arable land is at a premium with growing population pressure.
- SHP is vulnerable to climatic extremes (drought, excessive rainfall, frost and fire), with the majority of SHP's population having limited cash incomes to use as a buffer when subsistence food stocks run low.
- There are growing food security issues in parts of the Komo-Magarima, Mendi, Nipa-Kutubu and Koroba-Kopiago districts, due to growing population pressure, poor land potential and very low cash incomes. People in these areas were seriously affected by the 1997-1998 drought.

Trend

Depletion of existing renewable resource stocks is likely to lead to pressure to develop new resource projects to maintain the government revenue base. Clashes between customary and contemporary land tenure systems are likely to persist and any attempt to bring about land reform is likely to be strenuously resisted. Food security problems are likely to increase as population continues to grow and HIV/AIDs impacts upon adult population.

International factors

Assumptions

International isolation reduces the capacity of the international community to influence peace-conflict dynamics within a society; proximity to violent conflict in neighbouring states/provinces can also have a destabilising effect due to trans-border phenomena (such as people movement, small arms flows and participation in war economy), especially where ethnic affiliations straddle borders.

Lack of engagement with other donors

- Apart from AusAID, the only other donor significantly engaged in SHP is the ADB through a road upgrading project. However, this project has stalled due to lack of SHP government counterpart funding commitment.

Proximity to instability/conflict in neighbouring provinces

- Whilst widespread violent conflict is not a major problem in the provinces that share a border with SHP, neighbouring provinces, such as Enga, Western and Gulf also suffer from poor governance.

Illicit small arms/drugs trade

- SHP's porous borders can act as a conduit for weapons, drugs and people.

Conclusion

Analysis of CIFP findings suggests that governance failure is essentially at the root of SHP's current problems, leading to (and allowing to flourish) both greed and grievance-driven conflict. The lack of provincial government accountability (political and administrative), social-conflict inhibitors, and an effective law and justice sector has created a permissive environment which encourages the spread of corruption, violent conflict and crime ('greed-driven conflict'), while service delivery failure, economic inequality and the perception that the state is ineffective and unresponsive has fuelled resentment and inter-group tensions ('grievance-driven conflict').

ENDNOTES

[1] This assessment was prepared after the workshop and incorporates much of the material presented at the workshop. The views expressed by the author do not necessarily represent the views of the Australian Government

[2] This template was developed by the Norman Paterson School of International Affairs, Carleton University, Ottawa

An Inside Post-mortem on the Southern Highlands: A perspective from Tari[1]

Philip Moya

Background

The Southern Highlands Province (SHP) comprises eight districts and more than 14 linguistic groups. According to the 2000 Census, the province has a population of 546,256 and a landmass of 23,000 square kilometres. The population growth rate, at 3.4 per cent, is regarded as the highest in the country.

The 2000 Demographic Survey indicates that there has been no significant improvement in the economic, social and political status of the province. This is clearly evident as the serious law and order problems experienced in the province contribute to the massive decline and deterioration of services — health, education, infrastructure — and deprivation of goods and service delivery.

These poor conditions contribute to a low literacy rate of 20 per cent, low life expectancy of 52 years, increased infant, childhood and maternal mortality rates, and low or nil economic growth.

The political and bureaucratic structure has malfunctioned and ceased to operate. This is leading to a situation in which the general fabric of a constituted system is disintegrating. It will be an expensive exercise to rehabilitate and restore it.

The province has been in crisis and is at the crossroads of its destiny. It is been designated a 'dysfunctional province' by Minister for Inter-Government Relations, Sir Peter Barter. SHP is arguably the most resource-rich province in the country, yet there is nothing to show for that wealth in the way infrastructure and development for the 'grassroots' people of the province.

Years of political faction-fighting and corrupt, greedy and self-serving leadership at every level, from national MPs and local-level government (LLG) presidents, through certain public servants, provincial politicians and even some church leaders, has left the province and its administrative functions ineffective. This has served to create further political divisions amongst a population already bedevilled by traditional tribal divisions. Bribery, corruption and nepotism have been blatant, rampant and entrenched throughout the society. This province, the very last to be contacted by the outside world and brought under civil administration prior to independence, needs to develop a healthier respect for the rule of law and civil order.

Exacerbating the problems associated with the breakdown in law and order in the province, the court system is also corrupted and dysfunctional and in dire need of restoration to cope with crimes among village communities. The current provincial government will need to prove that the civil administration can undertake its duties, unfettered by political intervention, to restore good governance in the province and to re-establish the mechanisms of the *Organic Law on Provincial Governments and Local- Level Governments* (OLPGLLG) and ensure they are effectively implemented. Once peace, stability and fiscal accountability and transparency have been introduced, the duly elected and constituted authorities should be able to work together to rebuild the province.

Provincial governments have hijacked the due processes of planning, budgeting, accounting and reporting, as provided under the OLPGLLG. They have imposed their political will on these vital processes and derailed the proper constituted procedures and mechanisms to ensure that all stakeholders participate in the development planning process from bottom up; budgets have not been devised to ensure transparency and accountability in expenditure of public funds.

The losers have been the vast majority of the population. Good road networks, communications, education, health facilities, and goods and services have been denied to 85 per cent of the provincial population, who depend entirely on the subsistence economy. This is because direction, advice, assistance, education and training have not been instigated by our leaders or the Southern Highlands provincial administration. Provincial infrastructure (roads, buildings and public facilities) has been neglected and is in urgent need of repair. The province is too large to manage. The net outcome of these conditions is reflected in:

- poor political and bureaucratic leadership and management;
- tribal warfare, which is increasingly politically motivated;
- lack of employment opportunities for youth;
- insufficient access to quality education and post-secondary education for youth;
- declining education and health services, particularly in the rural areas;
- lack of social activities (e.g. sports and entertainment) for youth;
- a sharp decline in traditional social and moral values;
- endemic bribery and corruption at all levels of society;
- break-down in the court system;
- lack of capacity of within existing law enforcement agencies to cope with the ongoing law and order issues;
- diversion of development project funds from LLGs to the provincial government;

- diversion of recurrent budget funds for day-to-day operations of the provincial administration (divisions, districts, and LLGs) to the provincial government;
- total mistrust and suspicion of the elected leaders by the people;
- little or no respect for the rule of law and order;
- the obvious absence of transparency, accountability and good governance on the part of many senior and middle line public servants;
- lack of cooperation between national and provincial leaders;
- unfair distribution of scarce resources;
- poor human resource planning and management;
- misuse of selection criteria in the recruitment of public servants;
- political interference in the appointment of public servants;
- poor human resource strategic planning;
- poor planning and budgeting each financial year;
- poor financial management and accountability;
- poor organisational planning and management;
- serious law and order problems;
- take-over of state land and properties by landowners;
- need for infrastructure upgrading and development;
- stagnant economic growth;
- poor implementation of the local-level government reforms;
- poor legal advice on matters of importance;
- poor tendering procedures for the awarding of contracts.

These problems continue despite recent efforts to restore services, and are all the more disconcerting because the province hosts some of the country's largest natural resource development projects that are of importance to the nation and province. The wealth and income derived from these developments has not improved the general status of the province. This is a sad state of affairs, and leaders and people of the province should be made accountable.

The failure of the 2002 elections in the province, and related violence, has contributed immensely to the deteriorating law and order problems and to the province's inability to function administratively. This is seen as a result of political instability and poor administration and management of the province. Despite this, new elections were successfully conducted in the midst of these ongoing problems, with heavy security provided by the state.

On several occasions in 1994 and 2003 the national government has sent teams to conduct investigations into the affairs of the province, but no positive action has been taken by the respective line agencies to date.

In this context, *The Way Forward to Recovery* is designed to develop a program to restore and rebuild confidence in the governance and administration of the province, and ensure that trust is regained from the national government, the

Papua New Guinea Chamber of Mines and Industry, the international community, and the people of SHP and Papua New Guinea.

The way forward to recovery

This is seen as a vital strategy for moving forward, as the province is currently regarded as dysfunctional and there is a need to send the right signals to restore trust and confidence. The goals, objectives and strategies of the proposed program of action are set out as follows:

Goals:

1. To restore and rebuild confidence in the governance of the Southern Highlands provincial government and administration.
2. To improve the quality of life and raise the living standards of the people in the Southern Highlands Province.

Objectives:

1. To restore good governance in the Southern Highlands provincial government and administration.
2. To restore peace and normalcy in the province.
3. To review and develop five-year developmental rolling plans.
4. To formulate minimum standards for the province.
5. To restore essential government services.

Strategies:

*   identify why SHP has been dysfunctional;
*   strengthen provincial and district capacity;
*   review the existing plans, and update and develop five-year rolling plans (LLG, district, regional and provincial);
*   the selection and appointment of public servants should be done by the Department of Personnel Management (DPM) or an independent body;
*   strengthen the law-enforcing agencies — police, Corrective Institutions Service (CIS) and courts;
*   appointment of village court officials, land mediators and peace officers should be based on merit and not political influence;
*   establish a minimum standard district office complex;
*   establish an effective human resource management a development plan;
*   review the provincial administration structure;
*   upgrade the existing health facilities and three hospitals;
*   upgrade the existing education facilities;
*   reactivate the court system;
*   set up effective communications networks;
*   upgrade and renovate all the major trunk roads and bridges;

- upgrade senior management staff housing and establishment;
- purchase reliable plant and transport;
- strictly apply financial management procedures;
- purchase essential equipment;
- install reliable electricity supplies in the districts (e.g. mini hydro systems);
- establish Treasury offices;
- establish networks with NGOs and donor agencies;
- formulate an economic development plan;
- the Electoral Boundaries Commission to review the boundaries and establish two more electorates and Hela Province.

The Way Forward is intended to improve the quality of life and standard of living by restoring normalcy and good governance in the province. This will enable us to create a healthy and peaceful environment for all, through responsive, effective, accessible, affordable, and sustainable economic and social development that is acceptable and relevant to the majority of the people. To effectively achieve this, the province should give priority to five main program areas:

1. Restoration of confidence in the SHP government and its administration.
2. Restoration of law and order.
3. Restoration of education and health services.
4. Restoration and upgrading of existing infrastructure.
5. Restoration of sustainable economic development programs.

These priorities are equally important; one does not outweigh the other. They are briefly analysed below.

Program one: Restoration of confidence in the SHP Government and its administration

Governance in the SHP is vested in our leaders, but the need for close consultation in advising the leaders is important. This has been one of the major problems, as advice from the Provincial Management Team to the Provincial Executive Council has never been sought in order for our leaders to make decisions based on technical, economic and financial feasibility.

The need for our national members of parliament and the Provincial Executive Council to work together is also crucially important. It is felt that politics has been and remains the major factor that has destroyed this beautiful province.

The Southern Highlands Provincial Assembly and the Provincial Executive Council have not sat to address the issues of the province. This raises questions about whether the law has been contravened.

There is a need to have the Southern Highlands provincial government operate from a building other than the Agiru Centre. While the provincial government and provincial administration work from the same building, there is no clear way to distinguish what provincial government and administrative staff are doing. Prior to the provincial headquarters building being burnt down in 2002 there was a clear separation between the government and the administration.

Political fragmentation is rampant in all sectors of the society — clans, tribes, families, groups, regions, LLG presidents and councillors, and the public service. This is a serious issue and one which contributes to the problems experienced in the province. Indeed it is apparent that the province has developed a culture, embedded into the system, in which a small group of people with authority either in politics or the civil service has manipulated the system to their benefit.

The dysfunctionality of the public service, and the deterioration of services and serious breakdown in law and order are all side effects of this chronic disease, which is contributing to a downward spiral effect in the way the province has been governed and administered over the years, despite the recent efforts made by Minister for Inter-Government Relations, Sir Peter Barter.

The restoration and reactivation of the administrative system is crucial, as morale and functions have badly deteriorated over the years. This is the vehicle that will resurrect the province and determine its ability to restore and rebuild its services. It is evident that the province has failed to meet it constitutional requirements, and as such it has become a failed province. Restoring confidence in the provincial administration will require comprehensive reform.

Appointment of a provincial administrator

The province has had the experience of many provincial administrators and district administrators appointed to suit the national or provincial governments' political interests over the years, with disregard for established procedures. This has contributed to instability in the public service. Governments have simply employed political cronies and provided jobs for *wantok*.

It has become a tradition in the Southern Highlands provincial administration to have two or more people paid for the same position. As such, the province has regularly exceeded the staff ceiling and salaries bill over the years. The current provincial government has gone ahead to recruit more public servants, with the number in August 2004 at 1,336 people.

The creation of a Public Relations Division in SHP seriously violates administrative processes. It will not only cost the Southern Highlands provincial government dearly to create this division, but is an insult to the peace and good order committee members, village court magistrates, land mediators, peace officers and casual employees who continue to work throughout the province despite not having been paid their allowances or wages for several years. What is the justification for employing more than 500 staff in a new division?

2001 selection and recruitment

The recruitment of new personnel in 2001 created many problems in the provincial administration. It is said that many unqualified and inexperienced people were recruited into the administration, while good experienced civil servants were put into the unattached pool. People who were recruited in 2001 have failed to perform. Despite this experience, more and more people are being recruited today to facilitate political interests. This is a major problem, and nothing has been done about it.

Restructuring of the provincial administration

The division of the province into three zones should be given priority, as past experience shows that the administration has been able to deliver services effectively. In the past the province has been progressive and vibrant, with development taking place and services being delivered. This strategy was deployed to administer the province effectively, given its land mass, population and infrastructure. The need to revisit this idea is crucial to restoring confidence in the civil administration, without political interference.

Establishment of a human resource management development program

The human resource management division (HRMD) of an organisation is the engine room of that organisation. SHP's HRMD has not functioned effectively for the past ten years. Recruitment of qualified HRM officers is an important requirement if the problems experienced in the SHP administration are to be seriously addressed. The poor performance of the public service is a result of poor advice provided to senior management, and this raises questions about the competence of the HRM staff.

There is a need to conduct an audit of the staffing and payroll over the last three years. People have been employed without following standard procedures and a lot of staff have paid themselves large sums of money in the form of allowances or special pay. This is a form of corruption, which is quite rampant and should be investigated; those responsible should be dealt accordingly.

The degree of corruption in the SHP payroll system should be determined by an independent organisation. On completion of this exercise the Provincial Coordinating Unit (PCU) functions of the Department of Personal Management should be transferred to SHP and the following matters be considered:

- effective operational procedure should be put in place;
- people involved in defrauding the SHP by paying themselves salaries over the last three years should be exposed and charged;
- staff of the DPM involved in this also should be dealt with;
- HRMD should immediately establish a computerised HRM data system;

- an audit of the whole public service should be conducted;
- there is a need to retrench staff or retrain and deploy the excess staff;
- qualified and experienced HRM staff should be recruited;
- an effective career development plan should be established;
- the Provincial Disciplinary Committee should be reactivated.

Appointment and placement of public servants to be based on merit

The provincial public service has been politicised over the years, contributing to poor performance and low productivity. Machinery has ceased to operate. Many public servants are living in Port Moresby, Lae or Mount Hagen and collecting their fortnightly salaries. Further, some people are employed in other organisations but are still paid by the SHP.

Politics has eaten away at the fabric of civil administration, with appointments and resources allocated according to political influence. District administrators tend to spend 85 per cent of their time away from the district centres, and it is unclear what they actually do. Often they seem to be living with the MP and not attending to their duties.

My view, after 23 months working in the Hela region, is that this trend must cease, and district administrators and their staff should be at their place of work in the district. One of the major excuses given by district administrators is that they have to attend to joint district planning and budget priorities committee (JDP&BC) meetings which are held away from the district.

I should also note that district support grants, the key source of funds to district administration, are not being made available in the district. As a result district administrators spend a great deal of time chasing these funds. In theory district administrators should have full access to these funds. What then is currently being done with these funds?

In order to improve SHP's administrative capacity a performance appraisal of human resources at the senior level should be conducted so as to assess the qualifications and experience of managers in accordance with the duty statements of the position. Competent people must be appointed to positions of authority, without political influence, if the province is serious about restoring the public service. The Public Service Management Act and General Orders are usually ignored dealing with public service matters.

Reactivation of the district administration centres

The public service has ceased to function in the province, and nothing is happening. An assessment is urgently needed to establish what it will take to restore the capacity of the administration at the provincial headquarters and in the districts. This should include assessments of what is needed to restore trust and confidence in the administration.

Local-level government reforms

It is apparent throughout the province that no LLG meetings have been conducted since the failed elections of 2002. Added to this, there have been serious flaws in the election of some presidents, which have led to challenges in the courts. Serious questions have been raised about:

- the election of ward councillors and presidents;
- the appointment of LLG officers and staff;
- management of and accountability for LLG finances; and
- LLG reform policy implementation plans.

LLGs have been heavily politicised and their constitutional roles have been totally ignored. At this time, no LLG in the province is functioning as it should.

Review of provincial and district five-year developmental rolling plans

An immediate priority is to review the existing plans, if the province has any. If it does not, there is a need to obtain help from the Department of National Planning and/or a technical assistance package. The province has been operating without a vision and plan. This has led to the mismanagement of provincial resources. As a result the province is dysfunctional.

Effective management of and accountability for the province's finances

The province has experienced major increases in its revenues over the years, due to payments of royalties, taxes, dividends and development levies derived from the resource developments, amounting to millions of kina over the years. To date however, these funds have been poorly managed. Accordingly the wealth of the province has not been realised. Its infrastructure and services have substantially declined and there is no social and economical growth. Several factors influence the situation, among them the following:

- There are two sets of accounts: one for the Southern Highlands provincial government and one for the provincial Treasury. These operate separately with their own staffing and functions. The provincial Finance Division and the SHP Treasury should be amalgamated to overcome problems of poor control and accountability in the expenditure of funds.
- Expenditures are not based on provincial development plans but are determined by political influence and interest. This has resulted in a lack of accountability.
- Funds have been paid out on bogus claims and to buy political support.

- There are large expenditures on staffing, allowances, travel costs and air charters that are never budgeted. Large amounts have been committed to consultancies and for legal advice, from which the province has not benefited.
- Many of the people employed in the two offices are semi-qualified or unqualified to perform their tasks. A clear example is the recent appointments to provincial Treasury positions; these should be investigated.
- In the formulation of the annual provincial budget, the provincial management team is not consulted.
- There is no proper tendering for projects amounting to millions of kina. Bogus companies have been registered to undertake consultancies and provide infrastructure.
- Cases relating to misuse of public funds must be investigated and appropriate action taken.

Most importantly, a strategy should be clearly identified to ensure that finances are managed in accordance with procedures under the *Financial Management Act*. Every effort should be made to address the issues highlighted.

Program two: Restoration of law and order

Good order, peace and normalcy are the ingredients for sustainable societal development. Without peace and harmony there will be continued degradation of law and order, which will deter development and progress in the province. Law and order problems have a negative impact on new investment and expansion of business activities in both the formal and informal sectors, and notably in the tourism industry, which should be encouraged in the province.

Perceptions of law and order in the province should be assessed and analysed, as the province is experiencing serious break down in law and order. My experience over the years suggests that in addressing the problems of law and order the following issues need to be recognised.

Local disputes

Disputes may arise from minor issues: two children might be playing and one hits the other; or a pig's ear is chopped when it enters another person's food garden. These may appear to be trivial matters, but if they are not resolved immediately they can become bigger problems, contributing to instability within villages, clans and tribal groups.

Based on my experience of conflicts in the Hela region, the following are prominent underlying issues in a lot of local disputes, and tribal fights.

- Land disputes.
- Disputes over bride-price payments.
- Domestic violence.
- Rape and forced marriages.

- Stealing of pigs.
- Compensation demands.
- Criminal activities.
- Use of drugs, especially marijuana.
- Political disputes.
- Payback killings.

Tribal fights

Tribal fights have long been a way of life for the highlander, and traditional procedures for conflict resolution are still used today in some isolated parts of the province. However the use of modern, commercially produced and home-made weapons in tribal fights, as evident in recent fighting in the Unjamap/Wogia, Nembi Plateau/Utipia, Parita/Poroma, and Hela regions, is increasing. There is a need to acknowledge and understand the significance of tribal fights, in order for the government to develop strategies to address them.

Political rivalry

The province has had serious problems since 1994, when the Southern Highlands provincial government was suspended, deepening political divisions throughout the province. Politics has been a major influence contributing to the failure of governance in the province. Our leaders do not appear to be working together for the interests of the province; they have become a liability to the province and its people.

Criminal activities

Criminal activity along the Nipa-Tari road is a serious problem, and many people have become victims. The establishment of highway patrols will be an effective measure to police the roads in the province.

The effectiveness of government and the community justice system

Institutions, such as village courts, land mediators, peace officers and community leaders, which at one time were effective in addressing issues of law and order at the community level, are not functioning. The trust and confidence that was established for these vital systems to deal with law and order issues at the community level has eroded. Reactivation of those systems should be given the highest priority if the province is serious about addressing the breakdown in law and order.

Much of the continuing violence stems from the 1997 elections and the competition between former governors the late Dick Mune and Anderson Agiru. This is an issue that needs to be seriously addressed, as the Hela people are continually falling victims when travelling on the road from Nipa to Tari, and as a result are effectively being denied services. They have suffered for almost ten years, despite the fact that the Hela region hosts some of the largest natural resources projects in the country. This has given them the motivation for a separate Hela province.

Peace for development

Where electorates and communities are peaceful, services should be restored and developmental programs encouraged. This may provide a model for others in the province to follow. Places identified for such initiatives are Upper Mendi, Lower Mendi, Imbonggu, Ialibu, Pangia and Margarima.

Arms build-up

It is public knowledge that the SHP has modern weapons, and there is an ongoing arms build-up. The number of high-powered firearms coming to the province is alarming. It poses a serious threat to national security, and every effort should be made to establish where the arms are coming from. The experience of the 2002 failed election should be ringing alarm bells. Among the reasons for this trend:

- arms been brought in by people with power and authority;
- arms smuggling has been associated with drug trafficking;
- fear of being attacked by an enemy tribe is widespread, so guns are acquired for security;
- individuals, villages, tribes and political groupings gain power and status through having arms.

Agencies responsible for addressing these issues have not done enough; a weapons collection and disposal strategy must be developed.

Status of the law-enforcing system

The Royal Papua New Guinea Constabulary (RPNGC) is severely constrained in carrying out its constitutional functions, due to lack of funds. Staff housing is in an appalling state of disrepair, and there are not adequate funds for fuel for the aging fleet of police vehicles. It is difficult to attract serving members of the police force to transfer to the province, because of the housing situation and the negative image that has been projected by the recent killing of a policeman in Koroba and the law and order situation generally.

There are in fact only 195 policemen and policewomen to police what is a very large and heavily populated province. Indeed with only one police officer to every 2800 people policing is incredibly difficult, and even serious crimes may not be attended to.

The police force alone cannot restore law and order: a combined effort from all sectors of the government and community is required. Despite the impediments they face, restoration efforts by the RPNGC in the province are progressing well. The leaders of the province should be thankful that the police and the church have held the province together.

An increase in the deployment of police to the province is vital. However, strategies for addressing the breakdown of law and order in the province should be home-grown rather than derived from nationally-developed programs. The provincial police commander (PPC) has already taken some useful initiatives. Strategies might include:

* training of police recruits in SHP (an initiative developed by the PPC);
* revisiting the law on inter group-fighting;
* giving more powers to the police;
* heavier penalties for crimes such as murder, rape, robbery, and tribal fights;
* using the concept for *peace for development* as a tool in restoring services;
* introducing community policing;
* reactivating the national, district and village court systems;
* establishing three mobile squads, in Mendi, Tari and Ialibu;
* initiating massive awareness campaigns through community policing;
* networking with NGOs in the province;
* funding the peace and good order committee functions;
* improving police infrastructure and adequately supporting with logistics;
* developing a weapons collection and disposal strategy.

The court system

The court system in SHP has been crippled, with no resources and only one magistrate in the province during the last five years. There are no magistrates in any of the six districts except Tari.

Since there are no courts to deal with offenders, people who have committed serious crimes remain on the loose. For example, in the Hela region there are 162 murder cases outstanding. One of the major problems — as for public servants throughout the province — is housing for magistrates.

The reactivation of the court system, with support from the provincial government and the national government, is critical.

Corrective institutions

The two CIS centres in the province, Bui Yebi in Mendi and Hawa in Tari, must be made functional. Hawa was closed for a good number of years; it has been recently reopened but resources must be allocated to enable it to function effectively. The restoration of corrective services will be a step towards addressing the breakdown in law and order.

Program three: Restoration of education and health services

Education

The Education Division is the biggest division in the SHP administration. There are in the province over 300 elementary schools, 150 community schools, 75 primary schools, 12 provincial high schools, 3 secondary schools, 6 vocational training centres, and one agriculture and technical secondary school. The total enrolment of students at all institutions is 83,884, and the average student-teacher ratio is 466:1.

Like other line divisions in the SHP, the Education Division is not functioning effectively. I suspect that 85 per cent of all educational institutions in the province are not providing their mandated functions.

Education reform has contributed to the problems. On the one hand, there has been an overall improvement in accessibility to basic education; however, access in some areas has worsened considerably. This has to do with the fact that the location of schools, teacher appointments and the selection of students is now subject to considerable political interference.

It is also the case that education subsidies from the national government to the province have been poorly used and inadequately accounted for over the years. Recently the Southern Highlands provincial government adopted a 'Free Education Policy' in the province, which in my view is adding to the problems of a poor education system that is trying to deliver. This is a politically sensitive topic, but it is apparent that the 'Free Education Policy' is not achieving its intended outcome.

If lack of access to education at all levels is not addressed successfully, there are likely to be wider ramifications, including:

- a marked increase in law and order problems;
- a marked decrease in the enrolment of SHP students in higher educational institutions;
- lack of incentive for skilled and experienced people to stay in the province, due to poor opportunity and quality of lifestyle;
- a decline in the local economy, impacting on local entrepreneurs, and a lack of well educated and trained personnel to be employed in the SHP government and administration.

Currently in SHP there is a shortage of teachers, and educational infrastructure is in need of maintenance. The SHP's Free Education Policy should be assessed to determine its viability. There is urgent need to appoint a qualified education advisor to help provide leadership.

Health

The Division of Health is similarly compromised. Indeed problems in the health sector are evident throughout the province. The division employs about 315 people of the current 900 or so provincial manpower. There are two district hospitals, at Ialibu and Tari, and a provincial hospital in Mendi. A third district hospital was recently built at Koroba, but has not been commissioned due to lack of staff accommodation.

In addition to the three hospitals, there are 8 health care centres, 2 of which two are currently closed; 56 health sub-centres of which 12 are closed; and approximately 120 operating aid posts, of which 97 are closed for various reasons. There are 6 ambulances operating throughout the province, while several are out of service due to mechanical failure. Ideally, there should be 20 ambulances servicing the districts that have road networks, including 3 based in Mendi.

Mendi has a level 3 referral hospital, with approximately 200 beds. The hospital is run-down, but continues to function despite limited equipment and resources. There is an immediate need to maintain the Mendi Hospital as a referral hospital for the province. There is a further need to have Tari and Ialibu hospitals rehabilitated and functioning.

Tari Hospital, which provides hospital services for the Hela region, does not have a doctor, and there is a need to rectify this. The hospital is in need of major maintenance, and requires essential equipment and drugs.

The Rural Health Service has suffered severely over recent years. There has been a major decline in services and worse may be expected in the event of a major disease outbreak.

If health services are to be restored, though, careful attention should be given to priorities, as so much needs to be done.

Program four: Restoration and upgrading of the existing infrastructure

Upgrading and maintaining existing infrastructure should be prioritised over building new infrastructure. The current status of roads, bridges, administration facilities, public service housing, educational institutions, and health facilities needs to be assessed.

The Southern Highlands provincial government must realise that the infrastructure in the province requires major assessments not only of technical feasibility but also of social and economic returns and the impact on our people. The Tax Credit Scheme and bilateral aid might be utilised to help restore the province's aging infrastructure.

Program five: Restoration of sustainable economic development programs

There has been a substantial decline in economic growth in all sectors throughout the province. The revenues derived from non-renewable resources should be invested in renewable resources. This has been neglected by successive provincial governments. What happens when the natural resources of the province are depleted?

It is important that economic programs give priority to projects that offer a sustainable return. Some that come to mind include:

- coffee production, geared towards smallholder coffee rehabilitation and new development;
- food security development;
- eco-tourism development;
- eco-forestry development;
- Rural micro and macro credit facilities.

Conclusion

If the national government is serious about reviving the province, it must, as a matter of urgency, work with the provincial government and provincial administration to see that the five priority areas identified in this paper are addressed. Furthermore it must:

1. utilise resource people in the province as partners in the decision-making process;
2. develop an action plan;
3. develop a restoration program;
4. ensure that its policies are fully resourced; and
5. carefully monitor the implementation process.

The National Government has a constitutional and a moral obligation to ensure that the SHP restores good governance and sound administration for its societal development and sustainable progress so that the province can compete with the rest of Papua New Guinea.

ENDNOTES

[1] This chapter is based on a presentation to a ministerial delegation to the Southern Highlands Province in August 2004. The same paper was presented to the Central Agencies Consultative Committee at Kiburu Lodge on 16 April 2004.

Index